ON THE SQUARE

ALSO BY STEVAN V. NIKOLIC

Royal Art Of Freemasonry
The Purpose Of Freemasonry
Freemasonry In Serbia
Spiritual Guide To The Secret Of Birth
Star - The Book Of Life

ON THE

Decoding Freemasonry

SQUARE

STEVAN V. NIKOLIC

New York, Belgrade

ON THE SQUARE
Decoding Freemasonry
By: Stevan V. Nikolic

Copyright © 2013 by Stevan V. Nikolic
www.stevanvnikolic.net

Published by ISTINA, a co-publishing venture of the My Story Publishers Group, 1340 Stratford Avenue, Suite 3K, Bronx, NY, 10472

All rights reserved. No part of this book may be reproduced in any manner whatsoever without written permission except in the case of brief quotations embodied in critical articles and reviews. For information, please address My Story Publishers DBA, 1340 Stratford Avenue, Suite 3K, Bronx, NY, 10472
www.mystorypublishers.com

Cover design: © 2013 by Stevan V. Nikolic

ISBN-13: 978-0-9896962-0-3
ISBN-10: 0989696200

Printed in the United States of America

For Tamara

*"I will strive to live with love and care,
upon the level, by the square."*

Inscription on the brass square, dated 1517,
discovered in 1830 under the foundation stone
of the Baal's bridge in the City of Limerick, Ireland

CONTENTS

	ILLUSTRATIONS	xv
	A NOTE TO THE READER	xxi
1	INTRODUCTION	1
2	THE MEANING OF FREEMASONRY	7
3	THE VERY ESSENCE	17
4	MASONIC SYMBOLS DECODED	25
	- Preparation for the Journey	26
	- Entrance into the Temple	30
	- The Pillars	36
	- Mosaic Pavement and Tracing Board	38
	- Lights	40
	- The Volume of Sacred Law	43
	- The Builders Tools	46
	- The Stones	51
	- The Point within a Circle	53
	- The rite of circumambulation	60
	- The Mason's clothing	62
	- The Hiramic Legend	67
5	MASONIC DEGREES, RITES, AND RITUALS	70
	- The Apprentice	72
	- The Fellowcraft	75
	- The Master Mason	77
	- Rites and Rituals	80
	- The Ancient Accepted Scottish Rite	83
	- The York Rite	88

	- The Rectified Scottish Rite	90
	- The French Rite	92
	- The Ancient and Primitive Rite of Memphis-Mizraim	94
	- The Swedish Rite	96
	- The Schroeder's Rite	98
	- The Emulation Rite	99
6	**THE ORIGINS OF FREEMASONRY**	100
	- The Ancient Mysteries	102
	- Knights Templar	111
	- The Rosicrucians	118
	- The Three Stage Theory	123
	- The Age of Enlightenment	128
7	**18th CENTURY - ENGLISH BEGINNINGS**	137
	- England, Scotland, and Ireland	139
	- France	144
	- Germany	146
	- Belgium	146
	- Spain	147
	- Portugal	147
	- Switzerland	147
	- Italy	147
	- Denmark	148
	- Sweden	148
	- Russia	150
	- Poland	150
	- Austro-Hungarian Empire	151
	- Colonial America	152
	- Ordo Ab Chaos	154
8	**19th CENTURY - INSTITUTIONALIZATION AND GROWTH**	156
	- England	158
	- United States of America	159
	- Canada	163
	- Scotland and Ireland	163
	- Australia	164

	- Germany	165
	- Eastern Europe	166
	- France	168
	- Consolidation and growth	172
9	20th CENTURY - THE TURBULENT TIMES	174
10	THREE TRADITIONS AND TWO CONCEPTS	183
	- English Craft Masonry	184
	- American York Rite Freemasonry	186
	- European Traditions	190
	- Two different concepts	193
11	MASONIC SECRETS	200
12	ANTI-MASONRY	206
13	MORALS AND ETHICS	213
14	CHARITY AND COMMUNITY INVOLVEMENT	220
15	SOCIAL ACTIVISM	227
16	PRACTICAL PHILOSOPHY	234
17	WOMEN IN FREEMASONRY	243
	- Adoptive Freemasonry	245
	- Co-Masonry (Mixed Freemasonry)	250
	- Female Freemasonry	252
18	AT THE DAWN OF THE THIRD MILLENNIUM	255
19	INSTEAD OF CONCLUSION	271
	APPENDIX	275
	- Masonic Abbreviations	277
	- Masonic Calendar	280
	- Short overview of the Rites, Degrees, and Orders	282
	A) York Rite	282
	- Capitular Degrees	283
	- Cryptic Degrees	287
	- Chivalric Orders	290
	B) Ancient and Accepted Scottish Rite	293
	- Lodge of Perfection	294
	- Chapter of Rose Croix	297
	- Council of Kadosh	299
	- Consistory	302

- Supreme Council A.A.S.R.	303
C) Structure of the Rectified Scottish Rite	304
D) Structure of the French Rite	304
E) Structure of the Swedish Rite	305
F) Masonic Orders worked in England and Wales	306
G) Structure of the Antient and Primitive Rite of Memphis-Misraim	308
H) Other Rites and Degrees	312
- Famous Freemasons	316
- List of the Grand Lodges	327
- International Masonic Organizations	343
- Masonic Libraries and Museums	345
- Masonic Research Organizations	347
- Masonic Magazines, Periodicals, and Websites	349
BIBLIOGRAPHY	352
ABOUT THE AUTHOR	361

ILLUSTRATIONS

Picture 1. The brass square, dated 1517, discovered in 1830 under the foundation stone of the Baal's bridge in the City of Limerick, Ireland -page ix
Picture 2. *The Great Geometrician of the Universe*—acrylic painting on canvas by Tamara Nikolic, page xxiv
Picture 3. *From the Ceremony of the Opening of the Grand Lodge Annual Assembly United Grand Lodges of Serbia,* Photo©2010 UGLS, page 6
Picture 4. *Symbols of Freemasonry,* page 15
Picture 5. *Front Page of the Anderson's Constitutions of the Freemasons from 1723,* page 16
Picture 6. *The Universal Religion,* ©2007, By Tamara Nikolic, page 24
Picture 7. *The Chamber of Reflection,* page 29
Picture 8. *Solomon's Temple from a 1660 version of the King James Bible,* page 31
Picture 9. *The Floor Plan of the King Solomon's Temple,* page 31
Picture 10. *Masonic Temple – The Lodge room in the Masonic Temple in Belgrade (Serbia) United Grand Lodges of Serbia,* Photo©2010 UGLS, page 32
Picture 11. *The Pillars Jachin and Boaz.* From "The Compass of the Wise", Berlin, 1782., page 37
Picture 12. *The Tracing Board of the Third Degree* (Ancient Accepted Scottish Rite), page 39
Picture 13. *Masonic Lights,* page 42
Picture 14. *The Three Great Lights in Freemasonry-Holy Bible, Square, and Compasses* Photo © 2013 S. Nikolic, page 45
Picture 15. *Working Tools of Freemasonry,* page 47
Picture 16. *Bavarian Stonemasons* 1505 by Rueland Frueauf the Younger (1470–1545), page 50
Picture 17. *The Rough Ashlar and the Perfect Ashlar,* page 51
Picture 18. *Laying of the cornerstone of the Washington Masonic Memorial in 1925* , page 52
Picture 19. *Point within a circle* , page 53
Picture 20. *Ouroborus, also known as ANANTA—a serpent biting it's tale,* page 56

Picture 21. *Lord Shiva Temple from India -designed in the circular form*, page 56
Picture 22. *Stonehenge in England*, page 56
Picture 23. *The Center of the Universe.*, page 58
Picture 24. *Two Saint Johns', point within a circle with two parallel lines and the Holy Bible*, page 58
Picture 25. *Adam Kadmon - The Original Man, from the* 13th century manuscript, Italy ,page 59
Picture 26. *Vitruvian Man* by Leonardo Da Vinci, page 59
Picture 27. *Rite of Circumambulation as practiced in the Masonic Ritual*, page 61
Picture 28. *White Leather Masonic Apron*, page 62
Picture 29. *Past Master's Apron, (top) and Grand Officer Apron (left)* , page 63
Picture 30. *Masonic Dress Code: Morning Suite or dark suite, Collar, White gloves, and the Top Hat for the Worshipful Master.*, page 66
Picture 31. From seventeenth century northern Italy - Hiramic Legend depicted in *Raising the Master* by Il Guercino., page 69
Picture 32. *The Pyramid presentation of the Masonic Degrees Structure*, page 71
Picture 33. *The Initiation of the candidate to the Apprentice degree*—French gravure, 18th century, page 73
Picture 34. *Entered Apprentice giving the solemn Obligation (top), and Apprentice being conducted around the Lodge (right)*, page 74
Picture 35. *Tracing Board of the Fellowcraft (Second) Degree)* , English , late 19th century, page 76
Picture 36. *Some of the symbols of the Third Degree - Virgin with the pot of incense and the sprig of acacia standing in front of Broken column with the Holy Bible; Death behind her and the Hour Glass*, page 78
Picture 37. *Third Degree Ceremony, Rectified Scottish Rite,* French print etching, 18th century, page 82
Picture 38. *Emblems of the AASR degrees* , page 87
Picture 39 . *Four Bodies of the AASR Valley* , page 87
Picture 40 . *Four Hats of the AASR Masons* , page 87
Picture 41. *"The Ladder" of the York Rite Degrees*, page 89
Picture 42. *Tracing Board of the First Degree of the French Rite*, page 93
Picture 43. *The Grand Seal of the A.P.R.M.M. (top), Joseph Balsano, called Cagliostro , the founderof the Rite of Misraim (right)*, page 95
Picture 44. *The Swedish Rite Regalia*, page 97
Picture 45. *Masonic symbols*, page 101
Picture 46. *Tabula Smaragdina (Emerald Tablet)*, page 109
Picture 47, 48. *Alchemical Symbols*, page 109
Picture 49. *Mystery Schools* (top), page 110

Illustrations xvii

Picture 50. *"Understanding"* Acrylic on canvas, © by Tamara Nikolic (left), page 110
Picture 51. *Pilgrims under escort of Knight Templars in sight of Jerusalem*, by Eduard Zier, page 116
Picture 52. *Knight Templars flag*, page 116
Picture 53. *Knight Templars seal*, page 116
Picture 54. *Templar tombstone in Scotland*, photo© D. Garner, page 117
Picture 55. *Mysterious Rennes-Le-Chateau Parchment*, page 117
Picture 56. *"Rosa Mistica"*, page 121
Picture 57. *Collegium Fraternitatis*, by T. Schweighart, 1604, page 122
Picture 58. *Regius MS, 1390*, page 126
Picture 59. The antiquarian Elias Ashmole and the page from his diary from Oct. 16, 1646. (the original manuscript is kept in Bodleian Library at Oxford), page 127
Picture 60. *The front page of the book Bacon-Masonry by George V. Tudhope, claiming Francis Bacon to "be original designer of speculative Freemasonry"* page 136
Picture 61. *The Royal Society of London was founded in 1662*, page 138
Picture 62. *Anthony Sawyer, The first Grand Master of the Grand Lodge of England (Moderns)*, page 143
Picture 63. *The Goose and Gridiron Ale House in London where on June 24th, 1717 the Grand Lodge was founded*, page 143
Picture 64. *The Constitution titled <u>Ahiman Rezon</u>, written by Lawrence Dermott, Grand Secretary of this Grand Lodge Of Ancients*, page 143
Picture 65. *Lawrence Dermott*, page 143
Picture 66. *The Duke of Wharton, Grand Master of the Grand Lodge of France in 1728*, page 145
Picture 67. *Count of Clermont, Grand Master of the Grand Lodge of France from 1743 to 1771*, page 145
Picture 68. *The Rite of Adoption Ritual (18th century)*, page 145
Picture 69. *18th century Masonic items at the Château de Mongenan*, page 145
Picture 70. *Karl Gotthelf Freiherrn von Hund, known as Baron von Hund, founder of the Rite of Strict Observance*, page 149
Picture 71. *Hermetical symbols, an illustration from the so-called "clerical records of the Templars..." 18th century—Germany* (Source: History of Freemasonry in Gemany, by Ferdinand Runkel - Berlin, 1942), page 149
Picture 72. *Count Ivan Draskovic, founder of the Draskovic Observance*, page 151
Picture 73. *Benjamin Franklin became a Mason in Tun Tavern Lodge in Philadelphia in 1731.*, page 153
Picture 74. *Old Tun Tavern Lodge*, page 153
Picture 75. *Coat of Arms of the Grand Lodge of "Antients " and the Grand Lodge of "Moderns"*, page 158

Picture 76. *Captain William Morgan,* page 162

Picture 77. *Cover page of the book Illustrations of Freemasonry By W. .Morgan, 1827*, page 162

Picture 78. *The very first Masonic Temple in Belgrade (Serbia) -Lodge Ali Koch, 1848*, page 167

Picture 79. *The Archbishop of the Diocese of Karlovci (the Province of Vojvodina) Stefan Stratimirovic was a member of the Lodge Vigilantia in 1785, working under the protection of the Grand Lodge of Draskovic Observance,* page 167

Picture 80. *The Seal of the Grand Orient of France*, page 170

Picture 81. *House of the Temple, Washington DC- a Headquarters of the AASR Southern Jurisdiction USA,* page 172

Picture 82. *Grand Lodge of Pennsylvania, Masonic Temple in Philadelphia,* page 173

Picture 83. *Freemasons Hall in London - United Grand Lodge of England,* page 173

Picture 84. *The Masonic Service Association of the United States was established in 1919, and the first Conference of the Grand Masters of Masons of North America was held in 1909,* page 177

Picture 85. *The German Nazi poster from 1935—The text at the top reads: "World politics World revolution." The text at the bottom reads, "Freemasonry is an international organization beholden to Jewry with the political goal of establishing Jewish domination through world-wide revolution." The map, decorated with Masonic symbols (temple, square, and apron), shows where revolutions took place in Europe from the French Revolution in 1789 through the German Revolution in 1919.* page 178

Picture 86. *In 2010 Romanian Post Office issued stamps commemorating 130 years of the Freemasonry in Romania. Freemasonry was revived in Romania in 1989.* Page 181

Picture 87. *The Annual Assembly of the Serbian Freemasons in 2010.* Photo © UGLS, page 182

Picture 88. *A quarterly publication of the United Grand Lodges Of Serbia*, page 182

Picture 89. *The Grand Seal of the UGLS*, page 182

Picture 90. *Master Mason's Apron: American York Rite, English Emulation Rite, and European Ancient Accepted Scottish Rite,* page 183

Picture 91. *United Grand Lodge of England Annual Assembly 2008,* Photo © UGLE, page 185

Picture 92. *At the One Day Masonic Journey on Oct. 30, 2010, a total of 1,937 men were raised to the Sublime Degree of Master Mason. Many went on to join the Scottish Rite and the Shrine.* (Grand Lodge of Pennsylvania) Source: Freemason, Volume LVIII, Feb. 2011, No.1, page 188

Illustrations xix

Picture 93. *American Freemasons are particularly proud of the fact that fourteen American Presidents were members of the Brotherhood of Freemasons*, page 189
Picture 94. *Masonic Charities are big part of the activities of the American Masonic Institutions*, page 189
Picture 95. *The Headquarters of the Grand Orient of France in Paris*, page 192
Picture 96. *The Brotherhood of men under the Fatherhood of God—major slogan amongst Anglo-American Masons*, page 199
Picture 97. *Laïcité - concept built into the structure of the liberal Masonic teachings in Europe*, page 199
Picture 98. *Many try to profit from "exposing" Masonic secrets*, page 204
Picture 99. *UGLE Library and Museum - Many Grand Lodges offer regular tours of their buildings, lodges, and museums to the general public.*, page 205
Picture 100. *Masonic Rituals are performed in the privacy of the Lodge rooms.*, page 205
Picture 101. *Anti-Masonic stamps issued by the Serbian Post Office in 1942. commemorating Anti -Masonic Exhibition organized in Belgrade under Nazi occupation by German forces in Winter of 1941.*, page 211
Picture 102. *In 1738 Pope Clement XII issued his bull "In Eminenti" condemning Freemasonry*, page 212
Picture 103. *One of the most famous Masonic poems - "The Palace" by Rudyard Kipling, a poet and a Freemason*, page 219
Picture 104. *"Shriners of North America" own and operate nationwide 22 children's' hospitals for the treatment of children with orthopedic conditions, burns and spinal cord injuries. All of the services in the Shriners hospitals are completely free. Since the first Shriners hospital was opened in 1922, over 855.000 children have been treated in them.*, page 226
Picture 105. *Poster announcing the Public Conference organized by the GODF on the subject: "Citizenship, Republic and Freemasonry"*, page 232
Picture 106. *Masonic Code of Conduct (French)*, page 233
Picture 107. *Temperance, Prudence, Fortitude, and Justice - Four Cardinal Virtues of Freemasonry*, page 241
Picture 108. *Masonic Principles - Faith, Hope, and Charity*, page 242
Picture 109. *Order of the Eastern Star Emblem*, page 248
Picture 110. *Front Page of the Ritual of Adoption 18th Century, France*, page 249
Picture 111. *The Ritual Book of the Order of the Eastern Star*, page 249
Picture 112. *Le Droit Humain Emblem*, page 251
Picture 113. *Maria Derasmes*, page 251
Picture 114. *Le Droit Humain building in Paris (France)*, page 251
Picture 115. *Seton Challen, Grand Master of the Honourable Fraternity of Antient Freemasons, and her Grand Officers , 1938*, page 253

Picture 116. *Women's Grand Lodge of France announcing a public conference about the purpose and aims of their Grand Lodge,* page 253

Picture 117 –118. *Membership numbers from 1925 to 2006 in the USA and the rate of membership decline in past 50 years according to the Masonic Service Association. (Source: Masonic Business Review)* , page 263

Picture 119. *According to the <u>Masonic Press Agency (APMR)</u>, on November 27th 2012 in the European Union's capital was held <u>the traditional meeting of EU's leaders and Freemasonry's representatives of the Member States</u>. On behalf of the EU participated José Manuel Durão Barroso (President of the European Commission), Herman van Rompuy (President of the European Council) and László SURJÁN (Vice-president of the European Parliament) and on behalf of the Craft attended: Grand Orient of Belgium, the United Grand Lodges of Germany, the Grand Orient of France, Droit Humain (Belgium, France and Spain), International Masonic Order DELPHI (Greece), Women's Grand Lodge of Belgium, Women's Grand Lodge of France, the Grand Orient of Hungary, the Grand Orient Lusitano (Portugal) and the Grand Lodge of Italy. Freemasons of Europe discussed with EU's leaders on the establishment of parameters for the society of tomorrow in Europe,* page 269

Picture 120. *" Beyond Glory" , acrylic on wood by Tamara Nikolic,* page 272

Picture 121. *Symbols of the Royal Arch Degrees –Keystone on the top of the arch and the Ark of the Covenant,* page 285

Picture 122. *Royal Arch Apron (English),* page 285

Picture 123. *Royal Arch Apron (American),* page 285

Picture 124. *The Symbols of the Cryptic degrees,* page 289

Picture 125 - 128. *Knight Templar - American regalia (top left)*, *Knight Templar - English regalia (top right)*, *Breast Jewels of the Orders—Knight of Malta, Knight of the Red Cross, and Knight Templar (left)*, *The Emblem of the Order of the Temple (below)* , page 291

Picture 129. *Regalia of the Fourteen Degree—Perfect Elu,* page 296

Picture 130. *Regalia of the Eighteen Degree - Knight Rose Croix,* page 298

Picture 131. *Regalia of the Thirtieth Degree - Knight Kadosh,* page 301

Picture 132. *Regalia of the Thirty Second Degree - Master of the Royal Secret,* page 302

Picture 133. *The Emblem of the Thirty Third Degree- Inspector General,* page 303

Picture 134. *Swedish Rite Regalia,* page 305

Picture 135—136. *Royal Order of Scotland Regalia (top) and Royal Order of Scotland Seal (bottom),* page 315

A NOTE TO THE READER

In the past fifteen years I wrote numerous papers, essays, and books on the subject of Freemasonry. Certainly the most notable were books <u>Royal Art -Three Centuries of Freemasonry</u> (2006), and <u>The Purpose of Freemasonry</u> (2008). Both titles were well received by the Masonic and general public in the U.S. and abroad and affirmatively reviewed by a number of prominent Masonic scholars.

Today, as an author, I am turning more and more towards fiction writing based on my research in Alchemy and Astrology. Nevertheless, I feel need to close the circle of my endeavors in Freemasonry. Mark Twain once wrote: "The time to begin writing an article is when you have finished it to your satisfaction. By that time you begin to clearly and logically perceive what it is you really want to say." In the spirit of Mark Twain's wisdom, I offer to readers my final work on this topic - <u>On the Square – Decoding Freemasonry</u>. In its essence, it is a compilation of my previous writings, with a number of revisions and additions.

Masonic scholarship was, for a larger part of its history, victim of the circumstances and conditions that existed in the Masonic community worldwide. At the very beginning, three hundred years ago, scholars were struggling with the few available medieval manuscripts in order to come to the valid conclusions.

Today, authors are drowning in the volumes of accumulated material, trying to separate facts from fiction.

Additionally, the division between Anglo-American and French Freemasons, one hundred and thirty years ago, caused by different understandings of Masonic principles, resulted in the development of two parallel schools of Masonic thought. Each school was concerned with the study of their own strain of Freemasonry, completely ignorant of the existence and equally valid experiences of the other group.

In this book I tried to make an overview, as impartially as possible, of many different interpretations of the concept of Freemasonry, its symbolism, teachings, rituals, and history. Nonetheless, I could not escape the temptation of adding my own understandings, particularly in the chapters regarding different traditions and concepts (Three Tradition and Two Concepts), and the future of Freemasonry (At the Dawn of the Third Millennium). After all, the purpose of any scholarship is to add another spark to ever burn the flame of human desire of knowledge.

Not claiming to be an authority on the subject, but just a passionate seeker after truth, I humbly offer my thoughts to curious readers, with intent to provoke their further inquiry on this valuable topic. Some may be impressed and enriched or enlightened, others angered and disturbed, but I hope to leave no-one indifferent.

STEVAN V. NIKOLIC

ON THE SQUARE

Picture 2. *The Great Geometrician of the Universe*—acrylic painting on canvas by Tamara Nikolic

1

INTRODUCTION

It is exactly two hundred ninety six years since the "premier" Grand Lodge of Free Masons was founded in England. On St. John the Baptist's Day, in June of 1717, members of four London Lodges met at the "Goose and Gridiron" Ale House. The Assembly and Feast was held and the Grand Master was elected. This event, known among Masonic scholars as the "Revival of 1717" brought the society of Freemasons into the public prominence. Since that time more than sixty thousand titles were published on the subject of Freemasonry throughout the world. Statistically that would be one new book every second day. There were more books published on the history of Freemasonry than any other single historical subject in the same time period. One would think that this enormous amount of material written by Freemasons and non-Freemasons alike would by now have covered all aspects of the phenomenon of Freemasonry and satisfied the curiosity of the readers. Many believe this to be far from the truth. There are several reasons for such a position. The first one is in the relation to the authorship.

Some of the authors, who are Freemasons, lack adequate methodology and objectivity in their handling of the research material. This is particularly true of the works written in the eighteenth and nineteenth century, before the appearance of the so

-called "authentic" or "realistic" school of Masonic research. C.W. Leadbeater, noted Theosophist and Masonic scholar, tried in 1920s, to classified the study of Freemasonry in four basic schools of Masonic thought: The Authentic school – coming out of critical research based on the facts; The Anthropological school – where the results of the research in Anthropology were applied to a study of Masonry; the Mystical school – which examined Freemasonry as a concept of human's "spiritual awakening and inner development; and the Occult school – where the goal was attainment of the conscious union with God through the higher knowledge and mental, emotional, and physical training. This classification never took a hold, since most of the books written by Masons were, anyway, unbalanced mix of two or three of these tendencies in Masonic scholarship.

On the other hand, a number of the books written by trained researchers and professional historians, often lack the "insider's understanding" of important components of Freemasonry, only available to one who is initiated into, and instructed in its Mysteries. There are, as well, numerous books that could be classified as "anti-Masonic", where authors were trying, for various reasons, to represent Freemasonry to the reader in as negative a light as possible. As a matter of fact, one of the very first works written on the subject of Freemasonry could fit into this category.

In 1730, Samuel Prichard, an ex-Freemason, wrote the pamphlet **"Masonry Dissected"**, with the expressed purpose of *"preventing so many credulous Persons [from] being drawn into so pernicious a Society"* as the author clearly states in his *"vindication"*. It is ironic, to say at least, that Prichard's pamphlet, which contained written down and "exposed" early

Masonic Ritual, represents today one of the most valuable Masonic historic documents. In the same year, Martin Clare, a London schoolmaster and Freemason wrote **"Defence of Masonry"** as a prompt reply to Prichard's pamphlet.

The subject of Freemasonry is very complex. After almost three hundred years of Masonic scholarship, the seemingly simple task of defining Freemasonry proved to be so controversial endeavor that those who practice it never agreed upon any of the existed definitions as universal. Prominent Masonic scholar, H. W. Coil, Sr. wrote in his book, **Conversations on Freemasonry:** *"The more there are who attempt to explain what Freemasonry comprises or teaches or stands for, the more their disagreements seem to multiply and clash."* Perhaps the beauty and the reason behind the longevity of the concept of Freemasonry lies in its ability to provide different things and satisfy the needs of so many different people.

The meaning of Freemasonry and its philosophy is masterfully expressed using symbols. That everything is a symbol, with multiple meanings on different levels, is one of the very first lessons to students of the "Royal Art", as Freemasonry is called among those who practice it. Books on Masonic symbolism are like a never-ending story that does not teach but only inspire. To claim to have written a conclusion to such a book is to deceive oneself into achieving the impossible. To learn to open one's eyes and look inward, into deepest corners of our subconscious, is the ultimate goal.

Knowledge of Masonic Degrees, Rites (Degree Systems) and Rituals is essential to all aspiring Freemasons, and this subject is well covered by a number of Masonic scholars. At the same time non-Masonic writers generally appear confused in their writings on this subject, often mixing up meanings, overstating importance and misplacing the origins of different degrees and Rites. This is further complicated with differences in practice of the Ritual that exist between various Masonic organizations throughout the world. Often, books written by Freemasons practicing certain Rites would endorse only those particular Rituals they use, without ever mentioning the existence of other equally valid Rites in use by Freemasons elsewhere.

The question of the origin of Freemasonry is another intriguing point of interest for many authors. There are several theories in existence, but lack of material evidence prevents giving substantial advantage to any of them. More so, such situation opens up the doors for further speculation by imaginative writers, in some cases bordering on science fiction. Recent archeological discoveries proving that some Biblical stories may not be legends after all, gave rise to renewed speculations by a number of scholars regarding legends of the origin of the Craft.

Interestingly enough, out of the vast number of books published on Masonry, most of the written material is by Freemasons and examines the history of Freemasonry, generally outside of the context of the social, economic and political conditions of the given time and place. This approach puts Freemasonry into its own artificial vacuum of historical existence, as it is untouched and unchanged by contemporary events. At the same time, historians, while writing the history of the last three hundred years, were for the most part ignoring the existence of Freemasonry and its possible influence. One will seldom find that any historical event or personalities of this period were examined in the context of, or in correlation to, Freemasonry. It is only in last twenty years that phenomenon of Freemasonry is starting to be taken seriously by some in the academic community who are becoming more aware of its validity as a historical research subject. There is, of course, a third group of authors, who, in developing their "conspiracy theories", like to view Freemasonry as a major culprit in the history of the world.

Freemasonry today, structure of its organizations and its future is the subject least written about by the contemporary authors. So much has been said about the past and it seems as though many have forgotten that Freemasonry is in the present as well. Does Freemasonry have the same meaning to a man today as it had to a man of the early eighteenth century? Does it need to change or stay firm in its tenets, its principles, and Ritual? What is its place in the fast changing global society? Are Freemasons a secret society, with dangerous agenda, as their enemies would like to present or a philanthropic association of good men (and women) trying to become better and improve the society they live in? Can we subscribe to the controversial idea that the phenomenon of Freemasonry has a life of its own within our collective unconscious that sustains itself regardless of human destiny?

There are many unsolved conflicts within the worldwide Masonic community today. The question of territorial integrity of Grand Lodges has caused division between recognized and unrecognized entities. Different interpretations of teachings and principles of Freemasonry have caused division between "regular" and "liberal" Grand Lodges. Many Masons are completely ignorant of the fact that female Freemasonry and mixed groups of male and female Freemasons exist, and that are getting stronger. The number of independent esoteric groups and their membership claiming to be Masonic is on the rise worldwide. Membership in some Masonic organizations is declining while at the same time in others is going up. What can we learn from each other? What can Freemasonry offer to humankind in the future? At a certain point during the Masonic Ritual, the candidate going through the degree is asked: "Where are you going." His answer is "In search of Light in Freemasonry". Perhaps the question to be asked now should be "Is Freemasonry today in search of its own identity?"

Picture 3. *From the Ceremony of the Opening of the Grand Lodge Annual Assembly - United Grand Lodges of Serbia,*
Photo©2010 UGLS

THE MEANING OF FREEMASONRY

What is Freemasonry? Any Freemason could give a straightforward answer without too much doubt as to what it should be, but at the same time, he is aware that there are dozens of other Freemasons who, with equal certainty, would give completely different answers. Most likely all of the answers would be correct. The reason for this lies in the very nature of Freemasonry itself.

While for some it is the "very essence" of all religions, for some a bit religious, for others it is a set of lectures on morality and philosophy of life that has nothing whatsoever to do with religion. For some, who believe that Freemasonry is a school of Mysteries, the lodge room is a holy place; reincarnation of the Sanctum Sanctorum or Holy of Holies of King Solomon's Temple, where one enters upon the path of reunification with the Divine within himself. For others it is just a meeting room where members of the group, through the use of the symbols during the Ritual work, try to comprehend the psychology of our inner being and to convey lessons of morality to initiates in a closed private setting. There are even those who think that Freemasonry should be reduced to a social club or fraternity bound only to charity and community work. Contrary to this, there are those who believe that charity work should be eliminated or just limited to fraternal benevolence. All of these opinions one will find, possibly even within one single Masonic Lodge, among men who practice Freemasonry together in the same room, use the very same ritual, and govern themselves according to the same rules and regulations. So then, how one could come up with the correct definition of Freemasonry or explain meaning when, by its own nature, it allows so many different interpretations of its character.

We often come across the following statement, usually in pamphlets published by Grand Lodges, that Freemasonry is *"a peculiar system of morality, veiled in allegory and illustrated with symbols"*. In England, one would be informed that Freemasonry is *"secular, fraternal and charitable organization which teaches moral lessons and self-knowledge through participation in a progression of allegorical two-part plays."* For some Masonic organizations in continental Europe *"Freemasonry is an initiatory and philanthropic society open to men and women of good will and high ethical standards. Their methods represent an access to perfectibility and to self-discovery through the use of universal symbols."* In the United States *"Freemasonry is dedicated to the Brotherhood of Man under the Fatherhood of God"* and it is *"oldest philanthropic, community oriented organization in the world."*

Problem with the most of the definitions is that, by trying to express very complex nature of the certain concept in compact form of one sentence, they often miss the point. An additional obstacle in developing an official definition is in "political correctness" which most of the Masonic organizations observe in their social settings. Many members of the fraternity like to say that Freemasonry is a way of life, but the closest one could come to short correct definition is to say that Freemasonry is philosophical concept practiced by the members of the fraternal organization, who are brought together by shared ideals of both ethical and metaphysical nature.

It is obvious that the general definition of Freemasonry, given in one sentence, could not cover all of the properties of this phenomenon. Another problem with a general definition is the factor of time. Can we take the very same subject, unchanged and constant, place it in different periods, and expect it to be understood in the same way and have the same meaning or even expect it to stay unchanged? In addition, the final problem is that the very same Freemasons who were insisting on the "unchanged, constant nature of its teachings and character" constantly were changing Freemasonry through its history.

To define Freemasonry as a philosophical system we first have to remind ourselves about basic ideas behind the term "philosophy". Many scholars claim that Pythagoras was the first one to use this term, which in Greek means, "love of wisdom". It is understood as a study or *"methodical work of thought"* of the general questions regarding human life and universe. According to modern definition there are six fields of philosophical study. Logic-dealing with the concept of reason; Ethics-study of morality, human character and concept of "good"; Metaphysics - concerned with the nature of "being" including theology and cosmology; Psychology- study of the complex field of mental phenomena; Esthetics-dealing with the nature of beauty, harmony and elegance; and Epistemology concerned with the knowledge as an absolute form and with the concept of "truth".

Freemasonry could be understood as a practical or applied

philosophical system where those involved in, are trying to implement results of the abstract work - to their self-improvement; to the general perfection of their surroundings; and to the better understanding of many of their realities. Through the symbolic use of the working tools of Masonry, they are implementing Logic, norms of Ethics, and principles of Esthetics. Through the scenography and choreography of their Rites and Rituals, they are entering upon the fields of metaphysics and psychology. Through the scenarios of the various degrees, they are involved into Epistemology. One could say that a difference between traditional concept of philosophy and Freemasonry is in their position toward the object of research. While traditional philosophy speculates upon existing conditions of our realities, Freemasonry creates scenarios of various conditions in the closed setting of the Lodge room, in an effort to actively change our understanding and our position toward them; all in a belief that this will lead to self-improvement and attainment of absolute knowledge. This work of theirs, Freemasons call "Royal Art". The term first appeared in reference to Freemasonry in the **Constitutions** written by Dr. James Anderson in 1723. He never gave reasons for referring to Masonry as to a "Royal Art".

As an historical phenomenon Freemasonry is "an oath-bound fraternal order", inspired, among many other things, with the teachings and organization of the medieval fraternity of stonemasons. Freemasons like to refer to themselves as to "speculative Masons" in order to distinguish the nature of their work and association from the activities of those members of the Masonic guilds involved in the actual building trade, whom they called "operative Masons". There are two important characteristics of the connection between speculative Freemasons and operative stonemasons: first- requirement of an oath from a member; and second - fact that structure and traditions of the medieval guilds of stonemasons were used as a setting for philosophical speculations and not of some other group of medieval craftsmen, artisans or tradesmen.

As to the first question, having an oath as a condition to join any group means that there is a set of rules, teachings or some kind of concept, that one would need to subscribe to and hold to in order to be a member of the given group. An oath puts members of the group in a different relationship with each other and separates them from the world. A particular characteristic of the Masonic oath is that, besides being an oath binding each one to the other members of the group and to certain rules and teachings; it is an "oath of secrecy" as well. This indicates that there is some part of the concept that needs to stay private and not to be revealed to outsiders. That this part of the concept must be very important we can conclude from the severe physical punishments originally prescribed in the oath for any member who reveals the secrets and breaks his oath. One could understand the presence of the punishments in the oath of the medieval stonemasons. Breaking the oath and revealing potential secrets of the trade would be equal to "industrial espionage" today, where the professional prospects of the owner of the "know how" would be damaged by making it public knowledge.

In contrast, in "speculative Masonry" there are no "trade secrets". The subject of work of the speculative Masons is the man himself or rather his "non-physical side". What could be so immensely important about the concept related to such an abstract subject, to make it oath-binding, secret, and with the punishment of death for those who reveal it? There are two answers to this question. One relates to the socio-political conditions in which Freemasonry was developing, where religious dogmas were often the only accepted philosophy and prejudices of all kinds standard form of behaving. In such conditions any knowledge or understanding of human circumstances and his relation to the Divine, different from the accepted teachings of the official religion or State, expressed publicly, could potentially have severe consequences for those subscribing to them. This is easy to understand because even today we are not far from such conditions. Unfortunately, there are still places around the world, where those propagating equality of all people regardless of their religious beliefs, race or gender, would not live long enough to prove their point. Second answer refers to the symbolic nature of the punishments, where physical pain to the flesh is symbol of the self-inflicting mental pain that one may experience if failing to meet the ethical standards of his own conscience. Today, in number of Masonic organizations throughout the world, reference to punishment is dropped from the obligations and important symbolism connected to it is lost.

Let us look now at the second question: "Why guilds of stonemasons?" We know that speculative Freemasons of today are still subscribing to the "Ancient Rules, Regulations, and Legends of Origin" of the medieval operative stonemasons. The use of their working tools acquired new symbolic meaning in the teachings of speculative Freemasons. Just as operative stonemasons did in the past, Freemasons of today meet in Lodges, governed by a Master and Wardens, have secret passwords and signs and they subscribe to the observance of the principles of brotherly love, equality, mutual aid, and assistance.

There were few important characteristics of the medieval stonemasons. First, they were, for the most part, free men; free to travel around, free to learn by observation, through building experience and interaction with each other and be, thereby, free to communicate their knowledge to those whom they find worthy. Second, to be a stonemason and builder, even today, presupposes that one has to have a broad knowledge of the different arts and sciences to be able to put together a structurally safe, useful and aesthetically pleasing edifice. This means that the medieval stonemasons had to be very knowledgeable people for their time. Nevertheless, that itself does not explain their connection to Speculative Freemasonry. At the same time, there were other organized groups of men equally educated and even more knowledgeable. The answer lays in the nature of their knowledge. The art of building was the only field of human activity based exclusively on "reason". The only way to build any structure is through the applications of geometry, mathematical calculations, and physical laws of nature. The cathedrals, temples, and mosques were not built through the power of faith but through the power of reasoning. Stone was not sitting on the top of the stone forming a wall because Pope or Ayatollah issued an edict to that fact or Emperor ordered to be so, but because stonemason cut the stones square and placed them in balanced position one on top of the other by the aid of square, plumb and level. Somewhere in the process of building beautiful structures, that may be divinely inspired, but still in accordance with natural laws, somebody perceived that the reasoning behind the building art could be applied, with equal results, to the "building" of human mind and conscience. With this, speculative Freemasonry was born. The adoption of operative stonemasons as their forerunners was just a natural progression in the application of knowledge from concrete to abstract, from physical to spiritual and from particular to universal.

As an organizational concept Freemasonry is a complex network of Lodges subordinate to the Grand Lodges or Grand Orients (as they are called by some), spread throughout the world. Over the period of some three hundred years Grand Lodges (Grand Orients) became Sovereign institutions with their Constitutions governing Lodges and their members and with Rules and Regulations regarding every imaginable eventuality: from official teachings and Ritual to the mutual recognition and definition of Freemasonry. The majority of Grand Lodges prescribe through their Constitutions as a requirement for somebody to become a Freemason that he has to be a free man and "believe in One God and in the immortality of the soul". Belief in "One God" is closely connected with the acceptance of the "Holy Bible" as the "Greatest Light in Freemasonry" and with the requirement that the open Bible or some other "Book of Sacred Law" be present in the Lodge room during the time that the Lodge is at work. Grand Lodges and Grand Orients that subscribe to these principles consider themselves "regular". There are also Grand Lodges that do not subscribe to all of these principles. In these Grand Lodges requirement of the belief in God was, as a part of religious dogma, substituted with **"absolute Liberty of conscience and the solidarity of Humanity"** and the potential candidate is not asked about his religious beliefs. Use of the Bible or other "Book of Sacred Law" during the ritual was left to the discretion of the individual Lodges to decide. These Grand Lodges and Grand Orients call themselves "liberal" or "cosmopolitan".

All Freemasons, regardless of their strain of Freemasonry, agree that Freemasonry is non-dogmatic. It is not a religion, sect, social club, business network or political party. This gentle concept values freedom of thought among all human beings, regardless of their station in life. The language of symbols is used to search and lead one on the path to inner development. Freemasons of different ethnic origins, religious beliefs, and political opinions are all united in the fact that they are seekers after universal truths and self-perfection. While they are building their **"inner Temple",** they hope that **"as living stones"** they will fit themselves into that Temple of a more enlightened world, **"not built by hands",** but through practice of great principles of Love, Truth, mutual tolerance, and Benevolence for all human kind.

Picture 4. *Symbols of Freemasonry*

Picture 5. *Front Page of the Anderson's Constitutions of the Freemasons from 1723*

3

THE VERY ESSENCE

From the very beginning of organized Freemasonry in the early eighteenth century, some Masonic scholars were insisting on the very deep religious character of Freemasonry. Through comparative research in various religions they were trying to prove that the teachings of Freemasonry were nothing else but the basic teachings or the "very essence" of all major religions or as some of them used to call it, "universal religion". The religious character of Freemasonry was and still is one of the most sensitive questions of the nature of Masonic teachings. There are several issues one has to deal with here. The first one is certainly the religious references in the numerous Masonic Rites and Rituals (particularly in the Scottish Rite). The second issue is the writings of some prominent Masonic authors, like Albert Pike, Manly P. Hall, Arthur E. Waite, Albert Mackey, and Thomas M. Stewart, all of whom were strong proponents of the notion that Freemasonry is either a religion or a religious institution. The third issue has to do with similarities between Freemasonry and Deism, and the final question is the official position of the Grand Lodges regarding the relationship between Freemasonry and organized religion.

Freemasons meet in their Temple. Every Masonic Temple, when built, was properly dedicated with corn, wine, and oil. All

Temples are symbolically situated East-West. They are furnished with an Altar, on which are placed the Three Great Lights – Holy Bible, Square and Compasses. At the opening and closing of the Lodge and on other occasions during the ritual work, invocation for the blessing of the Most High and the prayers are recited by all present. Various Rites, similar to those in religious Temples and Churches, are performed. We ask of the Initiates their profession of faith in the Almighty before initiation and we ask them to bow with reverence and humility at his Holy name, while the Book of the sacred Law is open upon the Altar. Everything we have mentioned so far, except the presence of the square and compasses, could apply to practices of any other established religion. Even more so, in some of the Scottish Rite degrees and ceremonies, the Ritual performed is taken directly from the Catholic Liturgy or inspired by it. The search for the "Lost Word" in the degree of Rose-Croix is directly inspired by the teachings of the Christian Gospels. The Mystic Banquet in the Ceremony of the Feast of the Paschal Lamb is nothing else but a Masonic reenactment of the Holy Eucharist. The Lecture of the Holy Royal Arch Degree, or the lecture of the "Key-stone" from the Mark Master Degree, where "the stone that builders rejected has become the head stone of the corner" are nothing more than references to the traditional Biblical lessons. One can say, without too much doubt, that Rites performed in the Lodge rooms are no more than allegorical plays and prayers based on the Biblical lessons.

It seems that a number of Masonic authors were convinced that Freemasonry is a religion. The most notable was Albert Pike (1809-1891), who in several places in his book <u>Morals and</u>

<u>Dogma,</u> claims Freemasonry to be the foundation of all religions: *"It (Masonry) is the universal, eternal, immutable religion, such as God planted in the heart of universal humanity. No creed has ever been long-lived that was not built on this foundation. It is the base and they are the superstructure."* (Page 219) He also refers to the Masonic Temple as a religious Temple: *"Every Masonic Temple is a Temple of Religion, and its teachings are instructions in religion."* (Page 213)

Albert Mackey has a similar opinion in his <u>Encyclopedia of Freemasonry</u>: *"Masonry, is in every sense of the word, except one, and that its least philosophical, an eminently religious institution - that it is indebted solely to the religious element which it contains for its origin and for its continued existence and that without this religious element it would scarcely be worthy of cultivation by the wise and good."..."Freemasonry is NOT Christianity nor a substitute for it"..."But the religion of Masonry is not sectarian. It admits men of every creed within its hospitable bosom, rejecting institutions; and on this ground mainly, if not alone, should the religious Mason defend it."* (Encyclopedia of Freemasonry, Albert G. Mackey, Revised Edition, 1921, pages 618, 619) Arthur Edward Waite in his New Encyclopedia of Freemasonry has a very similar opinion: *"There is a fund of inconsequence which characterizes a great many good people under our various obediences who pass for serious, and they would- I presume – be astonished beyond words if they were told that apart from religion Masonry has no title to existence, because its much-lauded "system of morality" is either a gate which leads to religion or a gate which leads nowhere."* (New Encyclopedia of Freemasonry, A. E. Waite, 1996 Edition, Page 329)

Manly P. Hall goes even further, stressing the universal nature of Masonic teachings: *"The true Mason is not creed-bound. He realizes with the divine illumination of his lodge that as a Mason his religion must be universal: Christ, Buddha or Mohammed, the name means little, for he recognizes only the light and not the bearer. He worships at every shrine, bows before every altar, whether in temple, mosque or cathedral, realizing with his truer understanding the oneness of all spiritual truth."* (The Lost Keys of Freemasonry, Manly P. Hall, 33rd, page 65, Macoy Publishing and Masonic Supply Co. Richmond, Va., 1976.).

Thomas M. Stewart in his book Symbolic Teachings, published in 1915 in Cincinnati, probably presents the best case for Freemasonry as the "very essence" of all religions. He starts with the assumption that Freemasonry is as old as the human race. According to this understanding, once man was able of rational thinking, which separated him from the rest of the creation, Freemasonry was born. According to this understanding, the prehistorically original religion of men was nothing else but "Freemasonry". Everything else after that was just a build-up of the original understanding corrupted by ethnic, cultural, social, and political factors. The truth, if it is the truth, must be one and common to all religions. God, if it is God, must be One, the creation is one, (or otherwise it would be more than one world), Providence is One, and the Destiny of men is one. There are only many different interpretations of the very same truth, each with a claim to exclusivity. Freemasonry is the only all-inclusive teaching, the "custodian of truth", encompassing all of the existing religious teachings in one, universal truth. This is the basic understanding of those who believe that Freemasonry is the very essence of all religious teachings.

Let us look now at Deism and its similarities to Freemasonry. Deism is a religious movement and philosophy that became popular in France, England, and in North America in the 17th and 18th centuries. It exists to this day in the form of Classical Deism and Modern Deism. Deism derives the existence and nature of God from reason and personal experience, in opposition to the theism of religions like Judaism, Christianity and Islam, which rely on revelation in sacred scriptures or the testimony of the Prophets. Deism was never an organized religion but rather a movement of philosophers and free-thinkers. Efforts by some French Deists to transform catholic churches into Deistic Temples following the French Revolution ended up in great failure. Some of the prominent Freemasons of the eighteenth and nineteenth centuries were Deists. When one says that, it does not mean that they belonged to some church or organization of Deists, but just that their outlook on the nature of God and our whole existence was rather Deistic. Among them, we can mention Benjamin Franklin, Voltaire, George Washington, and Alexander Pope. Deists, like Freemasons, express belief in the existence of one and only one God.

God's powers are displayed in the world, created, sustained, and ordered by means of divinely sanctioned natural laws, both moral and physical. Like Freemasonry, Deism encourages the study of natural arts and sciences in order to understand better the divine plan and fit into it. For Deists, as well as Freemasons, the natural law requires the leading of a moral life, rendering to God, one's neighbor, and one's self what is due to each. Deists believe that "men have been endowed with a rational nature which alone allows them to know truth and their duty when they think and choose in conformity with nature. Likewise, Masons were symbolically given builders' tools to enable them to arrive at universal truth and knowledge of God and themselves, through rational thinking as well as faith. Deists, like Freemasons, believe that the soul of men is immortal.

Of course, there are significant differences between Freemasonry and Deism. For one, Deism (very much like other established religions) denies the validity of any other religious beliefs or practices conflicting with their tenets. For Freemasons, any true religion is compatible with Freemasonry. The practice of Prayer and the use of the Book of the Sacred Law in the Lodge rooms completely contradict deistic teachings. Furthermore, ritualistic practices in some of the Masonic degrees are much different in character than anything deists, with their rational mind, would ever subscribe to.

The official position of the established Masonic Institutions was from the very beginning of their public existence in 1717, that Freemasonry is not a religion, nor is it a substitute for religion. Even more so, efforts were made on several occasions, to purge the Rituals of explicit religious references. Some of the liberal Jurisdictions went even further with the exclusion of the belief in God as a requirement to become a Mason. The regular Masonic Jurisdictions require of their members belief in God as part of the obligation of every responsible adult, but advocate no sectarian faith or practice. Ceremonies in the Lodge room include prayers, but only in order to reaffirm each individual's dependence on God and to seek divine guidance. Freemasonry is open to men of any faith, but religion may not be discussed at Masonic meetings. Freemasons believe that there is one God, but accept that we all have our different ways to seek, and to express our knowledge of Him. Masons use the non-sectarian term "The Grand Architect of the Universe", when addressing or referring to Deity. By this, Masons of different faiths may pray and practice together. Official claims that Freemasonry lacks basic elements of religion could be summarized as:

(a) It has no dogma or theology, no wish or means to enforce religious orthodoxy.

(b) It offers no sacraments.

(c) It does not claim to lead to salvation by works, by secret knowledge, or by any other means. The secrets of Freemasonry are concerned with modes of recognition, not with the means of salvation."

These official claims are based on a very narrow definition of religion. Contrary to this, Albert Mackey in his encyclopedia of Freemasonry uses several definitions which are very affirmative in proving that Freemasonry is religion. Of course, regular Masonic institutions never fail to claim that they are far from indifferent toward religion. Without interfering in anyone's religious practices, they encourage all of their members to follow their own faith, and to place their duty to God above all other duties. Masons believe that their moral teachings are acceptable to all religions.

Unfortunately, most of the established religions never shared this opinion. Exclusive and sectarian in their nature, most of the religious institutions see in Freemasonry a competitive teaching that is trying to take away believers from their fold. The all-inclusive nature of Freemasonry is often seen as a false religion. The truth of the matter is that Freemasonry helps individuals to a mature appreciation of the religion of their choice. Often, that results in more active practice of their religion. In many Anglican, Lutheran and other protestant churches, one will find that the most active laymen are Freemasons. Not to mention, that many Priests, some very prominent in their churches, are members of the Brotherhood of Freemasons.

Picture 6. *The Universal Religion*
©2007, By Tamara Nikolic

4

MASONIC SYMBOLS DECODED

A symbol is a physical or abstract image that represents something different or more than the basic elements incorporated in that image. To most of the people symbols are a kind of "universal language" that enables them to function faster, understand clearer, and interact without difficulty with each other. We have to recognize, however, that often the very same symbol in different settings and for different groups has a completely different meaning.

In Freemasonry, symbols are much more than just a universal language. In the psychological inner world of human beings, symbols often represent important knowledge or power hidden deep within our unconscious, which one can intuitively reach but not verbally express or describe. In some of the Masonic Rituals, the candidate going through the initiation is told: *"Here, everything is a symbol."* In other words, it is said that only if one learns to look into the symbolic nature of everything, does one have a chance to comprehend the full meaning of many different levels of our constantly changing reality. In doing so, a person will enlighten oneself and learn the ultimate truth, or in the words of the Masonic Ritual *"gather, that which was scattered"* and *"find that which was lost"*.

A number of Masonic authors have tried to list the most important symbols used in Freemasonry and to explain their meanings. A. Mackey came up with 19 symbols, C. Hunt with 21 and H.W. Coil with over 90. This rather simplistic approach to Masonic symbolism often confuses readers more than helps. The reason for this is that, as it was to be expected, none of these lists matches. There are only five common symbols in the Mackeys' and Hunts' lists. Further more, just the ability to recognize the prescribed meaning of a particular symbol does not make a Freemason. Only by implementing an understanding of the nature of these symbols in everyday life and conduct, can one hope to perceive clearly and balance one's physical and abstract realities. Freemasons believe that in doing so, one necessarily places oneself on the never-ending journey from the dark of ignorance towards the light of truth; from meaningless prejudice towards meaningful loving kindness; from despair towards happiness and, finally, from the particular and natural towards the universal and divine.

PREPARATION FOR THE JOURNEY

This journey starts for the candidate with the decision to join the Order. Once somebody led by his intuition rather than rational thinking, steps on that misty path towards initiation into Freemasonry, knowingly or unknowingly he separates and isolates himself from his profane everyday life in order to examine himself. This natural need of the candidate is recognized and accommodated through the process of preparation for the initiation in the "Preparation Room" or "Chamber of Reflection" as it is called in some Rites.

We could learn from the pages of history that the Sages, Prophets and the Wiseman of Ancient times would give up all of their worldly possessions before they would start their own journeys towards enlightenment. After exchanging their clothes with those of the beggars, taking off their shoes, and in such condition, barefoot and dressed in rags, they would travel east, towards the Sun -source of light and life - through the foreign and harsh lands, in search of greater knowledge and inner peace. During these voyages, they would depend completely for their survival upon the mercy of unknown inhabitants of the countries through which they would pass. They would repay the assistance given them by sharing their acquired knowledge. In an exchange they would learn even more, all in the hope that one day, they would arrive at that "summit of human knowledge", and attain inner peace and perfection through the realization of absolute truth.

In the same way, the candidate for initiation is placed in the "Preparation Room", a small room adjoining the Lodge room, where he is "divested of all metallic substances" such as jewelry, watches and money, symbolically representing all the impurities of life. He is asked then to take off his clothes and put on the rags of the initiate to let him know that worldly riches and fancy clothes will not make a difference on the path that he is about to take. He is commanded to take off one shoe in order to go into the initiation wearing only one shoe. Symbolism of this act is dual. On the one hand the initiate identifies with the "seeker after that which was lost", like Jason – the man with one shoe in the ancient story of the Golden Fleece. On the other hand, he is reminded of the obligation, as in the Rite of Discalceation, to uncover the feet on approaching sacred ground. For this reason, in some of the Masonic Rites the candidate is barefoot on both feet. He is then blindfolded, as this was the state in which the candidate lived in his profane life - in complete darkness of ignorance. The only way to get to the light of knowledge is through the initiation conducted by fellow human beings in whom the blindfolded candidate has to place all his trust. The candidate is bound in chains or has a rope wrapped around his neck. In ancient times, it was often the case that one condemned to death was forced to carry the instrument of his death himself to the place of execution. Jesus carried his cross, so those condemned to death by hanging carried the ropes already wrapped around their necks. This was to teach the candidate that the road to enlightenment is often beset with difficulties, suffering and even death and that the difference between life and death lay in our fear of the unknown and not in the nature of death. For we know that death is the beginning of life as birth is the beginning of death. In order to be born, we first have to die.

The candidate, properly dressed for the initiation, as already described, is asked there to write his "Philosophical Will" to be read later in the Lodge. He is alone, seated at the table on which are placed a sheet of paper and a pencil, with a lighted candle providing the only illumination, a piece of bread, glass of water, hourglass, skull and bones and three small dishes, one containing salt and the other two sulfur and mercury. On the wall is a picture of a cockerel and the word *"Vitriol"* written in white letters on a black board. V. I. T. R. I. O. L. is an acronym for an expression in Latin urging one to examine oneself: *"Visita Interriora Terrae, Rectificando Invenies Occultum Lapidem"* (meaning: visit the center of the earth and through purification you shall find the hidden stone). The cockerel is there ready to announce the beginning of the new day and appearance of the Light with the rising of the Sun. On the same poster, two words are written: "Vigilance" and "Perseverance" - two essential characteristics of one desiring to reach the "Light of the new day". The hourglass reminds us of the passing and reversibility of time. As in alchemy, salt represents fire delivered from water. Bringing together salt and sulfur is a symbolic representation of opposites feeding each other; light and darkness, good and evil, life and death. Through all of these symbols the candidate is taught that nothing that exists in our reality is inherently bad or good. Only humans, through their actions and thoughts make and perceive things as such. Opposites are an essential part of our reality and by their interaction the energy - sustainer of life and all-out existence in the universe, is born.

Picture 7.
The Chamber of Reflection

ENTRANCE INTO THE TEMPLE

After the conclusion of his meditations, the candidate is led to the door of the Lodge room, where he is asked to give an alarm at the door to inform those inside that he seeks admittance. In some Masonic Rites, this alarm is given by three knocks at the door, which allude to the quotation from the New Testament that reads: *"Ask and it shall be given you; seek and ye shall find; knock and it shall be opened unto you"*. (Luke,11:9). In other Rites there is only one knock, after which the candidate is informed that upon entering he should stoop low because the doorway is very low. This testifies to the fact that the one seeking admittance is not yet initiated, and not entrusted with the correct manner in which to seek admission, but is a humble seeker worthy of being accepted.

There are many different meanings of the terms "Temple" and "Lodge" in Masonic terminology. Historically, Lodge was an organizational form of the medieval guilds of operative stonemasons. In the Seventeenth century, speculative Freemasons adopted this form, together with the legend of its origin. Practically, the Masonic Lodge is a duly organized group of Freemasons "in good standing", legally empowered by some Grand Lodge or Grand Orient to perform the approved Ritual and ceremonies. The Lodge room is the meeting place of that group, furnished in a particular manner necessary for the performance of these rituals and ceremonies. The Masonic Temple is the building where the Lodge room is situated.

Symbolically, the Lodge room is a representation of King Solomon's Temple. Through the symbols from the building trade and allegories connected with the Legend of the building of King Solomon's Temple, Freemasons are taught important lessons to help them in their individual quest for self-knowledge, moral, and spiritual perfection.

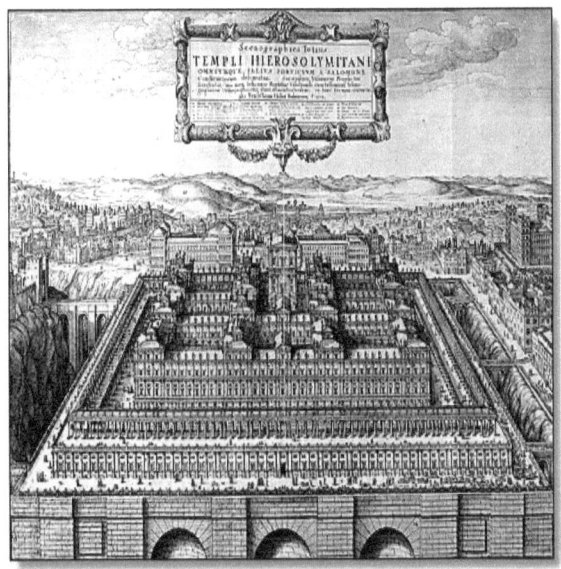

Picture 8. *Solomon's Temple from a 1660 version of the King James Bible*

Picture 9. *The Floor Plan of the King Solomon's Temple*

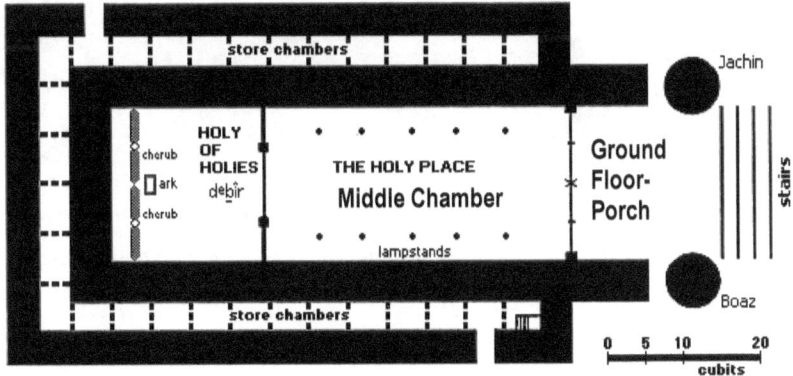

Philosophically, the Lodge room is a representation of the world we live in and the Temple refers to that inner Temple, *"that Temple not made with hands, eternal in the Heavens"*, which each of us must build within our hearts and consciences. In doing so, each of us is hoping to achieve inner peace, recognize and reconnect with the divine within and contribute to the more enlightened world.

Picture 10. *MASONIC TEMPLE – The Lodge room in the Masonic Temple in Belgrade (Serbia) United Grand Lodges of Serbia,* Photo©2010 UGLS

King Solomon's Temple, or the First Temple, as it is often referred to, was described in the Bible (1stKings 6:2) as the magnificent structure. It was located on the historical site of Mount Moriah. According to the Masonic legend, King David made a plan for the erection of the *"permanent dwelling place for the God of Israel"*, but permission from God was granted only to his son, King Solomon, to execute the work. He, with the assistance of Hiram King of Tyre, and his Master builder Hiram Abif, commenced the work in the *"second month of the fourth year of his reign"*. A large number of workers were involved in the construction of the Temple and they were divided according to the level of their skills in three groups.

The biggest group was that of Entered Apprentices – the lowest grade, whose duty was to cut and prepare stone for the building. To perform their duty they used the common gavel, chisel, and twenty-four inch gauge. The second group of workers was that of Fellowcrafts, who had to be more qualified because of the level of knowledge and skill necessary to perform the work assigned to them. The Fellowcrafts used the stones cut and prepared by Apprentices to build massive walls and columns. Their tools were the square, level, plumb, ruler and lever. The third, smallest and most skilled and educated class of workers were Master Masons. Their duty was to supervise the work of Fellowcrafts and Entered Apprentices. Only after being satisfied that the stones were properly prepared and placed with the greatest precision on their assigned places would they give permission for the mortar to be applied to *"connect different parts of [the] building in [to] one common mass"*. For this reason, the tools assigned to them were all of the tools of Masonry and particularly a trowel.

In charge of the whole project were King Solomon, Hiram King of Tyre, and Grand Master Hiram Abif, who drew plans and designs on the Trestle-board every day by the aid of a square and compasses. The Temple was designed so as to have three different sections: the Ground Floor, Middle Chamber, and the Sanctum Sanctorum. Entered Apprentices were allowed access only to the Ground Floor; Fellowcrafts were permitted to enter the Middle Chamber; while the Master Masons performed the work in the Sanctum Sanctorum or "Holy of Holies". The different groups of workmen could be recognized by the manner in which they wore their aprons. They could prove their membership in a particular class of workmen by certain secret signs, grips, and passwords belonging to each of the groups. Legend tells us that King Solomon, Hiram King of Tyre, and Hiram Abif were in possession of the secret Master Mason's Word which they promised to reveal to all "worthy and well-qualified" Fellowcrafts, but only when the Temple is completed and consecrated, and then only in the presence of all three of them. Otherwise, the "secret word" could not be communicated! Three Fellowcrafts, in an attempt to extort the secret word of Master Mason before the completion of the Temple from Grand Master Hiram Abif, became his assassins. They buried his body secretly and marked the spot with a sprig of acacia. The workmen later found his body and the assassins were caught and executed. But the "secret word" was lost, since it could no longer be communicated without the presence of all three: King Solomon, Hiram King of Tyre, and Hiram Abif. The body of Grand Master Hiram Abif was recovered and brought to the Temple for more appropriate burial. By the order of King Solomon, a substitute for the lost word was established for the use of Master Masons until, by the labor of future generations, the lost word could be found and its use reestablished.

The functions and names applied to these three groups of workmen established by King Solomon for the purpose of erecting the Temple were co-opted and adopted by speculative Freemasons to represent the three degrees (or grades) practiced in Freemasonry. When Freemasons meet as Entered Apprentices they are assembled in the Lodge of Entered Apprentices, which is a symbolic representation of the Ground Floor of King Solomon's Temple. Similarly, the Lodge of Fellowcrafts meets in a symbolic representation of the Middle Chamber and the Lodge of Master Masons in the unfinished Sanctum Sanctorum. Entered Apprentice, Fellowcraft, and Master Mason degrees are also called "Craft Degrees" since their lessons are based on the legend connected with the building of the First Temple. Lessons connected with the symbolic use of the tools belonging to a particular degree represent teachings of that degree. "Seven Liberal Arts and Sciences" (Grammar, Rhetoric, Logic, Arithmetic, Geometry, Music and Astronomy) are introduced in the Second or Fellowcraft degree in order to emphasize the importance of education in one's quest for personal enlightenment. The legend of the tragic death and reburial of Hiram Abif, known as the "widow's son", is used as an allegory in the Third (or Master Mason) degree to convey important lessons regarding life and death and the immortality of the soul.

THE PILLARS

On entering the Temple, the initiate necessarily has to pass between two pillars. The <u>Bible</u> informs us (1st Kings 7: 15-21; and 2nd Chronicles 3: 15-17 and 4: 11-13) that two pillars stood in front of King Solomon's Temple. The name of the one on the right was **Jachin** and that of the one on the left was **Boaz**. Scholars continue to question even today whether the left and right are determined by looking from inside or outside of the Temple. We can read in the Masonic Ritual that they were cast of brass and were *"hollow for the purpose of containing the rolls and records which comprised the archives"* of Freemasons. On the top of each of the pillars were chapiters decorated with leaves of lilies – symbolizing peace, a network - symbolizing unity, and the pomegranate - symbolizing plenty. Some Masonic scholars even suggest that the pomegranate might well be the forbidden fruit of the Tree of Knowledge referred to in Genesis. In an ancient Greek story, Persephone was seduced against her will after eating pomegranate seeds and through this the pomegranate became known as the fruit of error.

Two spheres or globes surmount these pillars: one on the top of Boaz - representing the earth, and the other on the top of Jachin - representing the sky and the universe. The two pillars are symbols of the binary nature of our reality. Jachin represents "establishment" but is also referred to as the "Royal pillar". This comes out of the Biblical promise of God to David that God would *"in strength establish"* his kingdom forever. Boaz is the symbol of strength and accordingly, although there is no reference in the <u>Bible</u> for it, it is called the *"Priestly pillar"* (for the strength is in keeping the law of Jehovah). It is also possible that these two pillars are symbols of the Pillar of Cloud and the Pillar of Fire mentioned in Exodus (Ch. 13 and 14). In books on Kabala, we read that the "Tree of Life" was the model for the ground plan of King Solomon's Temple. If we apply that understanding then Boaz would correspond to the Pillar of Severity and Jachin to the Pillar of Mercy. By placing himself between two pillars, upon entering the Lodge, the initiate becomes the third Pillar of Equilibrium and ultimately steps on the path to discovering and understanding the relationship between practical human experiences and the Absolute, Infinite, and Divine.

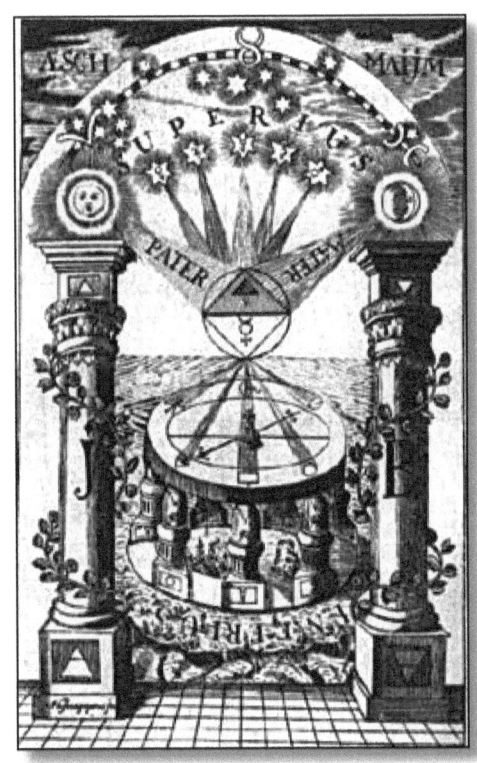

Picture 11. *The Pillars Jachin and Boaz.* From "The Compass of the Wise", Berlin, 1782.

MOSAIC PAVEMENT AND THE TRACING BOARD

In each Lodge room, on the floor, may be seen a mosaic pavement or checkered floor, which consists of black and white square tiles, very much as on the chessboard. Generally, the purpose of the black and white squares of the mosaic pavement is to inspire us into thinking about contradiction and the complimenting of opposites. In some Lodges, the mosaic pavement is surrounded with tiles forming a "tessellated border or indented tessel" and in the center is a tile in the form of a blazing star. According to the Masonic Ritual they are emblematical of human life checkered with good and evil - symbolized by the mosaic pavement; *"manifold blessings and comforts"* that are all around us -symbolized by the indented Tessel; and *"Divine Providence"* – symbolized by the Blazing Star.

In the center of each Lodge, on the floor, is placed the "Tracing Board" or Master's Carpet, which is a drawing of the Masonic symbols, particular to the given degree (grade). Originally, it would have been drawn directly on the floor with chalk before the Lodge started its work and it would be erased after the Lodge was closed. Later, it was drawn on canvas, blackboard or a piece of fabric or leather. In certain Rites it is required from the Apprentice to draw a tracing board of the first degree, from Fellowcraft to do the same on the second degree and Master Masons are responsible for the tracing board of the third degree. In some Masonic groups, it is an adopted practice of having permanent drawings of tracing boards that would be used as needed. Today in many Lodges in the USA and UK, a tracing board for a given degree is a chart with the emblems and symbols of that degree, framed and placed in the east of the Lodge room for the purpose of instruction only. In my opinion, there is much more to the symbolism and a higher purpose in drawing them on the Lodge room floor. By walking around and over it, candidate is positioning himself to receive "Masonic Light" contained in the study and understanding of the symbols drawn on the given tracing board.

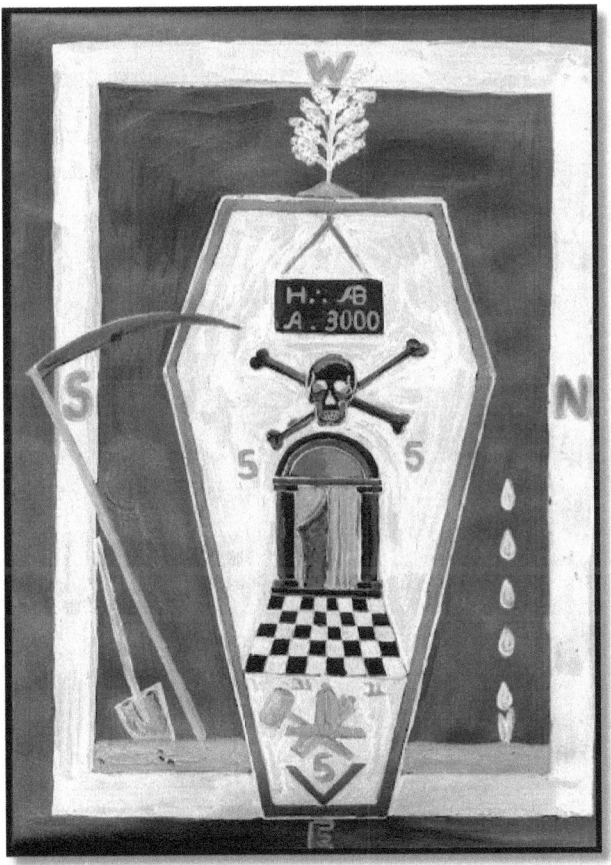

Picture 12. *The Tracing Board of the Third Degree*
(Ancient Accepted Scottish Rite)

LIGHTS

The word "light" has a number of meanings in Masonry. Generally, it is perceived as the light of knowledge and understanding, education, morality, and truth that one who seeks can find through the practice and study of Freemasonry. When the candidate is brought into the Lodge for the reception (Initiation) he is blindfolded. The reason for this is to impress on his mind that in his profane life he has lived in the *"darkness of ignorance"*. After he goes through the ceremony of Initiation and gives pledge respecting his duties as a member of the Fraternity, the blindfold is ceremonially removed and he is symbolically brought to Light. In some Masonic Rites this routine is repeated in the Second - Fellowcraft Degree and in the Third - Master Mason Degree to further stress the importance of the *"search for more Light in Masonry"*.

Often one can come across references to the "Three Great Lights". Most of Freemasons refer to the "Volume of Sacred Law", the "square", and the "compasses" as the three great lights. In every Lodge, while it is at work, there are present three great lights prominently displayed on the Altar, either in the east (Orient) or in the center of the Lodge room. The position of the Altar in the Lodge room and the understanding of that which represents the "Volume of Sacred Law" vary with respect to the Rite that is practiced and the traditions of the particular Masonic group. Most often, the Volume of Sacred Law is the Holy Bible, or a book that is recognized as having valid spiritual worth, such as Qur'an, Bhagavad Gita, the Veda or other such text. The candidate is informed that he should study the Volume of Sacred Law in order to use its teachings as the *"rule and guide for his practice, thoughts and belief through life"*. The square is given to him to *"square his actions"* and the compasses to *"circumscribe his desires"*.

Another group of symbols is called the "Three Lesser Lights". These are the Sun, Moon, and the Master of the Lodge. Associating the presiding officer with the Sun and the Moon is in order to stress the importance of the Office of the Master or as many refer to it in the working of the Lodge as "Solomon's Chair". Ritual tells us that, *"as the Sun rules the day and the Moon governs the night, so should the Master, with the same regularity, rule and govern the Lodge"*. The Master sits in the East (Orient) of the Lodge, which symbolically represents the "unfinished Sanctum Sanctorum" of King Solomon's Temple. The east is the place of light where the Sun rises. The east is the place where Cain, the first murderer, became the first builder (Genesis 4: 8-17). The east is the place where one gains understanding of the "things unseen". The Three Lesser Lights are represented in the Lodge by three lighted candles placed on candlesticks or pedestals, situated in the center of the Lodge room at the east, west and south corner of the Tracing board or the Altar if in the given Lodge the Altar is in the center. In some Masonic traditions these three candles symbolize Wisdom, Strength, and Beauty and are represented by the three principal officers: Master, Senior Warden, and Junior Warden. Often, the Master, Senior and Junior Wardens, Orator and Secretary are called "the Lights of the workshop". In a number of Masonic Rituals from various periods, we can come across different terms such as "fixed lights", "lights of the Lodge", "astral lights", "lights of freedom" and others. This just tells us about the great importance and constant presence of the term "light" in Masonic symbolism.

Picture 13. *Masonic Lights*

THE VOLUME OF SACRED LAW

The Volume of Sacred Law is and may be any book of sacred writings accepted as such by the members of the particular Masonic group. As mentioned previously, most commonly accepted as the Volume of Sacred Law are the Holy Bible for Christians, the Old Testament (Five Books of Moses) for Hebrews, the Qur'an for Muslims, the Veda for Brahmans, the Bhagavad Gita for Hindus, the Zend-Avesta for Persians, the Tao Te King for Taoists etc. The acceptance of all of these books as the Volume of Sacred Law is for the purpose of accommodating people of different faiths during the ritual work. All of the candidates going through the Masonic Initiation are required to give a solemn pledge regarding their conduct as members of the Fraternity. This pledge is given in the presence of the "Three Great Lights" i.e. on the "Volume of Sacred Law" of the candidate's choice and square and compasses. All members of the Fraternity are encouraged to read the Bible and/or other sacred writings, because they will find there *"those principles of morality which laid the foundation upon which to build a righteous life"*. This is the reason why we refer to the Volume of Sacred Law and particularly to the Holy Bible as the "Great Light".

Passive reading of the Bible or any other sacred text will not help us on our road towards enlightenment if we do not try constantly to understand and implement the true meaning of the metaphors, allegories, and lessons found there. Sacred books are collections of ancient wisdom transported through the ages by the worthy and unworthy, translated and re-translated, cut and modified, used, misused, and overused. The only way to keep them relevant is to practice in our daily life the true wisdom found there. Sacred writings are not relics with magical properties, as some would like to believe. *"The Law is living word of living God to living prophets for living men"*, is what Jesus told us in the **"Gospel of Peace"** (translated from the Aramaic by Edmond Székely, in 1936). The "Word of God" contained in the Scriptures is just a printed stack of papers, if not fully understood and truly accepted in the heart of a man. Only then can the "Volume of Sacred Law" become the Great Light. It is believed by many Freemasons that once we understand the true meaning of the wisdom found in the Sacred writings, we feel invited to add our own page to that ultimate book still waiting to be written and deposited in that *"Temple not made with hands, eternal in the heavens"*.

In a number of Masonic organizations it is accepted belief that the "Volume of Sacred Law", when displayed in the Lodge room, is the "Great Light" only if understood as a symbol of all of the true wisdom recorded through the ages in many different languages and cultures, in countless books, sacred and unsacred, which are all part of that ever-burning flame of knowledge. Still today, this is an open book written by the men and women from all over the world. We are invited to contribute our part in this important endeavor and through our life and conduct to write another page in the Great Book of Life deep in our hearts.

For this reason some Masonic groups allowed their Lodges to place on the Altar a book with blank pages as the symbol of all of the sacred texts ever written and as a challenge to the members to educate themselves, build their good characters in accordance with universal and true moral principles in order to be able to fill those blank pages when time comes. Understanding of the "Volume of Sacred Law" and of its place in Freemasonry is variously regulated in the Constitutions and Regulations of different Masonic Organizations throughout the world. Acceptance or non-acceptance of the "Volume of the Sacred Law" as a required great light became the cause for serious divisions among Freemasons, which still exist today.

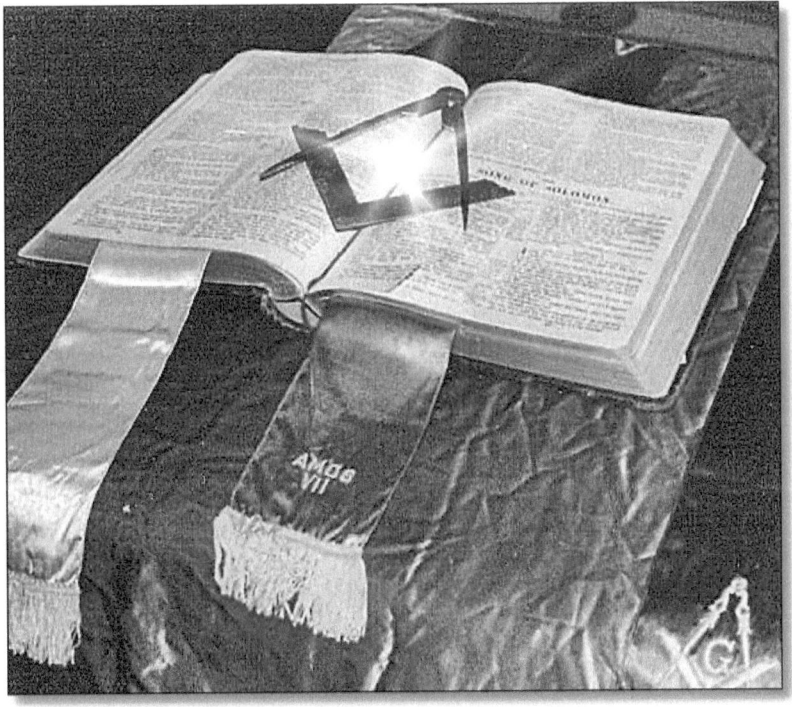

Picture 14. *The Three Great Lights in Freemasonry-*
Holy Bible, Square, and Compasses
Photo © 2013 S. Nikolic,

THE BUILDER'S TOOLS

In 1830, while rebuilding an ancient bridge near Limerick, Ireland, builders discovered under the foundation stone an old brass square, dated 1517, with the inscription: *"I will strive to live with love and care, upon the level, by the square"*. The expression "to live by the square" is recognized worldwide by Masons and non-masons alike, as a metaphor for an upright life and moral conduct. Mencius, follower of Confucius, in the sixth book of his philosophy writes: *"A Master Mason in teaching Apprentices makes use of the compasses and square. Ye who are engaged in the pursuit of wisdom must also make use of the compasses and square"*. In the Masonic ritual we are instructed *"to square our actions by the square of virtue"*. We are further told to use the compasses to *"circumscribe our desires and keep our passions in due bounds with all mankind "*.

In operative masonry, when a building is constructed it must conform to two lines: the line of the Plumb going downwards representing the centripetal forces of gravity, and the line of the Level extending horizontally, representing the centrifugal force of the earth's motion. Its stability is "proved" if these two lines are on the square, which is then called "building on the square". As the building not built on the square will be unstable and eventually will collapse, so human actions, conduct and thoughts not verified by reason and conscience, as being good and truthful will lead towards error and failure. This particular use of the building tools for verification through measurement is their key quality for speculative Freemasons.

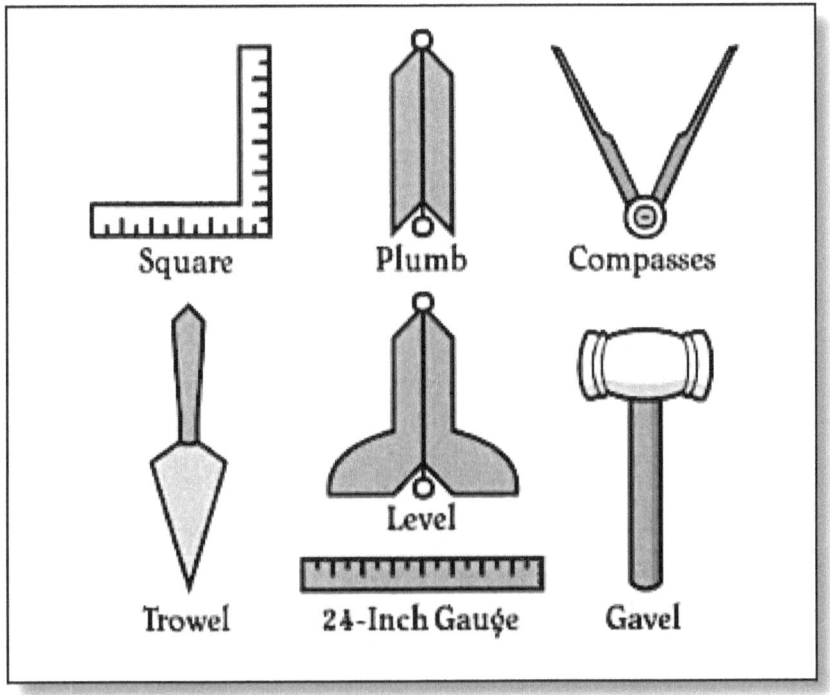

Picture 15. *Working Tools of Freemasonry*

Ruskin, in his **"Seven Lamps of Architecture"**, argues that the laws of architecture are moral laws, equally applicable to the building of material objects and character. According to him, these laws are Sacrifice, Truth, Power, Beauty, Life, Memory, and Obedience. Through the centuries, and particularly in the Middle Ages, human education has been based mostly on the different religious texts interpreted by priests and on superstitions and legends. Things were good or bad, right or wrong, divine or evil because the one wearing the crown and wielding the sword or presiding in the Temple of God said so, and not because it was proven through reason and conscience verification in accordance with true measurements. The only science that was, by its nature, outside the circle of human subjective way of thinking was geometry and with it architecture and the building arts.

From the first moments of Creation everything in universe exists, functions, and relates according to the perfect Laws of Nature. Man always had the desire to fit into that perfect circle of existence, not only physically, but also spiritually and mentally as well. In human nature, many forces need to be understood, controlled, and balanced. By use of the square and compasses in dealing with these forces, humans shape their reality through rational thinking and free themselves from the bonds of uncontrolled passion, prejudice, and ignorance. Only the true and good actions and thoughts can survive the material and conscience verification by the square of Virtue, and the universal and divine validation by the compasses.

In speculative Masonry, the Plumb line going downwards is the one going toward man's spiritual existence, his inner being, his understanding of the Universe and his relationship with the Divine, by suggesting truth through a profound knowledge of oneself. *"The Plumb admonishes usto walk uprightly"*- we are told during the ritual: *"Traveling upon the Level of Time – to that undiscovered country, from whose bourne no traveler returns"*. The Level line extends horizontally towards our everyday life, our neighbors and our fellow humans regardless of their position in life or society. The builders of men can never unbuild that which was erected on the level of time. Once done it is gone forever, so we always must be squared with the level of life on which we tread. This "Golden Rule" was well understood by the wise men thousands of years ago: *"Therefore all things whatsoever ye would that men should do to you, do ye even so to them; for this is the law and the prophets"* (Matthew 7:12).

The Ruler is the instrument used by operative masons to measure their work in order to fit them better. In Freemasonry it is the symbol of the importance of measuring and balancing our life and conduct through the application of the universal moral laws. In some Masonic Rituals, it is referred to as a "Twenty-four inch Gauge" instead of a Ruler and it is a particular tool of Apprentice. Another tool not mentioned in all of the Masonic systems is the Lever. This tool increases the strength of the man making it possible to act forcefully in the quest for good and truth. Its symbolism teaches us about the power of education. The Trowel in operative masonry is an instrument used to apply mortar, thereby connecting stones into one structure. By spreading plaster over the stones and covering their connections, we create a wall as a unit and not as a number of stones stacked together. We are reminded through the symbolism of the trowel of the importance of the fellowship and the community and of the rewards that one can receive in one's personal growth from the strength and harmony of bonding and support within a group.

The Gavel and the Chisel are used to impose the mason's will on the stone. By striking the stone with the gavel or forcing the chisel into stone with the Mallet we create the desired shape. The Gavel is the symbol of authority and the power of the will of the one using it. Consequently, it is assigned to the principal officers of the Lodge being the Master and Wardens of the Lodge. The Maul is the Gavel with a woodenhead and is often used for driving a chisel into the stone. The Setting Maul is a mallet used for "setting stones" by tapping them gently into the right position. It teaches morally how to *"correct irregularities and reduce man to the proper level"*. By observing the ways in which the gavel and chisel treat stones, we are inspired to think about the complementary nature of the active force represented by the gavel and the passive force, represented by the chisel. Symbolically, this passive force results from the *"advantages of discipline and education"*.

Picture 16. *Bavarian Stonemasons*
1505 by Rueland Frueauf the Younger (1470–1545)

THE STONES

In every Lodge, displayed in a prominent place in the east, we can find the Rough Ashlar or unfinished stone and the Perfect Ashlar or cubical stone. The Rough Ashlar is there to remind us of our rude and imperfect nature on which we have to work in accordance with the Moral Laws. Self-improvement through education and liberation from the impurities of our nature will enable us to come to the summit of human virtue. The Perfect Ashlar is the symbol of that summit, of that masterpiece of Creation, which we endeavor to become. The adjective "perfect" generally applies to the condition of the stone. In some Rites the term "cubical stone" is used which applies, not only to its condition but also to its dimensions. Here, qualities of the Square enter in three dimensions the material world of four elements. In some Lodges the cubical stone may be seen topped with a pyramid, which further deepens the symbolism of the Perfect Ashlar. Symbolism of the Perfect Ashlar is closely connected to the symbolism of the corner stone and the foundation stone.

Picture 17. *The Rough Ashlar and the Perfect Ashlar*

Picture 18. *Laying the cornerstone of the Washington Masonic Memorial in 1925*

The corner stone or the foundation stone on which the whole edifice rests is the most important stone. Everything about this stone has to be perfect, because on that depends the stability of the whole building. We can read in the Bible: *"Behold, I lay in Zion, for a foundation, a stone, a tried stone, a precious cornerstone, a sure foundation."* (Isaiah 28:16). Sometimes, blinded by ignorance, humans cannot recognize the corner stone: *"The stone which the builders refused is become the head stone of the corner"* (Psalm 118:22). Through the symbolism of the Corner stone, we are invited to lay the foundation of our own self-improvement; of that moral edifice built by the power of wisdom and faith in the divinely inspired goodness of man.

THE POINT WITHIN A CIRCLE

One of the trade secrets of medieval operative stonemasons was "proving of the square" by use of the "point within a circle". Indeed, if we make a circle, then draw the line through its center cutting the circle in half, at any point of the circumference (C) which we would connect with these two points (A and B) where line cuts the circle, we would form an angle of the square (Picture 19).

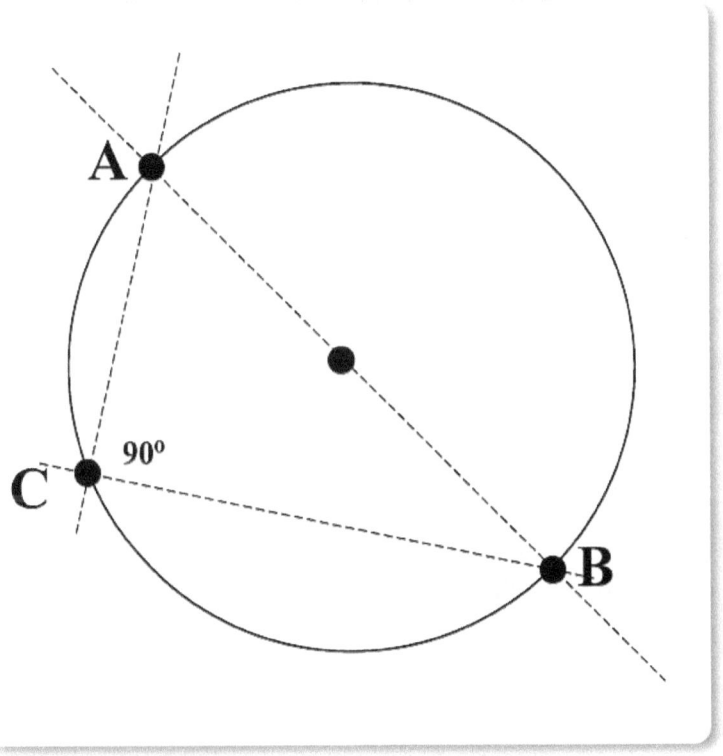

Picture 19. *The Point within a Circle*

The point within a circle is one of the most powerful symbols in Freemasonry. Its importance is not only in antiquity, which we may trace, neither in the bond between Speculative and Operative Craft, which this symbol makes, but also in many rich meanings, which a student of Masonry may read from it. As Manly Hall, in his book <u>The Secret Teachings of All Ages,</u> stated: "The keys to all knowledge are contained in the dot, the line and the circle. The dot is universal consciousness, the line is universal intelligence, and the circle is universal force - the threefold, unknowable Cause to all known existence."

Although undefined in geometry, a point can be described as indicating location with no size. Nothing exists without a center. From the nucleus of an atom, the center of planet Earth, the Sun in the solar system to the black hole in the center of the Galaxy, everything has a center. Even the abstract idea has a center because we consider it "pointless" if there is not a center holding it together. The fixed point is called the center of a circle. At times, it is synonymous with the circumference, just as circumference (distance around the circle) is often equated with the circular movement. It is very often an emblem of the Sun, or it stands for Heaven, perfection, or Eternity. Psychological study asserts that the discovery of the circle in humans arrives at the age when the child discovers himself ("I am"), and distinguishes himself from others. According to Swiss psychiatrist, Carl Gustav Jung (1875-1961), *"a circle represents the ultimate state of Oneness"*. To the ancient Greek philosophers, the circle was the symbol of the number **One**, since it was the source of all subsequent shapes. They called it MONAD, from Greek "monas" (oneness).

A circle, understood as a circumference, is a symbol of adequate limitation and of the inner unity of all matter and universal harmony. Enclosing beings, objects, or figures within a circumference has a double meaning: from within, it implies limitation and definition; from without, it represents the defense of the content of a circle against disintegration and chaos.

Origins of the point within a circle, as is the case with many other ancient symbols, are lost in the mists of antiquity. A point within a circle was the Egyptian, Chinese and Mayan glyph for "light". In many ancient myths and modern scientific theories about the beginning of the Universe, the universal creation process begins with the expansion from a Divine Center, or from the Big Bang, as in the very first words of God in Genesis *"Let there be Light"*. On early Egyptian monuments the circle can be found with two letters in the center of it and bordered by two parallel serpents symbolizing wisdom and power. According to some scholars, the letters in the center stand for "beginning" and "end", indicative of God or Creator. Some other similar Egyptian symbols known to us are ANANTA (meaning "eternity") – a serpent in the form of a circle biting its tale, and CRUX ANSATA - a cross within a circle, symbolizing eternal life.

In Hindu mythology, Brahma speaks aloud the word AHM -"I AM", a word made of the first, middle and last letters of the Sanskrit alphabet, which represents the circle's three parts: the center, the radius, and the circumference. The point represents our own spiritual center or God within us; the radius -our mental and rational limits of understanding of God and the circle the sphere of our material existence. We can find the "point within a circle" as a symbol of "Phallus" in some old Indian legends. In many countries around the world, remains of the ancient temples consisting of stones placed in a circle can be found, with a single stone in the center. Although, the explanations of the real purpose of these temples are still controversial, these are usually connected with Sun worship practices in some cultures. The best known examples are Druidic Temples in Great Britain.

Picture 21. *Lord Shiva Temple from India - designed in the circular form*

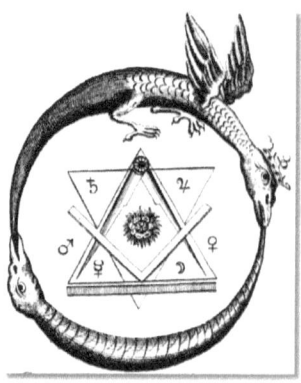

Picture 20. *Ouroborus, also known as ANANTA—a serpent biting it's tale*

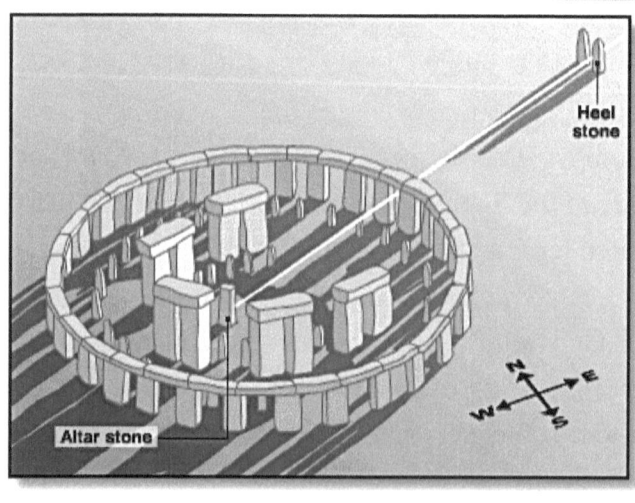

Picture 22. *Stonehenge in England*

In the Kabala, the point represents YOD, the creative knowledge of God, and the circle the space in which He creates. The two parallel lines are symbols of justice and mercy of God. They are equal and upright because they are regulated by His perfect Wisdom. Christian theologian Lucian (c.240-312) wrote in the third century: *"God makes himself known to the world; he fills up the whole circle of the universe, but makes his particular abode in the center, which is the soul of the just"*.

This symbol appeared in the Masonic ritual work, most likely, early in the 18th Century. The first Masonic record mentioning a point within a circle was Prichard's **"Masonry Dissected"**. Today, it is mentioned, either in the lecture of the First degree, or in the opening of the Third degree in most of the Rituals. By tracing the development of this symbol through different cultures around the world from time immemorial, we learn of various understandings of its meaning. There are three elements constantly present in all of the stories: God, Man and the Universe.

When we think about God, we often refer to Him as Creator of all things, Great Architect of the Universe, the One with many names, Divine Omnipresence or Ultimate Cause of Everything. If one would have to present graphically or to draw a picture that would represent God or the Ultimate Cause, and be understood and accepted as such by all human beings what would that picture look like? Is it possible to express the infinite nature of God by drawing a point within a circle on a blank sheet of paper? Many accept this possibility because they perceive Him as being the center of existence, with the whole existence emanating from His creative power. One can understand it as God or as the Big Bang, but it is still there and still the Absolute Force, or Power or Spirit that created the Universe - the point within a circle.

Is there any better way visually to present the Universe than by using a point within a circle? Through the ages this has been the prime choice of Philosophers, Magicians, Artists, Alchemists, and Scientists. The origin of the word Universe is Latin **unus versus**, meaning "one turn". The human mind is incapable of fully comprehending time and space without the help of this symbol, which exists because of man's effort to visualize more perfectly immeasurable and infinite that Universe represents.

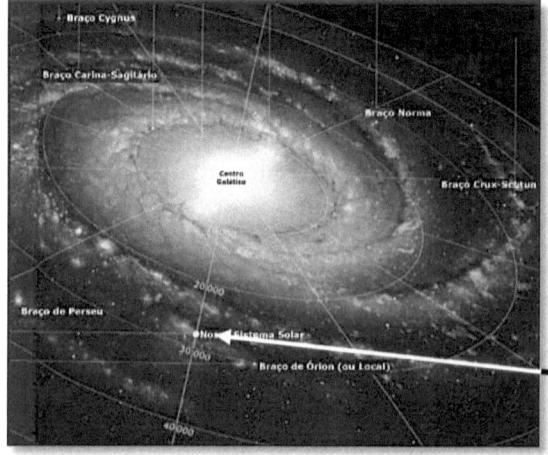

Picture 23.
The Center of the Universe.

Our Solar system

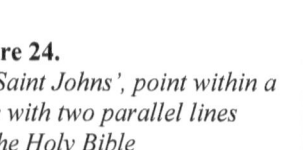

Picture 24.
Two Saint Johns', point within a circle with two parallel lines and the Holy Bible

Picture 25. *Adam Kadmon - The Original Man, from the* 13th century manuscript, Italy

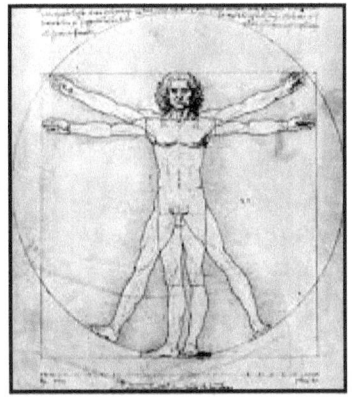

Picture 26. *Vitruvian Man- By Leonardo da Vinci*

Finally, we come to a human being, the point within its own circle of existence. This circle is one's family, neighbors, fellow workmen, Brothers or Sisters in the Lodge, community; all that surrounds one in the warm light of the Summer Solstice and cold light of the Winter Solstice, represented by two parallel lines. But then, a person is the eternal circle itself, trying to place in the center and keep in balance, the hidden point within, which then creates the puzzle, how can one draw a circle whose center is everywhere and circumference nowhere?

RITE OF CIRCUMAMBULATION

Continuing with the symbolism of the circle, the Rite of Circumambulation is the act of processing around the Altar or around other sacred object or space. Circumambulation was an important part of the Rituals and Ceremonies in Ancient Greece, in Rome, and in the Sun –worship Rituals of the Druids and of a number of pre-Colombian cultures in the Americas. Today, it is still used in Rituals of Christians, Muslims, Hindus and Buddhists. It is adopted by Freemasons for their Rituals and has a significant place in all of the initiatory Rites. The basic symbolism of circumambulation is an allusion to the course of the sun in the sky: from the east by way of the south to the west and by way of the north back to the east. By imitating the motion of the sun, one attempts to become part of that grandiose renewal of life, repeated by the sun day after day. From birth at sunrise in the east, to maturity at noon in the south, to old age in the evening in the west, to death in the darkness of the north to rebirth in the east, humans have always been fascinated by the ability of nature to make full circle of life over and over again. Circumambulation is often closely connected with the act of purification. In some Masonic Rites the candidate going around the Lodge room makes three circles, representing three symbolic journeys. During each journey he is purified by the elements of water, air, and fire. Cleansed of all impurities of life, he arrives at the east where he has a chance to enter into the dawn of his new existence.

In certain Masonic ceremonies, circumambulation is used to symbolically draw different symbols on the floor of the room, such as a rose or pentagram. In doing this, it is of great importance always to walk clockwise, i.e. with the right side closer to the center. This guarantees that the participant is moving in the direction of the sun. Through the ages, circumambulation was most often understood as a sacred procession, with mystical, even magical attributes. Psalm 26:6 read, *"I will wash mine hands in innocence: so will I compass thine Altar, O Lord."* One going through it would in doing so earn the favor of God and the right of passage. Each circle would bring a new revelation and the awareness of yet another circle. J. Bohme wrote in 1612, *"The essence of God is like a wheel"*. D. Mylius adds to this in his Philosophia Reformata in 1622, that rotations should be repeated, *"Until the earth is heavenly and heaven is earthly and connected with the earth, then the Work is completed"*. Whatever could be the reason for the performance of the act of circumambulation, one thing is certain: it is deeply embedded in human spirituality and gets activated whenever humans want to relate to things outside of our material reality.

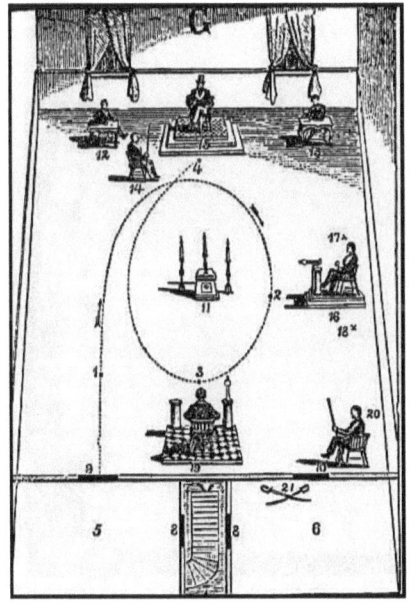

Picture 27. *Rite of Circumambulation as practiced in the Masonic Ritual*

THE MASON'S CLOTHING

In its general use, the apron is a piece of cloth or other material applied by various kinds of workers, including masons, to protect the clothing from being soiled during the work. The root of this word may be found in the French word "napperon" meaning placemat or table cover. It sounds very logical that, since operative masons wore leather aprons, speculative masons would adopt this custom and give it symbolic meaning. Freemasons, however, wear "white leather aprons", and that fact connects this practice more with the ancient Rites of Investiture than with the manner in which operative masons were dressed.

Picture 28. *White Leather Masonic Apron*

The Rite of Investiture is an act of placing upon the neophyte some form of white garment as a sign that he is purified and ready to proceed on his path. Israelite Priests wore the "abnet" or the linen apron during the investiture; initiates in the Mysteries of Mithras wore white aprons as well. Candidates for the Christian monastic order were dressed in white. The symbolism of the Masonic apron comes out of its two characteristics: the color and the material. There is some further symbolism connected to its form (rectangular or square with the triangular flap), but mostly from students interested in sacred geometry speculations.

Picture 29.
Past Master's Apron
(top)
And Grand Officer
Apron (left)

The color of the Masonic apron is white. White was, as the Masonic Ritual says *"an emblem of purity"*. We can read in the Bible: *"To him that overcometh will I give...a white stone."* (Revelations 2:17). The gift of white is the promise of Divine wisdom as well as an obligation to purity on the part of the recipient. It is an expression of hope after death. The Masonic apron is made of lambskin. The lamb was in many traditions accepted as a symbol of innocence. It was an innocent animal killed and burned as a sacrifice offered to God. In Judeo-Christian tradition, Isaac was almost that lamb (Genesis 22:8) and Jesus crucified was *"that spotless Lamb of God who was slain from the foundation of the world"*. The requirement that no one who was not pure and uncorrupt, can step on sacred ground or enter sacred spaces was present in many traditions as well as in the symbolism of Freemasonry where the white leather apron or lambskin is *"so essentially necessary to enter the Sanctum Sanctorum or Holy of Holies."*

Today, in Masonic Lodges, a white leather apron is presented to Entered Apprentices during the ceremony of Initiation. Once he reaches the rank of Master Mason he wears an apron that is lined with blue or red, depending on the traditions and regulations of the particular Masonic organization. He may also wear a sash or collar with the emblems of the rank. In the so-called "higher degrees" of different Rites aprons are decorated usually with the symbols of the particular degree. Those who hold higher offices in Masonic organizations often have aprons lined with purple and gold and made of silk. However, when the Entered Apprentice receives his apron, he is reminded that there is no higher honor that one can receive, than to wear the white leather apron or the lambskin.

Freemasons also wear white gloves while in the Lodge. In some Rites, in higher degrees they also may be red or black. Symbolism of the white gloves is closely connected to that of the apron. It is said that the works of the hands of Freemasons should be *"as pure and spotless as the white gloves given to them"*. We can read in the Bible:*"Who shall ascend into the hill of the Lord? Or who shall stand in his holy place? He that hath clean hands, and a pure heart"* (Psalm 24:3,4). We can perceive here white gloves as "clean hands" and the apron as a "pure heart". There is yet another reason for wearing gloves and that is to protect the hands of the worker from the sharp edges of the rough stones. This understanding carries further symbolism, referring to the impurities of the profane life. There is yet another practical purpose for the gloves. In many cases, in covering our hands the uniformity of the gloves makes all in the Lodge room equal. The hands of the carpenter and the prince, of the baker, and the general become all the same. The sash serves a similar purpose. In the Seventeenth and Eighteenth Centuries only the nobility wore the sash. The Masonic Lodge was the very first place where all, regardless of their social status, wore the sash.

It is a custom in some Lodges that the Master of the Lodge wears a hat. Usually he is the only one who has the right to have his head covered while the Lodge is at work. The hat is a symbol of royalty and could be well-explained if understood as the Kether sephiroth in the cabalistic Tree of Life. One wearing a hat is manifestation of that which "contains all that was, is and will be". The Master of the Lodge is elected to rule for the benefit of everybody and not to use the power of the ruler for his own selfish aims. He is to be a beacon of Light received and the keeper of higher ideals in the eyes of the Lodge members.

Dress code in the Lodge room varies from Lodge to Lodge. In the United States and Great Britain, usually black tie and dinner jacket or morning suit is required. The reason behind this requirement is again to make a point regarding equality. In some Rites it is required to wear black, white, or orange robes or even a blue chasuble over their regular clothes.

Picture 30. *Masonic Dress Code: Morning Suite or dark suite, Collar, White gloves, and the Top Hat for the Worshipful Master.*

THE HIRAMIC LEGEND

The Hiramic Legend or the story about the betrayal and death of the Master Builder of King Solomon's Temple, Hiram Abif, who appears in the third or Master Mason degree, is common in all of the Masonic Rituals all over the world. This story is the key point and essence of Masonic symbolism and philosophy that defines Freemasonry and sets it apart from all other similar systems.

Grand Master Hiram Abif was, according to legend, slain by three craftsmen because he would not reveal to them the secret word of a Master Mason before the Temple was completed. With his death the Master's word was lost. This story, in almost its contemporary form, is first given to us in 1730, in Prichard's "Masonry Dissected".

The historical identity of Hiram Abif is a very controversial subject. The few references in the Bible do not reveal much except that he was a master craftsman from Tyre, possibly related to the King of Tyre (father or son?) and that he was a "widow's son" (Kings 7: 13,14 and Chron.2:13,14). Even his appearance in the legend of the Craft is relatively confusing. Cook's Manuscript mentioned that "the son of the King of Tyre was his 'Master Mason'". Subsequent manuscripts mention him in passing fashion under different corruptions of the name Hiram. In 1726, it appeared in a London pamphlet for sale bearing the title, "The Whole History of the Widow's Son Killed by the blow of a Beetle" (setting maul). Even as late as 1738, the story was not completely set for we can read in revised Anderson's Constitutions, that Hiram Abif was killed after the Temple was completed and not before, as we have it today. But historical accuracy is not our primary interest. The historical name or origin of the person of the slain Master Builder is of minor importance. As with everything else in Freemasonry symbolism and the hidden meaning of the allegories is what practitioners of Freemasonry are after. Why did Hiram Abif had to die - is our primary question? Two of many symbols coming out of the Hiramic legend are a sprig of Acacia and a Broken Column. Acacia marked the spot of Hiram Abif's grave and as a plant surviving in the harsh conditions is a symbol of immortality. The Broken Column symbolizes the ruin of death of a Builder.

As already mentioned, in Masonry everything is a symbol. The universal world of symbols is a workshop of the Master Builder. This short review attempts to touch upon the possible meanings of just few of them and to bring to the reader some understanding of how the "language of Freemasonry" functions. Once somebody steps on that road and starts going through the degrees of the various Masonic Rites, he will discover a whole new level of existence in the different meanings behind everyday common things.

But the purpose of symbols is not only to help communicate to the one going through the ritual something that otherwise could not be communicated. It is also to train one to perceive things on a different level, to transcend the material plain and conscience and concentrate on the spiritual and unconscious. In other words, only if we are able to comprehend deeper meanings of our thoughts and actions, could we use their qualities in our spiritual growth. Most of the modern theories about the meanings of the symbols are inspired by or coming out of the work done by

Carl Gustav Jung. He believed that symbols play an important role in the processes that influence every aspect of human mental or physical activities. According to Jung, all human beings are born with "instinctive predispositions" towards qualities that make us human, such as truth, justice, wisdom, mercy, love and others. These "blueprints" or "archetypes", as he called them, are hidden deep within unconscious, but can be inspired to come out into consciousness in the form of symbols. Although, Jung gained his knowledge through clinical studies and scientific research of different myths and traditions, he was not the first one to understand the true character of symbols. In the Gospel of St. Philip (early Christian text found at Nag Hamadi in Egypt) words of Jesus Christ were recorded: *"Truth did not come into the world naked, but it came in types and images. One will not receive truth in any other way..."*

Picture 31. From seventeenth century northern Italy - Hiramic Legend depicted in *Raising the Master* by Il Guercino.,

5

MASONIC DEGREES, RITES AND RITUALS

"**Degree**" or "**Grade**" work in Freemasonry represents a certain esoteric ceremony, during which the candidate is entrusted with relevant information and advanced to the given rank. This knowledge, including lectures, secret signs, words and grips of the degree (grade) is not to be shared, discussed or revealed in any manner to anybody unless to a person of the same or higher rank (degree). Particular characteristic of the degrees in speculative Freemasonry is that they enable the initiate to transcend boundaries of different levels of human existence, thereby giving him a chance to understand and improve his inner and outer experiences.

Craft Degrees are three basic degrees of speculative Freemasonry, which originated in England and Scotland in the first part of seventeen century. Historic records are sporadic and blurry regarding their original rituals, but it seems that the very first Lodges of speculative Freemasons were conferring only two degrees (Apprentice and Fellowcraft), while the Master Mason Degree was, at first, conferred upon the presiding officer of the Lodge only as investiture into the chair. Some records talk only about "making Freemasons" without referring to a particular degree. It was not until the middle of the eighteenth century that finally the structure of the Craft degrees was stabilized.

Since then, candidates were initiated "Entered Apprentices", passed to the degree of "Fellowcraft" and raised to the "Sublime Degree of a Master Mason". As we already mentioned in the previous chapter, Craft or Symbolic degrees were so called, because the lectures of these degrees were based on the legends and symbolism surrounding the building of the King Solomon's Temple, also known in history as a "first Temple". These three degrees are contained and are conferred in all of the existing Masonic Rites. In Anglo-American Masonic traditions it is understood that there are no higher than the Craft Degrees. Other degrees are called "additional" degrees and their numerical superiority to the Master Mason or third degree does not mean that they are superior or higher in their substance or teachings but just an addition to the lessons of the three Craft degrees.

Picture 32. *The Pyramid presentation of the Masonic Degrees Structure*

THE APPRENTICE

Entered Apprentice degree is the degree of initiation (from the Latin *"initium"*- a beginning, a birth, a coming into being). It is a candidate's introduction into symbolism of Freemasonry and the work is symbolically taking place on the ground floor of the Temple. In many ways, we never leave the ground floor. We never stop being apprentices, until the *"work is completed"*. It is a place of the material manifestations of our mind and conscience. There we can still feel the ground beneath our feet. After the preparation, a candidate is brought from the darkness of ignorance of his profane reality into the Lodge room. He is received with the dagger pointing into his heart. It is to warn him of all of the dangers of the journey inward. Further on, there is a slight difference between various Rites. In some Rites, the candidate, after expressing his "trust" in One God, has to satisfy Wardens and Master that he is taking this step *"of his own free will"* and that he is *"properly prepared"*, before he is asked to take obligation of Entered Apprentice. In other Rites, the candidate is conducted before the obligation through symbolical journeys, where he is "tried" or "purified" with elements of air, fire, and water. After the Obligation of secrecy, candidate is symbolically brought to the Light. This is where the real work begins. Nevertheless, he is not overwhelmed; too much is neither given nor expected of him. He is introduced to the basic symbolism and moral teachings of the Craft, given a title "Brother" (or "Sister"-in female Freemasonry) and told that he is "three years old". He is given the seat into the northeast corner of the Lodge, which symbolically represents the place of darkness. His working tools are gavel and the chisel. (In American York Rite system, the apprentice has gavel and twenty-four inch gauge). He is to use them to work on the Rough Ashlars, which represents his earthly nature. In some Rites, the Apprentice is even not permitted to speak in the Lodge until he is passed to a degree of Fellowcraft. He has to learn the advantages of listening and appreciate the "sounds" of silence. Only those who listen carefully can think wisely and speak clearly. A primary duty of the Apprentice is to meditate on the lessons of the Degree and to hold to his vow of secrecy regarding Freemasonry.

Picture 33. *The Initiation of the candidate to the Apprentice degree -
French gravure, 18th century*

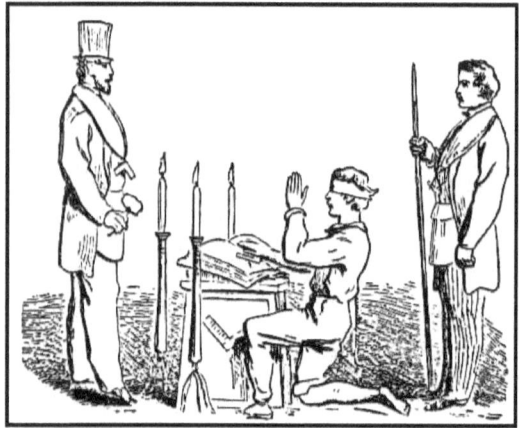

Picture 34. *Entered Apprentice giving the solemn Obligation (top), and Apprentice being conducted around the Lodge room (right)*

In most of the Masonic traditions, the Apprentice Lodge is a place where all of the Lodge business is done. Ritual tells us that the Lodge could be open when seven or more Masons are present. Lodges of Fellowcrafts or Master Masons are usually only open for degree conferrals and instructions. Contrary to this, most of the Lodges in the United States are conducting their business only on the third or Master Mason degree. This prevents Apprentices and Fellowcrafts from attending regular Lodge meetings until they are raised to Master Mason degree. A desire to bring candidates to the full membership in the Master Mason Lodge as soon as possible is probably one of the reasons behind the fast progress through the degrees in American Lodges.

THE FELLOWCRAFT

Fellowcraft degree is by many Freemasons underestimated as "just the intermediate" degree of passing between initiation and "sublime rising" in the third degree. We, however, cannot forget that Fellowcraft is a "Builder" in a true sense of that word. He is working with a perfect ashlar. To be a builder one has to possess a great knowledge, and this degree is all about advantages of education. While in the First degree, the candidate is received with warning; here he is received with instruction. In the York Rite he makes his way into the middle chamber of the Temple, by a way of the porch and between two Pillars. In other Rites he takes five symbolical journeys. There he learns about the meaning of the letter "G", about five human senses, Architecture, and about seven liberal arts and sciences: Logic, Rhetoric, Grammar, Arithmetic, Music, Astronomy, and particularly Geometry. He is also informed about five great Initiates: Moses, Pythagoras, Socrates, Jesus, and Mohammed.

Fellowcraft tools are square, plumb, level, ruler and lever. (in American York Rite - only square, plumb, and level). Without these tools no structure could be built stable and in balance. Here, one learns to be on the level with the fellow human being and on the square with all of the Creation. A work description is to obtain and comprehend the moral and intellectual truth. That is a purpose of a Fellowcraft degree. One's mind and conscience has first to be firmly established before the soul could pass beyond into the uncharted realm of the spirits. Fellowcraft is "five years old" and the wages paid to him consist of corn, wine and oil, whose symbolism is to teach him that the rewards of the true Builder are far greater that any reaches of the material sphere.

Picture 35. *Tracing Board of the Fellowcraft (Second) Degree)*
English , late 19th century

THE MASTER MASON

In many ways, all of the Masonic degrees have a similar form. They all have ceremonial entry, reception, a circumambulation or journeys, obligation, investiture, lectures and a charge. Third or Master Mason degree beside all of these elements has one unique element that puts it apart from other degrees.

That is a ceremony of rising. In the third degree, a candidate going through the ceremonies represents Hiram Abif-the widow's son. After refusing to reveal the secret word to three Fellowcrafts, he is symbolically killed by three blows of the setting maul to his forehead. He is then placed into the coffin or on the place representing the coffin or grave. The Master of the Lodge then ceremonially "raises" him with the secret grip of Master Mason and communicates to the newly raised Master Mason the substitute for the Masters word in the particular manner. With this, a Freemason completes his journey.

On that path, he progressed from his physical world of Apprentice inward towards the deepest parts of his soul as a Fellowcraft. From there, by crossing symbolically the boundaries from life to death and back, he was enabled to touch upon the world of "higher existence" and just for a moment to grasp the spark of *"that which was lost"*. Those who were fortunate enough to complete this journey are now ready to take part in the "Great Work" of *"erecting that edifice not made with hands"* in their hearts and consciences. A Master Mason is symbolically seven years old. After climbing over three, five, and seven steps of the winding stairs leading to the middle chamber, he came to the "Holy of Holies" or to the Gates of unlimited enlightenment.

Picture 36. *Some of the symbols of the Third Degree - Virgin with the pot of incense and the sprig of acacia standing in front of Broken column with the Holy Bible; Death behind her and the Hour Glass.*

The history of humankind is the story of the efforts to experience the continuation of existence beyond the boundaries set by the natural process of life and death. Hiramic Legend is just one in the line of similar stories from dawn of civilization dealing with this subject. Many details in the story, as it was told during Masonic rituals, point to the significant similarities of this legend and ancient "Bear-son" or "Year-King" myths. Nevertheless, the ceremony of rising represented by the story of Hiram Abif is much more complex than traditional "death" legends. It is not only about Job's question: *"If a man dies, shall he live again?"* It is not only about immortality of the soul. It is about human incapacity to grasp the concept of Creation. Through the advantages of their mental abilities, humans always felt their great superiority compared to the rest of the beings. This gave birth to the ideas of the "higher origin" of man. A desire to return to that "original state" was just an expression of the natural need for completion and of the desperate efforts to *"gather that which was scattered"*. As is case with most of the Masonic ritual, influences of the performed Rites upon one going through the third degree are multiple and the experience is very personal.

RITES AND RITUALS

"**Ritual**", in its general meaning, as a form of human behavior, is a set of prescribed actions repeated from time to time in the same manner. According to Jung rituals are *"physical enactments of journeys into the collective unconscious"*. On these journeys, body is the symbol of a spirit. From the early tribal societies, rituals were intuitively performed in an effort to connect with the sacred and change our consciousness from the mundane to the spiritual realm. Places where rituals were performed were understood as portals to the Divine realm, thereby being sacred grounds. In Freemasonry, Ritual is a preset form of conducting different Rites and ceremonies.

"**Rite**" is an act of performing sacred or solemn service or duty, as prescribed by custom or accepted understanding, or as established by law or religious or other teachings. Some of the earliest established Rites were "Rites of passage" performed by humans at the transitional points in life; such as birth, adulthood, marriage and death. Rites of passage are also called "Initiatory Rites" because they mark the "beginning" of a new stage in the life of the individual. There are number of different Rites in use in the Masonic Rituals. Some of them such as the "Rite of Circumambulation" and "Rite of Investiture" we already mentioned. The Rites are integral parts of ritual of any of the Masonic degrees. But this is just one of the two meanings of the term "Rite" in Freemasonry.

In the first part of the eighteenth century, French Masons started using "Rite" as a term to define a group of the degrees or grades *"under common control or administration or being associated in the succession of working"*. This understanding spread over period of time all over the Masonic world and today it is a standard meaning of this term. Originally, there was only one Rite, which consisted of three Craft degrees (Entered Apprentice, Fellowcraft, and Master Mason), but through the ingenuity of the eighteenth century Freemasons, particularly in France and the rest of the continental Europe, soon there were invented numerous, so called "higher" degrees, organized and practiced in a number of various Rites. This was done, either to further explain, deepen and advance the original body of Masonic knowledge coming out of the Craft Degrees, or to reunite Freemasonry with its eventual "originators". As a result of these efforts we have a number of Rites and "higher degrees" so designed to reconnect Freemasonry with Egyptian and other Ancient Mystery schools, Hermetic Philosophy, Kabala, Early Christian Gnostic Teachings, medieval guilds of operative stonemasons, Knights Templar, and Rosicrucians. Inspired with the teachings and traditions of various groups from the past, some Freemasons tried to prove the existence of the unbroken line of spiritual thought and practice coming down from the Ancient Egyptian Mysteries all the way to the Freemasonry of today.

Most often practiced Rites today in the Masonic world are the Ancient and Accepted Scottish Rite-consisting of thirty three degrees (most of the Europe and South America), American or York Rite - with thirteen degrees (mostly in USA), Schroeder's Rite- three Craft Degrees (mostly in Germany, Austria, Switzerland, Serbia, Montenegro, Croatia, Slovenia etc.), French (Modern) Rite - with seven degrees (France, Belgium, South America), Rectified Scottish Rite - with seven degrees (France,

Belgium, Switzerland) Memphis-Mizraim Rite - consisting of ninety six degrees (based in France with a number of Lodges practicing it all over the world), Swedish Rite - with eleven degrees (Scandinavian countries and Germany), and the Emulation Working-consisting only of three Craft Degrees (England, Australia, Canada).

Picture 37. *The Third Degree Ceremony, Rectified Scottish Rite*
French print etching, 18th century

THE ANCIENT ACCEPTED SCOTTISH RITE

The Ancient Accepted Scottish Rite (A.A.S.R.) is one of the most widely practiced degree systems in the world. Where the Scottish Rite originated is a question that Masonic scholars still cannot answer with certainty. The first reference to the Scottish Rite appears in old French records. During the second part of the seventeenth century, British Isles were torn by strife between opposing dynasties and many Scots fled to France. Some of them were very active in introducing speculative Freemasonry in France. Their influence may have contributed to the use of the word "Scottish".

In 1740, the Ecossaise (Scottish) Lodge "Parfaite Harmonie" was organized in Bordeaux, France. The membership included Scottish and English Masons. In 1761, the Masonic authorities in France granted a patent to Stephen Morin of Bordeaux to carry the "advanced degrees" to America. About 1763, Morin established these degrees in West Indies. Within few years, other degrees were added until the Rite had a ritual structure of 33 Degrees. Henry Andrew Francken (1720-1795) deputized by Stephen Morin, organized a Lodge of Perfection in Albany, NY, in 1767. During the Colonial Period, Deputies appointed by Morin organized Masonic groups conferring advanced degrees in many cities throughout colonies. As the growth of these groups continued and to bring order out of chaos, *(ordo ab chaos)* Supreme Council was founded in Charleston, South Carolina in 1801, to organize and control the activity of the Ancient Accepted Scottish Rite groups. This later became the Supreme Council for the Southern Jurisdiction of the United

States, also known as a "Mother Supreme Council of the World". Supreme Council for the Northern Jurisdiction of the United States was organized in 1813. The headquarters of the Northern Jurisdiction in Lexington, Massachusetts coordinates activities of Scottish Rite within 15 Northeastern, Middle Atlantic, and Mid-Western States. The Southern Jurisdiction headquarters, located in Washington D.C., covers the remaining 35 states. Supreme Council of France was founded in 1804 and the Supreme Council for England and Wales was formed in 1845. Today there are over forty independent Supreme Councils around the world governing Scottish Rite Bodies (groups) in different countries.

Ancient Accepted Scottish Rite has thirty-three degrees worked in few different bodies: Symbolic or Craft Scottish Rite Lodges - from the 1st to 3rd degree are under control of the Grand Lodges. Under control of the Supreme Councils are: Lodges of Perfection - from 4th to 14th degree; Chapters of Rose Croix, from $15^{th} - 18^{th}$ degree; Areopagus - from 19th to 30th degree; Tribunals - 31st degree; Consistory - 32nd degree; and 33rd degree-honorary. In the Southern Masonic Jurisdictions AASR for USA body conferring from 19th to 30th degree is called Council of Kadosh, and Consistory confers both 31st and 32nd degree. In the Northern Masonic Jurisdiction 15th and 16th degrees are conferred in the Council of Princes of Jerusalem while the Chapter of Rose Croix works only 17th and 18th degree. Consistory covers all of the degrees from 19th to 32nd. Scottish Rite bodies are usually administratively grouped in so called "Valleys". Each Valley, consisting of the Lodge of Perfection, Chapter of Rose Croix, Council of Kadosh and Consistory is subordinate to the Supreme Council, which established the Valley.

Similar to the Symbolic or Craft Lodges, there are different standards from Jurisdiction to Jurisdiction, regarding the time needed to go through all of the degrees. In most of the European Jurisdictions it takes anywhere from five to ten years to get to the 18th degree. Most of the Scottish Rite Masons remain there and only most dedicated proceed further. In the American Scottish Rite tradition fourth, fourteen, sixteen, seventeen, eighteen, thirtieth, and thirty second degree are usually conferred within one year (as required degrees) to enable candidates to be members of the Consistory where all of the regular work of the Valley is done. It is left to the persistence of the members to, through the established Schools of Instruction or on their own, perceives and comprehends all of the philosophical lessons coming out of Scottish Rite degrees. It is also required, like in the Northern Masonic Jurisdiction AASR of USA, that all of the degrees (from 4th to 32nd) be conferred in each Valley within the period of five years.

Over time, various Scottish Rite Jurisdictions have made significant changes in the rituals of the Ancient Accepted Rite they use. Although, the moral and philosophical lessons of the degrees remained more or less the same, scenarios and names were changed. A reason for this probably resides in the opinion that there is a need to "modernize" the ritual or bring it closer to the mind of the contemporary man. Most of the changes were made in the degrees of the Lodge of Perfection and in the degrees of the Council of Kadosh. The Old Testament stories or other originals scenarios were substituted with the stories based on the events from modern history.

The best example of such alterations is work of the Northern

Masonic Jurisdictions A.A.S.R. for the USA where in the twentieth degree "Master of the Symbolic Lodge", the original story was substituted with the story based on events from the American Revolution featuring George Washington and his contemporaries. The twenty-third degree "Chief of the Tabernacle", has a story based on the events from the Second World War. The twenty-fourth degree has a story featuring Native Americans, the twenty-fifth is centered on the life of Benjamin Franklin, and twenty-sixth became a "Lincoln" degree. Certainly, many would agree that the story or drama behind the Lessons is just a vehicle for transitions of the moral, philosophical, or symbolic teachings and as long as the message is untouched scenario is irrelevant. Nonetheless, many in the Masonic community are skeptical of any such innovations, which may disturb very settle universality of the Masonic lessons.

The meaning behind the symbolism and philosophy of the Ancient Accepted Scottish Rite was best expressed in the "Basic Principles" adopted at the international Convention of the Supreme Councils in Lausanne in 1875. *"To raise man in his own eyes, to make him worthy of his mission on earth, Masonry lays down the Principle that the Supreme Creator has given to Man a most precious thing, called Liberty; Liberty, a heritage to all Mankind, a ray coming down from on High, that no power has the right to extinguish, nor to kill off, and is the source of honorable and dignified feelings".* The Scottish Rite is a school of instruction of Freemasonry. It interprets the symbols and allegories of Masonry in the light of history and philosophy, using the words of the prophets and wise men of the great religions and ancient schools of wisdom. The universal moral values that existed in the ancient world are as valid today and will be even more important tomorrow.

Picture 38. *Emblems of the AASR degrees*

Picture 39. *Four Bodies of the AASR Valley*

Picture 40. *Four Hats of the AASR Masons*

THE YORK RITE

Under the title York Rite we can (together with the three Craft Degrees) include Mark Master Degree, Past Master, Most Excellent Master, Royal Arch Mason, Royal Master, Select Master, Super Excellent Master as well as the Orders of Red Cross, Malta, and Temple. Although, these degrees did not originated in York, the city of York is, according to legend, the place of origin of the First assembly of Masons back in tenth century. Some of the earliest references to Royal Arch degree in eighteen century came from the records of the Lodges from York. The phrase "York Rite" came in common usage amongst Anglo-Americans, particularly on the American continent, to define their degree systems, which were by the beginning of nineteenth century much different then those practiced in the continental Europe. There are two other terms often used to describe same systems: one being the "American Rite" which refers to the American version of this degree system, and the "English Rite" which usually refers to a three Craft degrees and Holy Royal Arch degree.

York Rite degrees are practiced within several different Masonic bodies. Craft degrees are conferred in the Craft lodge, which is often called "Blue Lodge" and is under control of a Grand Lodge. In the American version of the York Rite, Mark Master Mason, Past Master, Most Excellent Master and the Holy Royal arch degree, are conferred within the Chapter of Royal Arch. In the English System Holy Royal Arch is the only degree worked in the Chapter of Royal Arch, while Mark Master Mason degree is conferred within independent Mark Master Lodges.

Council of Royal Masters confers Royal Master, Select Master, and Super Excellent Master Degree. The Orders of the Red Cross, Malta, and Temple are conferred within the Commandeeries (in the United States) and Priories or Preceptories (elsewhere).

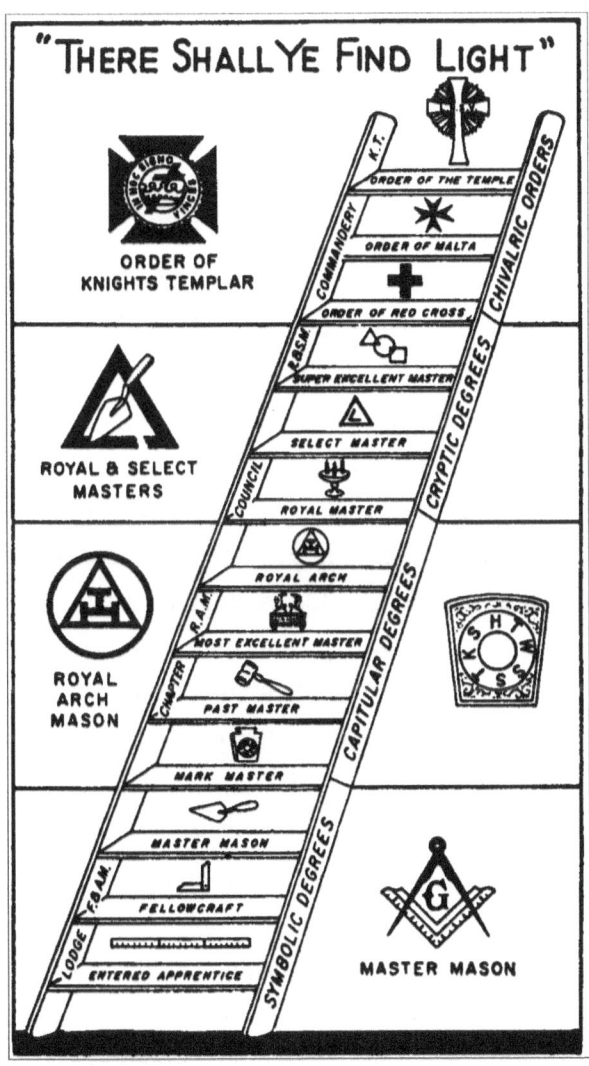

Picture 41. *"The Ladder"* of the York Rite Degrees

RECTIFIED SCOTTISH RITE

Rectified Scottish Rite (R.S.R.) is another degree system popular in the continental Europe. We can trace the origins of the Rectified Scottish Rite back to the System of Strict Observance, founded in 1756, by Baron von Hund. After his death, in 1776, there was a need to reorganize the system that was growing in popularity in France. At the initiative of Jean Baptiste Willermoz, a meeting was held in Lyon from November 25, to December 10, 1778. This meeting is known in the Masonic history as the "Convent of Gaul". A document titled "Masonic Code of the United and Rectified Lodges of France" was adopted and the Rectified Scottish Rite was founded. Willermoz, who is, together with Louis Claude Saint Martin and Martinez de Pasquali, considered a "spiritual father" of this Rite, wrote most of the Rituals. The main difference between the Ancient and Accepted Scottish Rite and the Rectified Scottish Rite is in their understanding of Templar traditions in the Masonic Teachings. While the A.A.S.R. based its degree structure and philosophy on the idea that Masonry has its roots in, and is continuation of the Order of Knights Templar, Rectified Scottish Rite was trying to restore the prominence of the Craft Degrees, keeping only pure spiritual lessons of the medieval Chivalric and religious Orders. The purpose of the Rite, in the words of its authors, was: *"To responds to the aspirations of many Freemasons, who hold to the traditions of pure Freemasonry, and desire to associate themselves with the glorious principles of the Freemasonry of 1717."* These principles would be self-improvement, intellectual advancement, practice of benevolence toward all men regardless of their status, subduing of passions and correction of faults, patriotism, as well as commitment to the spirit of Christianity and belief in One God.

The Rectified Scottish Rite is composed of Symbolic Lodges, the Prefectures and the Secret Order. They are the "Lodge of St. John" conferring Apprentice, Fellowcraft, and Master Mason degree; Lodge of St. Andrew conferring "Scottish Master" degree which is also considered Craft degree; the "Prefectures" conferring "Inner Order" degrees -"Ecuyer Novice" (Square Novice) degree and "C.B.C.S" degree ("Chevaliers Bienfaisants de la Cite Sainte" or "Knights Beneficent of the Holy City"). There is also a "Secret Order" consisting of "Professed Knight" (Chevalier-Profes) and "Grand Professed Knight" (Chevalier-Grand Profes).

Lodges of St. John or Craft Lodges practicing R.S.R. are under control of Grand Lodges. Today there are Blue Lodges in France, Belgium, and Switzerland practicing Rectified Scottish Rite. Lodges of Saint Andrew and the Prefectures are under the control of Great Priories. The most prominent one is Great Priory of Helvetia (Switzerland). There are Great Priories in France ("Great Priory of Gaul"), in Scotland, Belgium, England and Wales, Germany, Greece, Spain, Portugal, Australia, and elsewhere.

THE FRENCH RITE

Rituals of the Craft degrees of the "French Rite" have their roots in the original English Rituals, which were translated to French around 1725. In their general form, they were never significantly changed, which makes these Rituals some of the oldest authentic Craft Rituals still in use. The Grand Orient of France established the "French Rite" in 1786. The idea behind formulating this Rite was to bring down the number of the so-called "high degrees" and to keep only the important ones. Also, efforts were made to come up with Craft Ritual that would be official Ritual of the Grand Orient.

The "French Rite" has seven degrees. The first three Craft degrees are conferred in the Blue Lodge. The fourth degree "Elect", fifth degree "Scottish Master", sixth degree "Knight of the East" and seventh degree "Knight Prince of Rose Croix" are conferred in the Chapters. This Rite was one of the most often practiced systems in France and in Belgium, specially its Craft degrees. After 1877, French Rite was gradually "secularized" by omitting references to the "Great Architect of the Universe and immortality of the soul" from the ritual and particularly from the Obligations. These changes made higher degrees of the French Rite (4th to 7th) unattractive to a majority of Masons. Some of them, after completing three Craft degrees in the French Rite, would often continue their education in other Rites, like Ancient Accepted Scottish Rite. Under the name "Modern Rite" it was re-introduced in its unaltered original form in 1979, in couple of the Lodges of the National Grand Lodge of France, where most of the subordinate Lodges are practicing

Rectified Scottish Rite. Since that time, we can say that the French Rite is experiencing revival in France and Belgium. Because of its seven degrees, spiritualism, deep esoteric content of the lessons of higher degrees, and its antiquity and authenticity as the oldest French Craft Ritual, it became again very attractive for the seekers of the Masonic enlightenment in France. The French Rite is practiced in France, Belgium, and a number of Jurisdictions of South America.

Picture 42. *Tracing Board of the First Degree of the French Rite*

THE ANCIENT AND PRIMITIVE RITE OF MEMPHIS-MIZRAIM (A.P.R.M.M.)

The Ancient and Primitive Rite of Memphis-Mizraim and its ninety-six degrees have unique place among Masonic Rites. Since the "revival" of 1717, there were always Masons who were not very interested in the higher or additional degrees. Their understanding was that one could find all of the guidance necessary in the lectures and ceremonies of the Craft degrees and that there is no need for additional degrees. This is certainly not a case with the founders and practitioners of the Memphis – Mizraim Rite.

Joseph Balsano, called Cagliostro founded the Rite of Misraim, sometime around 1788. The Rite was spreading quickly through the Northern Italy and South France, just to be forbidden by state authorities in 1817, following some questionable events. Brothers Bedarride developed the Rite of Memphis in 1813 in Paris. Jacques Etienne Marconis de Negre was made "Grand Hierophant" in 1838. In 1841, Lodges become dormant until 1848, when their work was revived. In 1850, this Rite was introduced in England, where they worked in French. In 1856, De Negre brought this Rite to the United States where it became very popular, particularly under H. J. Seymour, who in 1862, took over its activities. In 1873, the Rite was introduced in Egypt where it was worked under direction of S. A. Zola. In 1888, through the efforts of General Garibaldi, the two Rites merged in what would be known as Memphis-Mizraim Rite.

There are three levels of teachings in this Rite. From the First to the Third degree, it is Symbolic Masonry, where symbolism is researched and candidates are introduced to the basics of Masonic philosophy. From the Fourth to the Thirty-third, it is considered Philosophical Masonry. Through the study of philosophy, history, and myths, one tries to comprehend causes and effects in human destiny. From Thirty-fourth to the Ninety-fifth, it is Hermetic or Esoteric Masonry. Here, one studies religious myths, mysticism, Alchemy, and different currents of the spiritual and esoteric traditions. Today, this Rite is practiced in France, Spain, Switzerland, Scandinavia, USA, Brazil, Argentina, Chile, Uruguay, Martinique, and Mauritius.

Picture 43.
The Grand Seal of the A.P.R.M.M. (top)

Joseph Balsano, called Cagliostro, the founder of the Rite of Misraim (right)

THE SWEDISH RITE

In 1774, Duke Karl of Soedermanland, Grand Master of the Grand Lodge of Sweden (founded in 1759), who will later become King of Sweden Karl the 13th, decided that all of the degrees practiced in Sweden should come under the control of the Grand Lodge. Through his efforts, the Swedish Rite was founded. In the following years, he revised the system and expanded it to the eleven degrees that it has now. The three Craft degrees are conferred in the Lodge of Saint John. "Apprentice and Companion of Saint Andrew" and "Master of Saint Andrew" are conferred in the Lodge of Saint Andrew. The 7th degree (Very Illustrious Brother-Knight of the East), 8th degree (Most Illustrious Brother-Knight of the West), 9th degree (Enlightened Brother of St. John's Lodge), and 10th degree (Very Enlightened Brother of St. Andrew's Lodge), are all conferred in the Capitular or Provincial Lodges. The Grand Lodge confers the eleventh degree (Most Enlightened Brother-Knight Commander of the Red Cross). At present time, there are only about sixty Masons holding this rank.

One of the important characteristics of this Rite is in progression of the degrees. Each sums up the lessons of the preceding degree and leads to the next one. Advancement through the degrees is not automatic. It depends on one's efforts, knowledge of Freemasonry, proficiency, and dedication. In 1811, King of Sweden established the "Royal Order of King Karl the 13th". It is a civil Order conferred by King on Freemasons holding the Eleventh degree, and is limited to thirty-three members. This Order is, however, not considered a Masonic degree. Today,

Swedish Rite is practiced in Sweden, Finland, Norway, Denmark, and Germany.

Picture 44. *The Swedish Rite Regalia*

THE SCHROEDER'S RITE

Schroeder's Rite is a Ritual of three Craft degrees written by Friedrich Ludwig Schroeder and adopted for use in the Grand Lodge of Hamburg in 1801. F. L. Schroeder was one of the greatest actors of his time in Germany, Director of the Municipal Theater in Hamburg, as well as accomplished Masonic scholar and the Grand Master of the Grand Lodge of Hamburg.

Masonic Rituals in use in the Germany at the close of the eighteen century were very esoteric in their content, with ever-new higher degrees, inspired with Hermetic Philosophy, Rosicrucianism, and Alchemy. Many in the Masonic community were of the opinion that Masonry should consist only of three degrees, as it appear in its original form in England, and that nothing else belongs to it.

For this reason Schroeder composed the Rite of three Craft degrees (Apprentice, Fellowcraft and Master Mason), based on his translation of early English Rituals, primarily ritualistic exposure "Jachin and Boaz" from 1762, by Goodall. For those interested in the higher degrees he founded "Select Historical Union" open only to Master Masons and for the purpose of studying other Rites and degrees. It took Schroeder almost two decades to complete the final form of his Rituals, but it was worth it. This Rite became very popular, and still is practiced in Germany, Austria, Croatia, Serbia, Slovenia, and Montenegro, as well as some Lodges of the Grand Lodge of Switzerland - Alpina.

THE EMULATION RITE

Emulation Rite or most commonly known among Anglo American Masons as Emulation Working or Emulation Ritual, founded in 1823, was a product of a number of Masons, who were members of the "Emulation Lodge of Improvement". The purpose of this Lodge was to teach the Ritual of the three Craft degrees which was adopted, after number of revisions, following the unification and establishment of the United Grand Lodge of England in 1813.

Emulation Ritual is the most popular ritual of the United Grand Lodge of England, which came as a product of an attempt to standardize rituals used in English Lodges and to make it universal by taking out some of the pure Christian references. "Emulation Lodge of Improvement" still works in London and is open to Master Masons. It does not confer degrees, but just exemplifies the work of three degrees and the Ritual of Installation of a Master. This Rite is practiced, not only in England, but also in Lodges in France, Switzerland, Australia, Africa, New Zealand, India, and Canada. Many Lodges in England kept their traditional Craft Rituals, so today we still have, beside Emulation, several other rituals in use; such as Oxford, Domatic, Stability, Logic, Aldersgate, Bristol, Universal, North London, and Taylor etc.

6

ORIGINS OF FREEMASONRY

What are the origins of Freemasonry? As we already mentioned, historians and Masonic scholars have different ideas about what Masonry is. There are also disagreements as to where it came from. When the Premier Grand Lodge of 1717 was established, founding members adopted "Legends of Origin" from the guilds (or companies) of medieval operative stonemasons, as their own. For many years, these legends were part of the official general history of Freemasonry, which entertained the theory that finds roots of speculative Freemasonry within the traditions of the medieval operative stonemasons. Even with the blessing of the Masonic authorities, this remains only one of the many theories.

Other most popular theories derive origins of Freemasonry in the Ancient Mystery Schools; in the organization, teachings and practices of medieval Knights Templar; in the philosophy of the secret order of Rosicrucians; or in the ideas of the men of the Age of Enlightenment. All of these theories have their own arguments which, when taken separately, seem credible and make each theory possible. Nonetheless, the lack of written records and other material evidence prevents giving advantage to any of the theories.

There was never much doubt as to the origins of the organizational structure of the fraternity of speculative Freemasonry itself. Problem arises when we try to connect its speculative philosophical concept to the teachings of operative stonemasons. There is absolutely no evidence in the manuscripts predating formation of the Premier Grand Lodge of 1717, pointing to speculative content of their instructions. Some Masonic scholars are of the opinion that we should look for the origin of philosophical concept of speculative Freemasonry within the context of Western Hermetic Philosophy in the time of Renaissance. Any way we look, we would necessarily have to come back in our research to the original "accepted" members of the seventeen-century Lodges, for within their intellectual affinities and practices lay the answer to our question. By looking at the nature of the Masonic Rites and Rituals, one cannot but notice the fusion of so many different philosophical traditions. Such synthesis could chronologically appear only in the Age of Enlightenment, when all the components were available.

Picture 45. *Masonic symbols*

ANCIENT MYSTERIES

The claim that Freemasonry is nothing else but a School of Mysteries is again very popular among Freemasons. As a philosophical concept, Freemasonry is concerned with man's inner being, his spiritual personality, and absolute truths regarding his destiny and role in the universe. One of the conditions for advancing on the path of sacred knowledge is to practice virtue and to maintain the integrity of the true wisdom. Freemasonry teaches us the unity of God and natural laws, and the resurrection of man to eternal life. It is an initiatory order, for to become a Mason, one has to go through the Rites of initiation. The nature of Masonic association is private. Its modes of recognition, oath, and teachings are secret. Everything we have mentioned so far is characteristic of the ancient Mystery schools. It would be natural to conclude that there must be some intimate connection between Freemasonry and the ancient Mystery schools.

All great teachers agreed that the "higher knowledge" must be presented concealed by symbols in order to be understood. It is logical to conclude that Freemasonry which uses the language of symbols in its rituals is searching for higher knowledge. There were many speculations about the nature of this higher knowledge. Is our Age the only Age of Knowledge? Is it possible that before our prehistory, there was another age with its own advanced knowledge and its own history? Some believe that to be true. There are also claims of the existence of the "sacred truth of Nature" concealed in the ancient mysteries and perpetuated in the Rituals and Rites of Freemasonry. It is an obligation of every initiate to search for that truth. Manly P. Hall calls Freemasonry "the science of the soul" and "the expression of Divine Wisdom" liberated from any creed or doctrine. The only chance to advance in Freemasonry is to understand it as a pathway to a higher "cosmic knowledge" with the realization of spiritual enlightenment as the final destination.

As human beings, we are connected in many ways to each other, to the nature that surrounds us and to the outermost parts of the Universe. Our existence is not manifested only on the visible physical level, but on many other levels. In the occasional excursions to our collective unconscious through dreams and altered states of mind, we realize that there is much more to our destiny then what we see when we open our eyes in the morning. The whole universe lives one life, breaths at the same speed the air of Divine creation. It is not necessary to peek through powerful telescopes or to send modules in space to realize this universal fact. The ancient sages proclaimed in the writings on the Smaragdine Tablet: *"True, without error, certain and most true; that which is above is as that which is below, and that which is below is as that which is above..."* The clues to the nature of the Universe, of the Divine, and of the whole existence are hidden deep within ourselves. The ultimate duty and the ultimate goal are to find within, and to live in accordance with the great truths, to build the inner Temple to the glory of Creation. When a Mason walks into the Lodge room, he is not entering the meeting place of the fraternity of builders. He is coming to the portal, to the entrance of the celestial Lodge of Wisemen and Sages from time immemorial. There, in that simple room, in the columns, furnishings, and ornaments, behind the symbols of Masonry, are inscribed directions to the "place not seen and to the things hoped for." An initiate is faced with several mysteries and experiences of the soul, once he steps on the path into Masonry: Mystery of Initiation, Mystery of Life, Mystery of Death and Resurrection, and the Mystery of Communion with God.

There are two problems with describing the ceremony of the Initiation of the Adept into Masonry. The first one is connected with our inability to express in words all of the experiences that one goes through during initiation; and the second has to do with the oath of secrecy of every new initiate. Masonry, like all other Schools of Mysteries, conceals its secrets from all profane and uninitiated and uses false explanations and misinterpretations of its symbols. Truth is not for those who are unworthy or unable to receive it, for they would distort it and destroy it.

The process for the new Initiate starts much before he knocks on the door of the Lodge room to be received. It has to be an act "of his free will and accord"- he has to have a sincere desire for true knowledge, not to be pressed or pushed into it; he must be "worthy and well qualified"- only those who possess virtue can step on the path of self-discovery; he must be "duly and truly prepared"- one has to be ready to relieve himself of all of the superfluities of life in order to enter his higher conscience.

Once the Adept enters the Sanctuary, he starts a new life, but he does not realize the meaning of the experience yet, nor there are assurances that he will ever understand it. As with any other Rite of Passage, he holds in his own hands the ends of the blindfold covering his inner understanding. It is up to him and up to his efforts to remove the blindfold and expose his eyes and his mind to true enlightenment. The same is true of Baptism. How many of those baptized in infancy ever grow up to realize the meaning of the initiation that they have undergone?

The Initiate then starts his symbolical voyage. There he is purified with the elements of air, water, fire and earth. Then he is given the symbolical tools of the Masonic trade. His attention is called to the two stones sitting one next to the other in the sanctuary. One is the rough stone of his own nature, rough with bad habits, heavy with passions and prejudice, brittle with fear and confusion, hard and often invisible. The other is the perfect stone- the stone we need to attain, the stone of loving kindness toward oneself, our neighbor and the whole of Creation, the stone of all things hoped for.

But this is just an opportunity; there are no guaranties or promises. As it is written in the books of the sacred knowledge - "many are called, but few are chosen." The road is long, often dark and treacherous, with many obstacles; even one's life could be threatened. But help is there. A fellow human being, Brother and friend, who walked the same way before, is offering his guiding hand without any desire for reward. He can advise, point, warn, and help when one falls, but the work has to be done by the Initiate alone.

Every initiate is bound by the oath of secrecy. This is his first duty to the Brothers of the Lodge and to himself. The search for the higher truth cannot be done in the public eye, in the presence of the profane and unworthy. It cannot be transmitted, unless concealed by symbols, handed over from one Great Teacher to another, from one age to another. Every Great Teacher was once a humble initiate. Every Great Teacher never stops being a humble Initiate. And every humble Initiate has a chance to be a Great Teacher. One of the Great Unknown Masters Oscar Ernst Bernhardt (1875-1941), known as Abd-ru-shin, in his work <u>In the</u>

<u>Light</u> of <u>Truth:</u> <u>The</u> <u>Grail Message</u>, wrote: *"The Message of the Son of God pointed out the way once before. But in his eagerness to show how clever he was, man interpreted it wrongly in many respects and consequently misplaced the signposts, thereby misleading the human spirit and preventing it from rising!....Therefore I call out once more: Take all these things as factual, as real, and no longer regard them as figurative! Then you yourselves will become living realities instead of the lifeless shadows you now are! Learn to understand Creation aright in its laws! Therein lies the way upward to the Light!"*

The mystery of creation and existence of life is the first question the student of Freemasonry must face. He is introduced to reason and advised to study the seven liberal arts and sciences. His tool is reason; his laboratory is Nature. He himself is a researcher and the subject of research. He cannot come up with false results; he cannot deceive himself, for it defeats the purpose. The very first thing he learns is that taking a degree does not make a Freemason. A Mason is not made; he is just given a chance and he must understand that the position he holds in the exoteric lodge or in the profane life means nothing compared to his position in the spiritual lodge of higher existence. He must forever abandon the idea that he can be told or instructed in the Great Mysteries or that his being a member of Brotherhood of Masons makes him better in any way. Manly P. Hall tells us: *"He (Initiate) must realize that his duty is to build and evolve the sacred teachings in his own being: that nothing but his own purified being can unlock the door to the sealed libraries of human consciousness, and that his Masonic rites must eternally be speculative until he makes them operative by living the life of the mystic*

Mason. His karmic responsibilities increase with his opportunities. Those who are surrounded with knowledge and opportunity for self-improvement and make nothing of these opportunities are the lazy workmen who will be spiritually, if not physically, cast out of the temple of the king." (The Lost Keys of Freemasonry, Manly P. Hall, Macoy Publishing and Masonic Supply Co. Richmond, Va., 1976.)

All those joined together in the chain of union of the Masonic Lodge are not there for social, political or commercial reasons. They are there to unlock the mysteries and to learn to apply the principles of Freemasonry to their everyday life. They become the practitioners both of occult Rites and of practical philosophy. The ultimate goal is not only to become better, smarter or happier, but to contribute their part to that great edifice called Human kind and to that eternal celestial Lodge, of which we all hope to become worthy members. The rich are not those who accumulate, but only those who give. The blessed are not those who give, but only those who receive. The history of human kind is the story of our efforts to experience the continuation of existence beyond the boundaries set by the natural process of life and death. Each of us carries in his mind Job's question: "If a man dies, shall he live again". This is not a question about the roots in the human incapacity to grasp the concept of creation. Desire to "find that which was lost" and "gather that which was scattered" is ever present; for the ultimate goal is the completion- return to the original "higher state of man".

In the third degree of Freemasonry, the candidate going through the Rites, represents one of the three Master Builders and is symbolically killed by three fellow workers. His body is discovered by another three workers, who bring his body back to the Temple. After three attempts his body is raised by one of the Grand Masters. Through this ceremony, the candidate symbolically goes from the world of living, to the world of dead, and back.

Now he is an experienced journeyman. He is given the secret word, and he can start his new life without the fear of death. As Jesus of Nazareth said: *"That which is born of the flesh is flesh; that which is born of the spirit is spirit. Do not be surprised, therefore, when I say unto you, than except man be born again he can not see the Kingdom of Heaven."* Master Mason is also obligated not to waste his life, but to use it for the benefit of the mankind. He is now a Master Builder. He rules not only in the Lodge room, but in the profane world as well. In the Gospel of Thomas we read: *"Whoever has come to understand the world has found a corpse, and whoever has found a corpse, is superior to the world"*

The repeated presence of the number three in this story seems to be the most intriguing. From the three-fold principles of Creation in the ancient mysteries, to the Holy Trinity of Christianity, the number three is the number of the completion of all things. It is the number of birth. Opposites are balanced by a third. Iablichus (c.250-c.330) Greek Neo-platonic Philosopher notices that: "The *Triad has a special beauty and fairness beyond all numbers, primarily because it is the very first to make actual the potentialities of the Monad."*

It seems to me that Ancient Mysteries, Religion, Science, and Art, persistently repeat the importance of trinities for one and only reason: The Tripartite nature of the universe is in constant touch with the archetypal roots within us. It is a continuous

TABVLA SMA-
RAGDINA HERMETIS TRIS-
megisti 제일 χυσίας. Incerto interprete.

erba Secretorũ Hermetis, q̃ scripta erãt in tabula Smaragdi, inter manus eius inuenta, in obscuro antro, in q̃ humatum corpus eius repertũ est. Verũ sine mendacio, certũ, & uerissimũ. Quod est inferius, est sicut q̃d est superius. Et q̃d est supius, est sicut q̃d est inferius, ad ppetrãda miracula rei unius. Et sicut oẽs res fuerũt ab uno, meditatiõe unius. Sic oẽs res natæ fuerũt ab hac una re, adaptatiõe. Pater eius est Sol, mater eius Luna. Portauit illud uentus in uẽtre suo. Nutrix eius terra est. Pater omnis telesmi totius mũdi est hic. Vis eius integra est, si uersa fuerit in terrã. Separabis terrã ab igne, subtile à spisso, suauiç cũ magno ingenio. Ascendit à terra in cœlũ, iterumq̃ descẽdit in terrã, & recipit uim superiorũ & inferiorũ. Sic habebis gloriã totius mundi. Ideo fugiet à te omnis obscuritas. Hic est totius fortitudinis fortitudo fortis, qa uincet omnem rem subtilem, omnemq̃ solidam penetrabit. Sic mundus creatus est. Hinc erunt adaptationes mirabiles, quarũ modus hic est. Itaq̃ uocatus sum Hermes Trismegistus, habens tres partes philosophiæ totius mundi. Completũ est, q̃d dixi de operatiõe Solis.

Picture 46.
Tabula Smaragdina (Emerald Tablet)

Picture 47, 48.
Alchemical Symbols

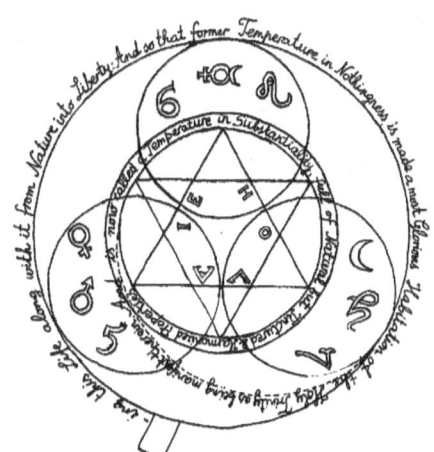

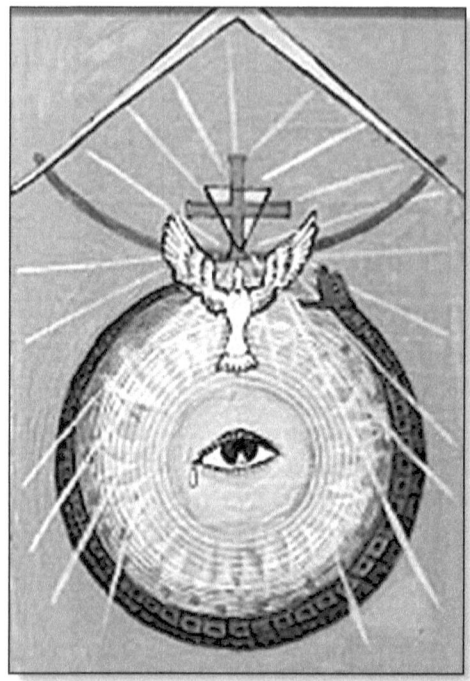
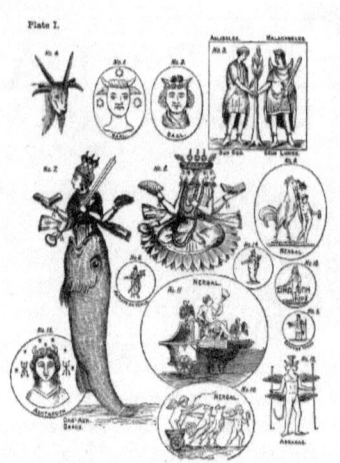

Picture 49. *Mystery Schools* (top)

Picture 50. *"Understanding"* Acrylic on canvas, © by Tamara Nikolic (left)

reminder that we are inseparable part of the great and eternal whole. Here in the third degree the doctrine of the new birth becomes the story of the awakening from the material life to the higher reality of our inner being. Here we experience the communion with God – the return to the birth place of our soul. Here is also the place where the real work is just about to begin. There are no more excuses. We are the Master Builders responsible for the true work. Challenges of the profane world and of our physical nature are many. But we are Adepts of the oldest School of Mysteries. Our strength is in Providence. We are not alone on our quest for the better world. Invisible forces of the Universe are here with us every step of the way. And the great question still remains: Does a man hold the keys to his future?

KNIGHTS TEMPLAR

In 1737, Chevalier Andrew Ramsey, Freemason of Scottish birth and Grand Chancellor and Orator of the Provincial Grand Lodge of England in Paris, wrote a discourse in which he developed a theory of origin of Freemasonry from the medieval Order of Knights Templar. In his famous "oration", he exclaimed: *"During the time of the holy wars in Palestine, several principal lords and citizens associated themselves together, and enter into a vow to re-establish the temples of the Christians in the Holy Land; and engage themselves by an oath to employ their talents and their fortunes in restoring architecture to its primitive institution. They adopted several ancient signs and symbolic words drawn from religion, by which they might distinguish themselves from the infidels..."* According to speculations of some Masonic scholars, based on the Chevalier Ramsey's speech, the Order was in possession of the secret arcane knowledge, which they acquired during their stay in Jerusalem, and was preserved in the teachings of the Brotherhood of Freemasons.

Nine French Knights founded the "Order of the Poor Fellow-Soldiers of Christ and the Temple of Solomon", which was their full title, in 1118 in Jerusalem. They were permitted to take lodging in the quarters erected at the site of King Solomon's Temple. After ten years of protecting pilgrims who were traveling to the Holy Places in Jerusalem, this Order suddenly became very influential, with special status and privileges granted by the Pope. Growing in numbers, through generous donations from Christian nobility, it became immensely rich. After almost 180 years of existence, they owned over nine thousand castles across Europe and became biggest landowners. Revenues from their properties were used for the operation of the largest banking system in Europe at the time, run by Templars.

After being driven out of Palestine, with the rest of the Crusaders, the Order continued its growth in their bases throughout Europe until 1307, when its Grand Master, Jacques de Molay, and many members of the Order were arrested by the French King Philip the Fair, and brought to trial on made-up charges of blasphemy and sorcery. In 1312, the Pope Clement the Fifth officially dissolved the Order and in 1314, Jacques de Molay was burned at the stake. Knights Templar were persecuted all over Europe by order of the Pope. Some of the Knights, according to legend, found sanctuary and protection in Scotland, far from the reach of the Catholic Church. The Order continued to exist there in seclusion for centuries and their secret knowledge was apparently preserved and transferred to the Fraternity of Freemasons.

As the theory goes, while in Palestine, the Knights Templar came in possession of great knowledge, which if revealed, would destroy the foundations of the medieval Catholic Church and its dogmatic teachings. Apparently, this knowledge has been found in the written form of scrolls buried in the secret vault under King Solomon's Temple together with many other riches like the Ark of the Covenant and the Holy Grail. These scrolls also contained secrets of different arts and sciences, particularly those of geometry and architecture. According to theory, this would explain the great knowledge of Cathedral building by Knights Templar and later by Freemasons, who used the designs of these edifices as a code to symbolically preserve their secret knowledge and, point to the few chosen ones, the place where all "treasures" were hidden. There are variations of this theory regarding the content of the treasure or secret knowledge discovered by Knights Templar. According to some, these secrets are about the truths of the origin of man and his place in the Universe. Others believe that it concerns the name of God, his essence and his relationship to humanity. In some interpretations, it is all about magical and scientific secrets of immense power. Still, there are those who think that the secret knowledge is related to the destiny of Jesus Christ and the Holy Grail.

According to this theory, Christ was married to Mary Magdalene who bore him a child. After Mary Magdalene left Palestine, she went to live on the Mediterranean coast of France, where their child grew up. It was claimed that the Merovingian Kings of France were direct descendants of Jesus and Mary's offspring. A medieval sect of Cathars was brought into picture as a possible link between early Christian Gnostics and Templars. All of these theories, which make entertaining evening reading material, put Freemasons as possessors of secret knowledge, owners of the treasures with miraculous properties, and protectors of the "Holy Blood Line".

There is a much easier and more logical way to connect medieval Knights Templar and Freemasons, maybe not as direct descendants, but as individuals of the same mind-set and Societies with similar values. Poor Fellow-Soldiers of Christ and the Temple of Solomon were brutal monk-warriors with strict monastic and military rules of life and conduct. The very idea of being both monk and warrior at the same time was itself a controversial one, which placed these men in an odd position to start with. The Order existed in Palestine for almost two hundred years before Ottomans pushed it out of the Middle East.

Palestine of the twelfth century was a colorful mix of many ethnic groups with different customs, cultures and religions. Among them were various Christian, Jewish and Muslim Sects, which did not subscribe to the official teachings of any of their religions. We know that, because such sects still exist today in the modern Middle Eastern countries. Some scholars believe that Knights Templar, while involved in the bloody warfare in the name of their God, to whom they committed their lives as monks, had to answer themselves conflicting questions regarding their acts, faith, purpose, and existence. It is just possible that some of the answers, instead of being in the dogmatic teachings of the medieval Catholic Church, were found in Gnostic teachings of different Christian or Manichaeans sects, or in the scrolls written by the members of the Jewish sect of Essenes, or even in the writings of Muslim Sufi Mystics. There is historical evidence that members of the Order were influenced by the cultures and customs with which they were surrounded. Maybe they brought back to Europe, to the great displeasure of the Pope and ruling Royal Houses, among other things, ideas, culture, and philosophy that did not fit well into the realities of the thirteenth century Europe. The question remains, did this contribute to their tragic end and their dissolution by Pope Clement V in 1312? What would be the parallel between the Knights Templar and Freemasons that attracted the latter to adopt the former as their ancestors ...for one, its position towards the dogmatic teachings of the Catholic Church?

In many ways, the Order of the Templars was an independent

organization within Catholic Church, practicing its religion in seclusion, only nominally responsible to the Pope. This independence was probably very attractive to the men of the early eighteenth century trying to free themselves from the pressures caused by constant religious conflicts in Europe. In the age of Enlightenment, men entering a new era in history needed examples from the past, to help them on their path and to strengthen their conviction for the progress of humanity.

Let us try to analyze the eighteenth-century men, particularly a Freemasons, and try to find answers to questions such as: What did they believe in? What were their hopes and fears? What was their attitude towards fellow men of different religions, women, or wealth? What was their understanding of life and death? In answering these questions, we would most certainly come up with a picture of a very confused individual, who had lost his way and was in urgent need to make sense of his existence and find a path towards a higher truth and towards "Paradise Lost". In the eyes of the eighteen-century men, the Knights Templar with their "chivalric quest" would perfectly fit into this profile as well: - Monks who committed their lives to Christ, took up swords, used them to savagely kill in Christ's name, fought gloriously for a Christian Kingdom in Palestine, and were defeated. They returned to Europe but were never fully accepted, questioned their own teachings, and finally were destroyed by the Church, which they served. Yes, they must have been very confused and in desperate need of answers. It was almost necessary for the Order of Templars to be reborn in the minds of romantic men of the age of Enlightenment. For them, the Templar ideal was the only encouragement that their new ideas based both on the ancient teachings and new philosophical and scientific speculations completely outside of Christian Church dogma, would survive the test of time.

Picture 51. *Pilgrims under escort of Knight Templar in sight of Jerusalem , by Eduard Zier*

Picture 52. *Knights Templar flag*

Picture 53. *Knights Templar seal*

Picture 54. *Templar tombstone in Scotland,* photo© D. Garner

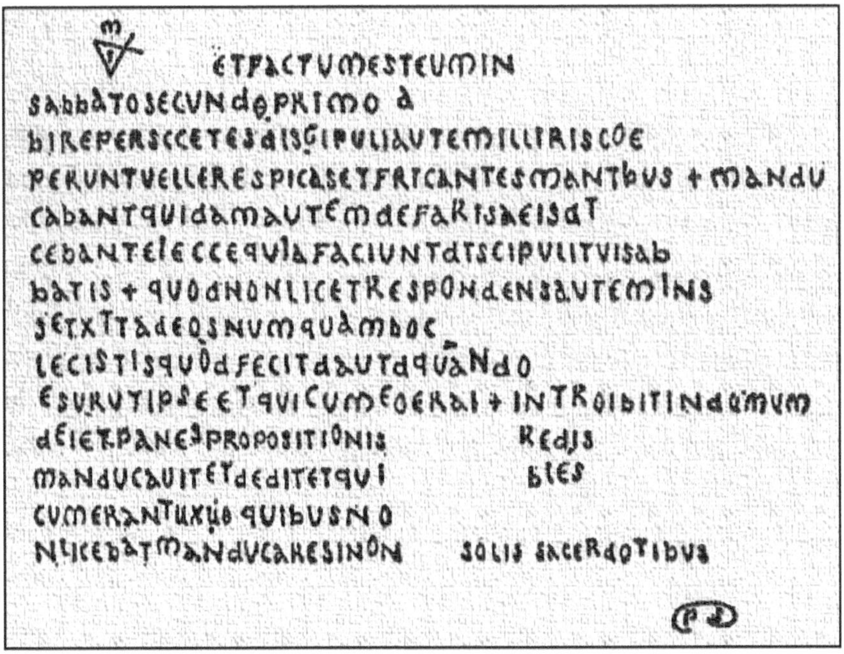

ET FACTUM EST EUM IN
SABBATO SECUNDO PRIMO A
BI REPERSCCETES DISCIPULI AUTEM ILLIRIS COE
PERUNT VELLERE SPICAS ET FRICANTES MANIBUS + MANDU
CABANT QUIDAM AUTEM DE FARISAEIS AT
CEBANTELECCE QUI A FACIUNT DISCIPULI TUI SAB
BATIS + QUOD NON LICET RESPONDENS AUTEM INS
SE TXT ADEQS NUM QUAM HOC
LECISTI SQUOD FECIT DAUT A QUANDO
ESURUT IPSE ET QUI CUM EOE RAI + INTROIBIT IN DOMUM
DEI ET PANES PROPOSITIONIS   REdIS
MANDUCAUIT ET DEDIT ET QUI   bIES
CUM ERANT UXQE QUIBUS NO
NLICEBAT MANDUCARE SI NON   SOLIS SACERDOTIBUS

Picture 55. *Mysterious Rennes-Le-Chateau Parchment*

THE ROSICRUCIANS

The Secret Fraternity of the Rosy Cross is another group mentioned as originators of the concept of speculative Freemasonry. In 1614, the pamphlet *"Fama Fraternitatis"* was published by an anonymous author in Germany as part of a bigger volume entitled <u>Universal and General Reformation of the whole wide world, together with the Fama Fraternitatis of the Laudable Fraternity of the Rosy Cross.</u> Soon after two other pamphlets, *"Confessio"* and *"Chemical Wedding"* appeared, and these three make, what is popularly known as the <u>Rosicrucian Manifestos</u>. Although the author is unknown, it is believed that Lutheran theologian Johan Valentine Andréa wrote them. The appearance of the Rosicrucian Manifestos represents the first reference to the Brotherhood of the Rosi Cross.

In the "Fama Fraternitatis" we find the allegorical story of Christian Rosenkreutz, mythical founder of the Rosicrucian Brotherhood. He was an "illuminated man", who traveled to the East where he learned "Magia and Cabala" from the wise men who deemed him worthy of transferring their knowledge to him. From there he traveled first to Spain and then back to Germany, where he founded, at first with only three helpers, the Fraternity of the Rosy Cross. Their main duty was to tend the sick free of charge and to spread the knowledge that they gained in their constant travels. They were obligated to be humble, dressed according of the customs of the country where they were staying, and meet once a year at their House of the Holy Spirit. The Fraternity grew in numbers and in the second Rosicrucian paper *"Confessio",* readers learned more about their philosophy and teachings, which call for the universal reformation of the religion and moral norms of European society through the application of the newly-acquired knowledge, mainly along the lines of the Protestant Reformation. The story also tells us about the discovery of the tomb of Christian Rosenkreutz by his disciples, 120 years after his death, filled with miraculous alchemical and cabalistic symbolism. The third romantic novel, <u>Chemical Wedding of Christian Rosencreutz</u>, represents further deepening of the same philosophy through an allegorical story. The <u>Rosicrucian Manifestos</u> bring to the reader a message of enlightened men who travel around inspired by the Divine, learning from Nature, teaching and healing people, and doing all kinds of good works, in the hope to bring themselves and humanity back to the lost original state of higher conscience, universal harmony, and perfection.

There is no proof that the secret Fraternity of the Rosy Cross, as presented in <u>Rosicrucian Manifestos</u>, ever existed, but again if one group wanted to remain "secret" and anonymous it would try probably not to leave too much evidence of its existence. There is, however, a lot of evidence of men of the seventeenth and eighteenth centuries trying to find and join this secret Order. This situation resulted in the formation of many "secret societies", subscribing to the teachings from the "manifestos" as they understood them, and claiming to be its direct descendants. According to writings by J. G.Buhle from 1804, and an essay by Thomas De Quincey, published in <u>London Magazine</u> in 1824, the Society of Freemasons is one such group, which "arose out of Rosicrucian mania". There are even earlier references placing the Freemasons and "brethren of Rosy Cross" in the same context, like the poem published at Edinburgh in 1638 mentioning the "masons word":

"For what we do presage is not in grosse,
For we be brethren of the Rosie Crosse:
We have the MASONS WORD and second sight
Things for to come we can foretell aright..."

In 1676, one of the first printed references to "Accepted Masons" refers to "Ancient Brotherhood of the Rosy Cross" as well. It goes as follows: *"To give notice, that the Modern Green-ribbon'd Caball, together with the Ancient Brotherhood of the Rosy Cross; the Hermetick Adepti and the company of Accepted Masons intend all to dine together on the 31st of November next..."* In 1730, a satirical letter was published in the English <u>Daily</u> <u>Journal</u> stating that Freemasons had based their ceremonies on those of the Rosicrucians. In the second part of the eighteenth century in France appeared a "new" Masonic grade called "Rose Croix" grade inspired by Christian Mysticism and Chivalry. This was followed by a number of esoteric Masonic groups proclaiming to be the true heirs of the Brotherhood of the Rosy Cross, whose teachings were intimately connected with those of the Freemasons. Such Masonic groups still exist today, mainly as unregulated and officially unrecognized groups by the major Masonic organizations throughout the world.

What are the similarities between Freemasonry and the Rosicrucians? Both Brotherhoods are involved in the search for the universal hidden wisdom, in building virtues in individuals, and in the practice of benevolence towards mankind. The fact that the "original" Brotherhood of the Rosy Cross probably never existed, loses its importance in view of the power of inspiration which their <u>Manifestos</u> had on the men of the age of Enlightenment in their pursuit of knowledge in the arts and sciences, and in the forming of the organizations committed to the "Advancement of Learning" such as the Royal Society, where many of the founding members were known to be Freemasons. This certainly points to the great importance of the Rosicrucian teachings in the development of speculative Freemasonry, but is far from anything that might support the theories rooting the origin of Freemasonry in the Rosicrucianism.

Picture 56. "*Rosa Mistica*"

Picture 57. *Collegium Fraternitatis,* by T. Schweighart, 1604

Count Goblet d'Alviella, in his comments on the paper presented in Quatuor Coronati Lodge No.2076, in 1919, wrote the following *"To sum up, I will not go so far as to pretend that speculative Masonry, as we know it, is the direct child of Rosicrucianism, but I uphold that it is the legitimate offspring of the fruitful union between the professional guild of medieval masons and a secret group of philosophical Adepts, the first having furnished the form and the second the spirit. The first parent died a natural death shortly after the birth of the child – unless we see its survival in the Trades Union of our time; the other is as lively and prosperous as ever, although confined for more than a century to the upper floors of the common mansion"*(AQC Transactions, London, Vol. XXXII, 1919, p.47).

THE THREE STAGE THEORY

For a very long time, the idea of the origin of Freemasonry from the medieval guilds of operative masons was the most supported theory among Masonic scholars and accepted as the "official" story of the origin by all major Masonic organizations. According to this theory, there were three stages in the development of Freemasonry as we have it today. First, as the Lodges of strictly operative masons whose origin we can trace back to the fourteenth century in the British Isles. The second stage being that of the "transitional Lodges" -Lodges of operative masons who were accepting as members men who were not masons or involved in any way with the building trade - records for which exist back to 1600 in Scotland. Third, Lodges of "accepted" (speculative) masons – of which we have records back to 1641, in England. There are numerous written records and "manuscripts", which document practices, organization, and development of the medieval Masonic guilds, particularly in Scotland. The oldest of these manuscripts, known as "Gothic Constitutions" or "Old Charges", came from the late 1300s (Regius Poem-1390), but most were dated after 1600. According to these documents, Masons were organized in Lodges, governed by Masters and Wardens, and they were regulating their trade, professional conduct and mutual relationship according to certain rules. From some of the documents related to the Scottish guilds, it is obvious that certain forms of ritual work were performed during the Lodge meetings. Admission of men who were not masons into Masonic guilds was well-documented, and we can clearly see from some of the records the gradual rise in numbers of so-called "accepted" masons in the Lodges of operative masons, to the point that some of them had membership consisting completely of accepted or speculative masons. To many students of Freemasonry, explanations and evidence that this theory offers would be sufficient to close the question of origins as answered.

There are few problems with this theory as well. The first one relates to the ritual of the eighteenth century Lodges. The first information on the ritual was found in 1730, in the pamphlet "Masonry Dissected" written by Samuel Prichard. Yet, there was very little evidence that would connect this particular ritual to anything practiced in the operative lodges before that time.

Second, with regard to "accepted" or speculative masons as members of operative Masonic lodges, the question as to what induced them to join guilds of operative masons was never satisfactorily answered. It is quite understandable that a prominent public person might join or accept an honorary membership in a trade organization in order to show support for whatever such trade organization does or stands for. However, to have men of different classes, political and religious backgrounds, joining the very same operative Lodges, there must be a much stronger reason than that of merely identifying oneself with the building trade.

The next problem relates to the differences in development between Lodges in Scotland and Lodges in England. The records tell us that operative Masonic guilds were developed much earlier and were stronger in Scotland than England. The first appearance of the "mason's word" or of the modes of recognition in Scotland was accepted as an undisputed fact. There was evidence of the initiation of prominent personalities in Lodges in Edinburgh in early 1640. There were claims of Edinburgh masons demonstrating two Masonic degrees, those of Entered Apprentice and of Fellow of the Craft, to English Freemasons in York in 1615. Yet, none of these arguments gave us solid proof of the existence of speculative Lodges or one predominantly speculative prior to 1717, to enable us to claim that Modern Freemasonry originated in Scotland.

On the other hand, many scholars subscribe to the theory that speculative Masonry started in England. Most often mentioned, as evidence, is the initiation of the antiquarian Elias Ashmole into the Lodge at Warrington, Lancashire on October 16, 1646. In his diary, the original manuscript of which is kept in Bodleian Library at Oxford, he wrote, " *4.30 PM. I was made a Free Mason in Warrington in Lancashire, with Col. Henry Mainwaring of Karnicham...*" He did not mention Freemasonry in his diary again until 1682. There are records of other prominent Englishmen of the seventeenth century who were speculative Freemasons, like Randle Holme III, antiquary and genealogist, Dr. Robert Plot, "Natural philosopher" and secretary of the Royal Society in 1682, Sir Christopher Wren, professor of astronomy and mathematics, and many others. In Anderson's <u>Constitutions</u> of 1738, we can find the claim that Sir Christopher Wren held the office of Grand Master prior to 1700, but because of the neglect of his duties, a new Grand Lodge had to be founded and a new Grand Master elected. In spite of all the information that we have in archives, libraries, and museums throughout England and Scotland, and many other claims of continental Freemasons trying to connect speculative Freemasonry with medieval operative masons in Germany and France, a few basic questions regarding these theories remain unanswered.

First and foremost is the question of origin of the esoteric content of Masonic teachings. Second is why all of these prominent and for their time extremely well educated men were seeking admission into the guilds of operative stonemasons. What kind of ritual did these men find in the Lodges they joined? Did they change or add parts of it? What were the qualifications for membership? We have surviving meeting minutes and regulations of the operative Lodges of this period but no written records of the speculative Lodges prior to 1717. Is there something in the whole story that we are missing? Bernard E. Jones wrote in his book Freemasons Guide and Compendium on this subject *"We can not read the story of the emergence of the symbolic Masonry and escape the conviction that between its lines there is another story, one that we should all like to read. Is there much hope that it will ever come to light?"* Can we hope one day to have the Masonic equivalent of the "Dead Sea Scrolls" discovery?

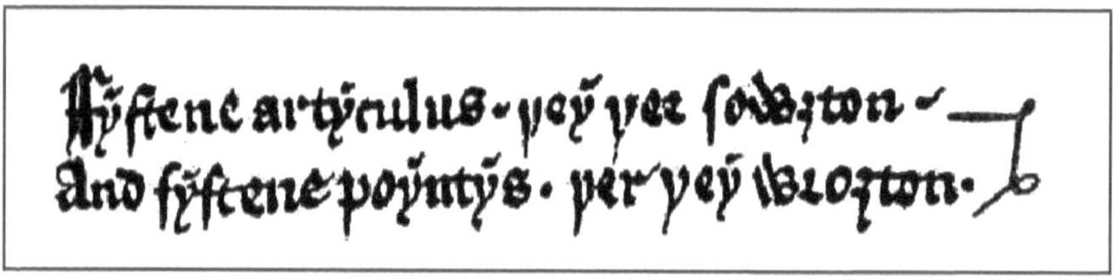
Fyftene artyculus þey þer soȝton
And fyftene poyntys þer þey wroȝton

Picture 58. *Regius MS, 1390*

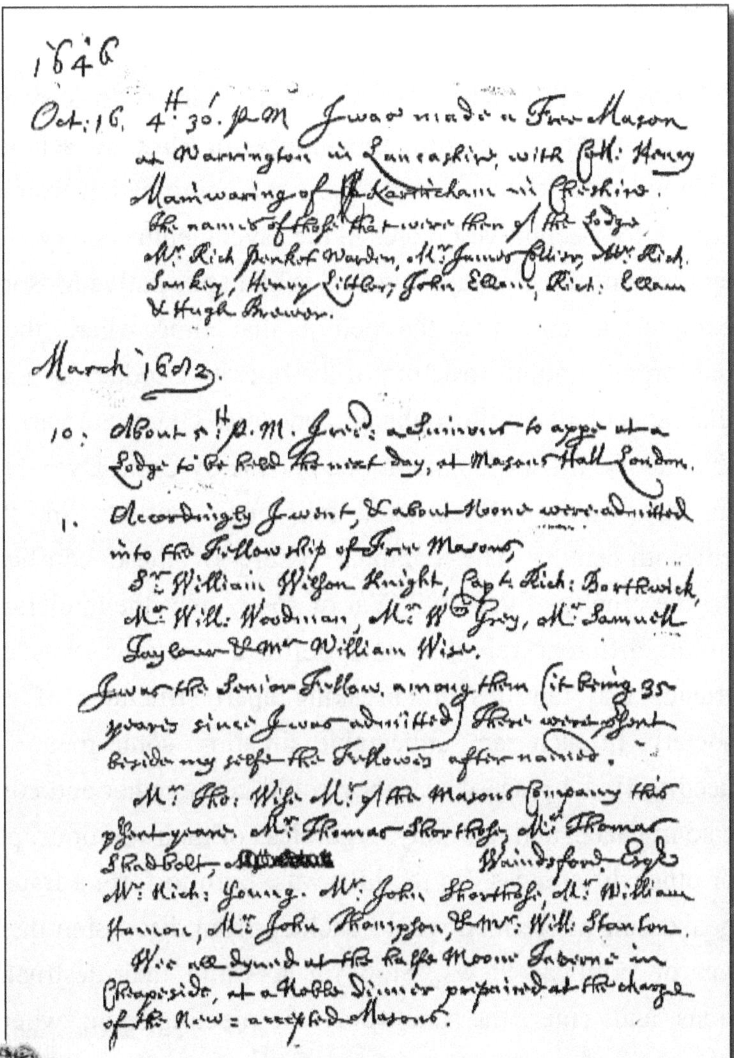

1646

Oct: 16. 4H 30' p.m. I was made a Free Mason at Warrington in Lancashire, with Coll: Henry Mainwaring of Karticham in Cheshire. The names of those that were then of the Lodge, Mr Rich Penket Warden, Mr James Collier, Mr Rich: Sankey, Henry Littler, John Ellam, Rich: Ellam & Hugh Brewer.

March 1682.

10. About 5H p.m. I recd: a Sumons to appr at a Lodge to be held the next day, at Masons Hall London.

11. Accordingly I went, & about Noone were admitted into the Fellow ship of Free Masons, Sr William Wilson Knight, Capt Rich: Borthwick, Mr Will: Woodman, Mr Wm Grey, Mr Samuell Taylour & Mr William Wise.

I was the Senior Fellow among them (it being 35 years since I was admitted) There were present beside my selfe the Fellowes after named. Mr Tho: Wise Mr of the Masons Company this present yeare. Mr Thomas Shorthose, Mr Thomas Shadbolt, [illegible] Waindsford Esqr Mr Rich: Young. Mr John Shorthose, Mr William Hamon, Mr John Thompson, & Mr Will: Stanton. Wee all dyned at the halfe Moone Taverne in Cheapside, at a Noble Dinner prepaired at the charge of the New-accepted Masons.

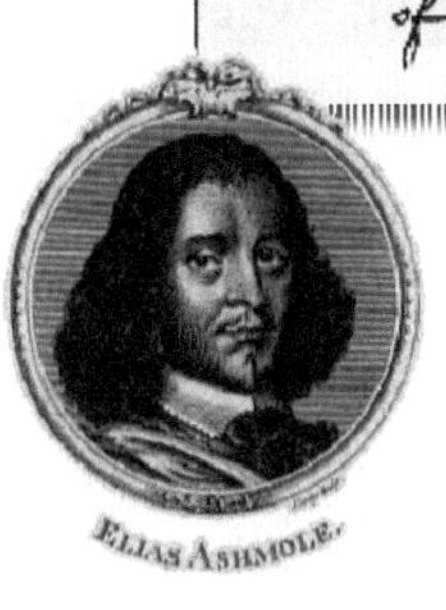

Picture 59. The antiquarian Elias Ashmole and the page from his diary from Oct. 16, 1646. (the original manuscript is kept in Bodleian Library at Oxford)

THE AGE OF ENLIGHTENMENT

There is yet another theory, which attempts to answer all of these questions. According to a number of Masonic scholars, the "Three Stage" theory failed to prove a continuation from the operative to speculative Lodges in the seventeenth century. The general idea of most of these writers is that speculative Masonry is a complete invention of the men of that time, where they used the organizational structure of the operative lodges as a shell for their speculative philosophical concepts. There are variations of this theory. Most often mentioned is one by Colin Dyer. He based his ideas on the political and religious conflicts in the seventeenth century. The complex nature of these conflicts, such as the cruelty of the Civil War of 1642, and the intolerance between different religious and political fractions, was dividing friends and families and breaking apart structures of civilized society. In such an unbearable situation, some men felt the need to find a place where they could get together and communicate in peace and harmony, regardless of their religious, political, or other differences. So the idea was born to form a fraternal organization where men would exclude from discussion their religion or political views. Stop for a while their destructive actions, and enter the sanctity of the meeting room, where they would, in the presence of God of all, try together to understand their reality and try to "build" and improve themselves for their own benefit and for the benefit of the society in desperate need for such solutions. Operative Masonic lodges gave the perfect cover for their organization with their building traditions. After all, these men wanted to rebuild the most important edifice on earth, destroyed by years of senseless, religious wars – MAN himself. The symbolic use of working tools and building practices in trying to develop their philosophy was a safe way of transmitting their ideas without using the symbols of any existing religions. Reference to God as the Great Architect of the Universe and the presence of a Volume of Sacred Law, was to assure their aim to always hold to the highest, most universal, moral and philosophical principles without ever subscribing to any particular religion or sect.

As an example of such an association, we can again refer to the initiation of Elias Ashmole in 1646. His initiation took place during the Civil War. Ashmole was a Royalist, captured and imprisoned by the Parliamentarians. Col. Henry Mainwaring was on the side of Parliament. He also happened to be Ashmole's father in law. These two men were initiated together in the presence of seven other Masons, - neither was operative and they belonged to the different sides in the Civil War. To understand the character of these associations, we could quote from the pamphlet "The Defence of Masonry" published in 1730. *"Others wonder at their admitting Men of all professions, Religions and Denominations: But they don't consider that Masons are true "Noachides" and require no other Denomination (all other Distinction being of Yesterday) if the new Brother is a good Man and True... Some observing Masons are not more religious, not more knowing, then other men, are astonished at what they can converse about in Lodge Hours! But tho' a Lodge is not a school of Divinity, the Brethren are taught the great lessons of the old religion ... .Morality, Humanity and Friendship, to abhor and to be peaceable subjects under the Civil Governments wherever they reside: and as for other Knowledge, they claim as large a Share of it, as other men in their Situation"*.

One of the major questions regarding this theory of origin is where did the Rituals come from? Were Rituals created consciously by one or more enlightened individuals, with a clear idea of what it was they wanted to achieve? On the other hand, are Rituals a collection of different teachings, ceremonies and philosophies with similar concepts, which solidified into one form over a period of time and through the interaction of individuals from different groups? There are those who believe that for the origin of the teachings and rituals of Freemasonry we should be looking among many students of Kabala, Alchemy, and Christian Mysticism in England of that time.

Kabala (meaning in Hebrew –"to receive") is secret Jewish mystical doctrine handed down and received through oral tradition. It is a system of religious philosophy. These teachings consist of four distinct parts: Practical, Literal, Unwritten and Dogmatic Kabala. Jewish Mystics, who lived in Spain in the middle Ages and had great influence on the work of some Christian theologians and philosophers in the time of Renaissance, introduced it into Europe. Many members of the early English speculative Lodges were familiar with the writings of most of the representatives of the Neo-Platonic and Hermetic philosophical schools. They were passionate readers of the Ficino's translation of <u>Corpus Hermeticum</u>, Mirandola's <u>Nine Hundred Conclusions</u>, Boyle's <u>Invisible College</u>, Comenius <u>Via Lucis,</u> and works by Dee, Fludd, and Hartlib. The works of great thinkers like Locke, Bacon, Descartes, and Newton influenced and inspired them. In the phase in European history of the so-called "Scientific Revolution", these men were equally concerned with their spiritual illumination as well as with the advancement of intellectual knowledge.

Regardless of the origin of rituals and teachings of the Lodges of speculative Freemasons, many are convinced that their Lodge practices had nothing to do with those of operative stonemasons. Whatever it was, it must have been very upsetting to some people according to the anti-Masonic leaflet published by M. Winter in Holbourn in 1698. *"Having thought it needful to warn you of the Mischiefs and Evils practiced in the Sight of God by those called Freed Masons, I say take Care lest their Ceremonies and secret Swearings take hold of you; and be wary that none cause you to err from Godliness. For this devilish Sect of Men are Meeters in secret which swear against all without their Following. They are the Anti Christ which was to come leading Men from Fear of God. For how should Men meet in secret Places and with secret Signs taking Care that none observe them to do the work of God; are not these the Ways of Evil-doers?"*

Reasons for such comments could be diverse. Either the author of this leaflet did not like the fact that men of different religions were sitting together in love and unity or he did not like whatever topics were discussed or the simple act of meeting in private did not sit well with this man. Whatever the reason, it was enough for him to refer to them as the Anti-Christ and Evil-doers. However, one thing is certain, if these men were performing the ritual of operative Lodges and discussing matters of trade; they would not have brought on themselves much wrath from an outsider.

So much has been written and said about the origins of Freemasonry and still it seems that we will never know the right answer. Maybe, just maybe, all of the answers are correct. Is it possible that everything from the Ancient Mysteries, early Christian Gnostics, Knights Templar, Rosicrucians, Cabalists, Alchemists, Neo-Platonists, operative stonemasons, to the enlightened men of the seventeenth and eighteenth centuries, played a part in the great design of Freemasonry? Many think it is a distinctive possibility.

Did Dr. James Anderson, when referring to Freemasonry as to a "Royal Art" in the first edition of his <u>Constitutions</u>, gave a hint about the origin and the content of the concept of Freemasonry. Could tripartite division of the Alchemy, which was also known as Royal Art among Hermetic Philosophers, be applied to Freemasonry? According to it, the part corresponding to the soul existed already in Egyptian Mystery Schools, particularly those from Alexandria. Its body came out of the wealth of knowledge accumulated through the ages by the Arab scholars. Its spirit was to be found within the work of natural philosophers of Ancient Greece. In the poem about the meaning of the Royal Art, published in Germany, in 1785, one could learn that the body gives form and constancy, the soul "doth dye and tinge it", and the spirit makes it fluid and penetrates it. The Art cannot survive in one of these three parts alone. "The greatest secret" cannot exit alone; it must have body, soul and spirit. Same way, the secret Word of Master Mason could not be communicated without presence of all three Master Builders. Once Hiram Abif was killed, the Word was lost. Earlier we mentioned the Chamber of reflection, where candidate, in the presence of salt, sulfur, and mercury, was advised to "visit the center of the earth, and find the hidden stone". What one could learn from it?

The major difference between humans and all other living beings on this planet is in their relationship to the mutual surroundings and to their destiny. While all forms of living organisms, somehow, by God's Divine Plan or through the laws of nature (whichever title one wishes to give to Great Architect of the Universe and his actions) adjust to the nature and to their destinies without consciously trying to change them, and thus become part of the great circle of life in the universe; humans were from the very beginning trying to modify, control, and conquer nature. Science will tell us that most of the living beings are not able to change their conditions willingly and significantly due to their physical and mental limitations and that our mind and conscience are what separate us from the rest of the nature in very special way.

Are our intelligence, along with our will and ability to influence and modify natural processes of Creation a blessing or a curse? Did they bring us closer to understand Creation or put us on the path of self-destruction? In the development of our civilizations, the advancement of knowledge of how to control natural resources and to best use them for the benefit of individuals and groups was an "easy" part. There were, however, and still are, processes and things that man could not control or modify; questions that he could not answer and answers that he could not understand. Three major unanswered questions were origin of Creation or nature of God, origin of man, and his place in Creation and the meaning of death.

Inability to have final answers to these questions made man feel tragically incomplete and insecure about his destiny. There he was, the most advanced being on the planet and even more, the conqueror and self- proclaimed owner of everything that surrounded him, but still unhappy, still in fear from unknown and in search of something, that he felt, he had at some point. Man was always trying to answer these questions, find that missing part of him, which had been lost, and understand his own death, so he could finally fit with the rest of the nature in the universal circle of existence.

Very early on, humans understood the workings of the nature and circular motion of life, where everything in nature is born, live, die, and then is born again. The only instance where man could not consciously comprehend that circle of life was in his own experience. We would be born, live, come to the gates of death, die and not have the memory of anything after. The understanding of that circle of existence, that we so desperately need to complete in order to be in balance with the rest of Creation, is missing. This unbalance is a major cause to yet another inability: to understand the essence of God and the origin of Creation. As a result, we constantly change and modify our concepts of God, Nature, Universe, good and evil, religious beliefs, moral and ethical convictions; all in hope that we will find the missing part and finally come to peace with ourselves.

There were individuals throughout history who felt a need for that inner balance more than others did. Following their instincts, intuition, and knowledge hidden in the deepest parts of their inner beings, they developed philosophy, teachings, and different rituals to help themselves understand universal truths and, thus, complete their journey towards full understanding of human identity. They tried to spread their knowledge, only to realize that there were necessary conditions under which one could be instructed in the higher truths. In Freemasonry, those conditions are defined as "purity of life and rectitude of conduct so essentially necessary to enter…" Practice of virtues and subscription to the highest universal moral standards were always prerequisites for one to be able to receive higher spiritual knowledge.

The search for our own identity is the process that keeps repeating in different times and different cultures over and over again throughout the history. It always appears in times after human disasters like wars, famine, and the end of Empires, and generally, whenever men are faced with death and temptations of their virtues. The search becomes less important and weakens in the times of prosperity and abundance.

The same conditions cause the appearance of identical experiences. The idea of building a bridge over river, when faced with that obstacle on the road in our physical world, is not necessarily a result of the acquired knowledge through study of the similar experiences; it is most often expression of our inherited ability repeatedly to react identically to the same conditions or challenges. Many believe the same about the realm of our inner being; we reach for the very same symbols, as men ten thousand years ago, in order to deal with the very same questions.

In summary, Freemasonry has its origin in intuitive need of human beings to complete themselves. Where to look for the vehicle that transports all that inner knowledge, philosophy and ritual practices in almost identical form, from one age to another, is yet another question. Is it written in our genetic code or DNA? Is it hidden deep within our collective unconscious, as Carl Gustav Jung proposes? Or is it the unbroken, invisible chain of individuals (Unknown Philosophers) through the centuries whose sole destiny is to keep that spark of light called "humanity" alive forever?

Picture 60. *The front page of the book Bacon-Masonry by George V. Tudhope, claiming Francis Bacon to "be original designer of speculative Freemasonry"*

7

18th CENTURY - ENGLISH BEGINNINGS

In 1662, the Royal Society of London was founded for the purpose of publishing scientific papers and organizing scientific debates. Newton published his *Principia* in 1687, and three years later Locke his "Essay Concerning Human Understanding". It was the time of Industrial Revolution followed by the Age of Enlightenment. Educated men entered into the eighteenth century with belief that the methods of natural sciences should be used to examine and understand all aspects of life. The concept of "reason" was born.

This was the time of great minds like Baron de Montesquieu, Voltaire, Diderot and Rousseau. In his writings, Voltaire often connected the advancement of science with the betterment of human beings. He despised religious intolerance, which was the cause of all savage and inhuman actions and glorified "piety and loving kindness" as embodied in Christ's words to "love God and your neighbor as yourself". Diderot and D'Alembert published their Encyclopedia in 1751 and Rousseau presented his Social Contract ten years later. The eighteenth century was also a time of enlightened Absolutist Monarchs such as Frederick the Great in Prussia, Catherine the Great of Russia, and Joseph II in Austria. Unfortunately, it was a century of constant wars over the domination in Europe and the colonies. It started with the War of the Spanish Succession, continued with the War of Austrian Succession (or King George's War), War of Jenkins Ear, Seven Years War (or French and Indian War), and finished with American Revolution leading to Declaration of Independence in 1776, and French Revolution from 1789 until 1799.

In England, Dutch Protestant William of Orange (William III) replaced the Catholic King James II in 1689, in the so-called "Bloodless revolution". Scottish and Irish Catholic loyalists of James II, unhappy with these developments, organized a series of bloody and unsuccessful uprisings, known as the Jacobite Rebellions. Some Jacobites found protection on the French Court after their defeat. Many of them did not perceive the union of Scotland with England and Wales of 1707 as a process of harmonization, but as Scottish capitulation to English political and economic power.

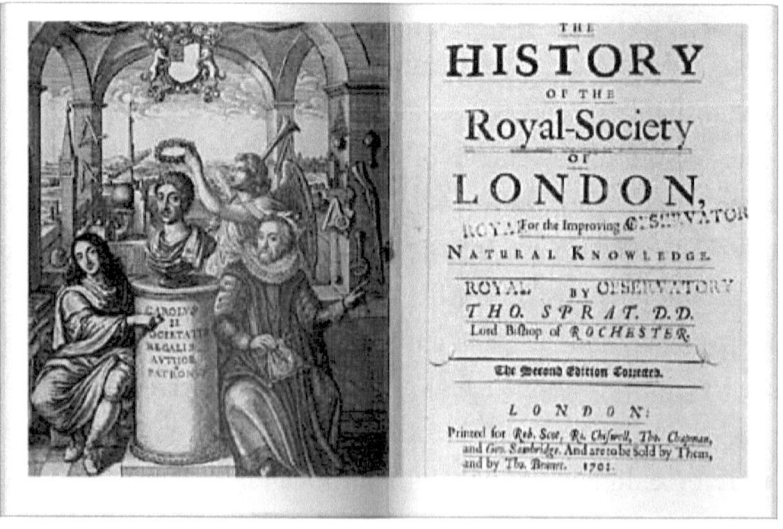

Picture 61. *The Royal Society of London was founded in 1662*

ENGLAND, SCOTLAND, AND IRELAND

At the beginning of such an exciting century, a group of Freemasons in London decided to reinvent themselves. In 1716, members of four Lodges "finding themselves neglected by Sir Christopher Wren" met in the Apple Tree Tavern in London to discuss their future. After placing the oldest Master Mason present in the "Master's Chair", they constituted themselves "Grand Lodge pro tempore". The plan of work was made and St.John the Baptist's Day, June 24, 1717, was chosen as a date for their founding conference. On that given day, they met again at the Goose and Gridiron Ale House. Anthony Sawyer had been elected and installed as the first Grand Master. Henceforth, St. John the Baptist's Day was designated as the day of annual communication of the Grand Lodge. Originally, this Grand Lodge controlled only few Lodges from London and Westminster. It would take number of years before a larger number of the existing Lodges accepted them as the authority and came under their protection.

Significant efforts were made to collect all of the documents and records relevant to the activity of Freemasonry in England from previous years. The Grand Lodge asked Dr. James Anderson, a Doctor of Philosophy and Minister of the Presbyterian Church in London, to use these materials as a guide, in order to write a Constitution and the history of their organization. Dr. Anderson submitted his work in 1722 to the Commission of the Grand Lodge, who approved it. On March 25, 1723, the Grand Lodge accepted this document titled, *"The Book of Constitutions for Freemasons, containing the History, Charges, and*

Regulations, etc., of that Most Ancient and Right Worshipful Fraternity, for the use of the Lodges". From that day on Freemasonry has been on the solid foundations, and would continue its progress and growth over the following centuries.

Today we know with certainty that speculative Freemasonry existed in England and Scotland early in the seventeen century. Few of the available written records are sufficient for such a claim. Anderson told us in his own writings that Sir Christopher Wren was the Grand Master at the close of the seventeenth century, but that he "neglected his duties", which prompted some Masons to establish the Grand Lodge of 1717. For many scholars remains unanswered question why did they decide to go public with their Assembly? Some think, that they were encouraged to announce their existence from the fear of being wrongly accused of political conspiracy against the Government or Ruling House, if they continued meeting in private (or secrecy). That is possible if we take in account that a number of Freemasons involved in the foundation of the Grand Lodge of 1717 were personally on the "wrong side" of the political divide at the time and most likely many of their actions could be misunderstood. There were other answers as well. It appeared from the records that the organization of the Lodges and their mutual relationship was very loose and mostly unregulated at the beginning of the century. If some group wanted to take matter "in their hands", assume authority, and regulate the system, the only way they could do so, was in public. As in everything else, if there was unclaimed inheritance scattered around, whoever claimed it first and in public had the biggest chance to collect it.

The following chain of events proves their actions correct. In spite of all the counterclaims of antiquity and seniority, from the groups from York or Scotland that came in the following years, the Grand Lodge of 1717, after unification of 1813, called United Grand Lodge of England and Wales, remained the "Mother Grand Lodge" of the world and unquestionably the greatest authority in Freemasonry worldwide. Soon enough, new claims of authority arose. Freemasons from York founded in 1725, the "Grand Lodge of All England". Due to its historical location, they gained authority over some Lodges, but their concept did not survive and they ceased to exist around 1792. The activities of the London Freemasons certainly had inspired their Scottish and Irish Brothers to remodel their groups in the similar manner.

The Dublin Weekly Journal reported of the meeting of the Grand Lodge held in Dublin on June 24, 1725, when the new Grand Master, Richard 1st Earl of Rosse had been elected, in the presence of the representatives from six Lodges. According to some authors, the Grand Lodge of Ireland was established four years later, when the Viscount Kingston was elected Grand Master. The following year, 1730, they published the Book of Constitutions.

On November 24, 1736, the representatives of thirty-three Lodges in Scotland met at the General Assembly for the purpose of organizing new Masonic authority. At this occasion, "The Grand Lodge of St. John of Scotland" has been founded. Baron Sinclair of Roslin, hereditary Grand Master of the ancient Grand Lodge of Scotland, had been elected as its first Grand Master.

After its foundation in 1717, the Grand Lodge in London introduced a number of innovations in the practices of the Lodges under their control. This caused resentment among some Masons, who in 1751 established "The Most Ancient and Honorable Fraternity of Free and Accepted Masons According to the Old Institutions". In 1756, they adopted the Constitution titled *Ahiman Rezon*, written by Lawrence Dermott, Grand Secretary of this Grand Lodge at the time. According to their Constitutions, the Royal Arch degree was recognized as an essential part of the Ancient Craft Masonry and Lodges were empowered to confer it as a fourth degree. Over the years, those who believed it to be more true to the ancient rules of Masonry used the term "Ancients" when referring to this Grand Lodge. Contrary to this, they would refer to the Grand Lodge of 1717 as "Moderns" due to the innovations they introduced. This division between two London Grand Lodges has intensified when the Grand Lodges of Scotland and Ireland recognized "Ancients" as the only legitimate power.

Two other Grand Lodges existed for a while in the second part of the eighteenth century in London. The "Supreme Grand Lodge" which seceded from the Grand Lodge of "Ancients" in 1770, lasted for about seven years and closed down in 1777. The Lodge of Antiquity broke away from the Grand Lodge of "Moderns" and founded the "Grand Lodge of England South of the River Trent" in 1779. Ten years later, three Lodges consisting this organization, reconcile with the Grand Lodge and, with this, their secessionist body expired.

The activities of the English, Scottish, and Irish Grand Lodges were not confined to Britain and Ireland. Freemasonry has been spreading like the wild fire to every civilized corner in the world.

Picture 62.
*Anthony Sawyer,
The first Grand Master
of the Grand Lodge
of England
(Moderns)*

Picture 63.
*The Goose and
Gridiron Ale
House in London
where on June
24th, 1717 the
Grand Lodge was
founded*

Picture 65.
Lawrence Dermott

Picture 64.
*The Constitution titled
<u>Ahiman Rezon</u>, written
by Lawrence Dermott,
Grand Secretary of this
Grand Lodge
Of Ancients*

FRANCE

The first Masonic Lodge in France was established in Dunkirk in 1721 under the name *"L'Amitie et Fraternite"*. Lodges in Paris followed in 1725 and in Bordeaux in 1732. The *"Grande Loge Anglaise de France"* was founded in 1743 and few years later dropped *"Anglaise"* from its name. By 1740, higher degrees were appearing in France and in 1754, Chevalier de Bonneville founded near Paris the "Chapter of Clermont" for the work of those degrees. Soon after, in 1761, "Emperors of the East and West", at that time one of the governing bodies for the high degrees in France, issued a Patent to Stephen Morin, giving him authority to confer degrees of the "Rite of Perfection", following which he left for West Indies. In 1773, the "Grand Orient" of France was established as a part of the complicated power-sharing governing body of the Grand Lodge of France.

Freemasonry in France became very popular among the nobility and intellectuals. Those involved were very serious and passionate about it. Even the women were trying to find ways to be able to participate. This led to the formation of the "Rite of Adoption" in 1774 to accommodate women desiring to practice Masonry. Groups practicing this Rite were usually a mix of men and women. The Ritual practiced, although similar to Freemasonry, was not considered Masonic. In spite of resistance from some, the Grand Orient took control of this Rite under condition that all male members should be Freemasons and that a regular Lodge supervised each Rite of Adoption body. Before the end of the century, "Rite of Adoption" would spread to neighboring countries.

Picture 66.
The Duke of Wharton, Grand Master of the Grand Lodge of France in 1728

Picture 67.
Count of Clermont Grand Master Of the Grand Lodge of France from 1743 to 1771

Picture 68. *The Rite of Adoption Ritual (18th century)*

Picture 69.
18th century Masonic items at the Château de Mongenan

GERMANY

The first Lodge of speculative Freemasons in Germany was founded in Hamburg in 1734 and the first Grand Lodge seven years later (National Grand Lodge of Saxony). The Rite called "Strict Observance", founded by Baron Von Hund around 1742, dominated Freemasonry in Germany for a large part of the 18th century. This Rite had three Craft degrees and four higher degrees. It was called "Strict Observance" because those who belonged to it would have to pledge and observe "strict" and unconditional obedience to the superiors and particularly to the "Unknown Superior-Knight of the Red Feather". By the time Baron Von Hund died in 1776, this Rite spread through France and much of Central Europe. Many of those who practiced it thought that it needed to be reorganized. It was finally transformed and used as a base to what was to be known as the Rectified Scottish Rite in France. Some of the Rituals of the Strict Observance also inspired founders of other Rites, like Zinnendorf Rite in Germany and Swedish Rite in Scandinavian countries.

BELGIUM

There were claims of existence of the Lodge in Mons as early as 1721, but the first written records of the Lodge in Belgium came from 1765. The Belgian Lodges were under protection of the Grand Orient of France and other Jurisdictions until 1833, when the Grand Orient of Belgium was founded.

SPAIN

The Lodge "St. John of Jerusalem" was founded on Gibraltar in 1728, which represented the beginning of Freemasonry in Spain. The Grand Lodge of Spain was founded in 1767 only to change its name three years later to "Grand Orient".

PORTUGAL

The first Lodge in Portugal received its Charter in 1736. Due to the strong opposition from the Catholic Church and Inquisition, which was still active in this country at the time, Lodges had to work in great secrecy. The Grand Orient of Portugal was founded around 1825.

SWITZERLAND

The first Lodge in Switzerland was established in 1736 in Geneva and the first Grand Lodge in 1769. Until 1844, when the Grand Lodge "Alpina" was formed, Lodges in Switzerland were working under several different authorities.

ITALY

Freemasonry came to Italy in 1733 when the first Lodge was open in Florence. It would take thirty years before the first Grand Lodge in Italy was founded, which was soon followed by appearance of other Grand Lodges competing for the control of Freemasonry. This would continue until 1864, when the three biggest Obediences united into Grand Orient of Italy, with Giuseppe Garibaldi as a Grand Master.

DENMARK

Freemasonry was introduced into Denmark in 1743, by Baron Munnich, a member of the Lodge "Three Globes" from Berlin and Secretary of the Ambassador of Russia. The name of the first Lodge was "St. Martin". The Grand Lodge of England, in 1750, established The Provincial Grand Lodge in Denmark. The Rite of the Strict Observance was most dominant until 1785, when majority of the Lodges returned to the English form of Craft degrees and practice of the Rectified Scottish Rite in higher degrees. The Royal Family recognized Freemasonry in 1792, and it was decided that the ruling Prince of the country would be hereditary Grand Master. With this, the Grand Lodge of Denmark was created.

SWEDEN

The first Lodge in Sweden was founded in Stockholm in 1736. New Lodges were subsequently established and, by 1759, the Grand Lodge was organized. The Rite of Perfection was introduced from France and the Strict Observance, with much less success, from Germany. In 1756, Carl Fredrik Eckleff, together with six brethren, founded the Scottish Lodge *"L'Innocente"* in Stockholm working in the, so-called, Scottish St.Andrew's degrees. Three years later, he established a Grand Chapter in Stockholm. King Gustavus the Third and his brother, the Duke of

Soedermanland, were initiated in 1770. Three years later, Duke Karl of Soedermanland became Grand Master and in following year started solidification of the degree systems in Sweden, which resulted in the establishment of the Swedish Rite.

Picture 70.
Karl Gotthelf Freiherrn von Hund, known as Baron von Hund, founder of the Rite of Strict Observance

Picture 71.
Hermetical symbols, an illustration from the so-called "clerical records of the Templars..." 18th century—Germany
(Source: History of Freemasonry in Gemany, by Ferdinand Runkel - Berlin, 1942)

RUSSIA

The Grand Lodge of England opened the first Masonic Lodge in Russia in 1731. In 1740, General James Keith was appointed Provincial Grand Master. There were about dozen Lodges working different Rites throughout Russia by the middle of the century. The National Grand Lodge of Russia was formed in 1776. Lodges under its protection were practicing a system of seven degrees. Russian Freemasons, like the French, were passionate about their Masonic work and philosophy. From the very beginning, they were impressed with the high degrees and esoteric and mystical side of Freemasonry. By the end of the century, the Empress Catherine, prompted by turbulent political situation, outlawed Freemasonry and ordered Lodges to be closed.

POLAND

According to some scholars, the first Masonic Lodge on the Polish territory was "*La Confrérie Rouge*", which already existed in 1721. The existence of the Lodge in Poland with completely developed structure, only four years after foundation of the Grand Lodge in London, is very interesting fact for research. The name ("Red Brotherhood"- *La Confrerie Rouge*) suggests Rosicrucian connection. Another Lodge appeared eight years later under the name " *Aux Trois Freres*" and worked in the French language. Membership of the early Polish Lodges consisted of aristocracy exclusively. By 1788, there were twenty-three symbolic and four Scottish Rite Lodges in Poland under the

Grand Orient of Poland. The end of the century brought the breakup of the country, which caused a decline in Masonic activities and the collapse of the Grand Orient in 1794.

AUSTRO-HUNGARIAN EMPIRE

Francis, the Duke of Lorraine, received his third degree in 1731, from Dr. Desaguliers in London. A few years later he married Maria Theresa, who became Empress of the Austro-Hungarian Empire in 1740. Soon after, the Lodge "Three Firing Glasses" was opened in Vienna. The Lodges in Prague and elsewhere throughout Bohemia followed. In 1775, Count Ivan Draskovic founded his own Grand Lodge from the four Lodges of Croatia and Hungary. They practiced their own form of the Strict Observance Rite, consisting of three degrees. In spite of the official ban on Freemasonry by the Pope's Bull, Lodges were thriving. By 1785, when the Grand Lodge of Austria was formed, there were already over twenty Lodges in existence. The end of the 18^{t}h century brought turbulent political times to Austro-Hungarian Empire, which caused, in 1798, all Fraternities and Secret Societies to be declared illegal.

Picture 72.
Count Ivan Draskovic, founder of the Draskovic Observance

COLONIAL AMERICA

According to Emmanuel Rebold, by 1740, Grand Lodges from Great Britain and Ireland established Lodges in most of the British colonies around the world. The very first Masonic Lodge in the American Colonies was active in Philadelphia in 1730. A year latter, Benjamin Franklin became a Mason in "Tun Tavern" Lodge in Philadelphia. There are references to the Masonic activities in Boston in 1730s. In 1733, the "First Lodge" (St. John's Lodge) was established in Boston. Daniel Cox received a commission in 1730 as a Provincial Grand Master of New York, New Jersey, and Pennsylvania, but it appeared that he never exercised his authority. The first Lodge in Savannah, Georgia was open in 1733, by James Oglethorpe. In following years, until the American Revolution, the Provincial Grand Lodges were established in several colonies. It is interesting to note that both, the Grand Lodge of "Moderns" and the Grand Lodge of "Ancients" had commissioned Provincial Grand Masters for New York, Pennsylvania, and Massachusetts. During and after the conclusion of the American Revolution, independent Grand Lodges were established in newly formed States. Vermont formed the Grand Lodge in 1774, Massachusetts in 1777, Virginia and North Carolina in 1778, Maryland in 1783, Georgia, Pennsylvania, and New Jersey in 1786, and New York in 1781.

Henry Andrew Francken, authorized by Stephen Morin, organized a Lodge of Perfection in Albany, New York, in 1767. This represents the beginning of the Ancient Accepted Scottish Rite in the American Colonies. The next thirty years saw an expansion of the Scottish Rite, which would culminate with the foundation of the Supreme Council of the 33° AASR in Charleston, South Carolina. The very first reference to the conferral of Royal Arch degree came from the Lodge in Fredericksburg in 1753. In 1775, Prince Hall and several other men of color were made Masons in the Irish Military Lodge No.441 in Boston. Nine years later the Grand Lodge of England (Moderns) chartered the African Lodge No.459.

Picture 73.
Benjamin Franklin became a Mason in Tun Tavern Lodge in Philadelphia in 1731.

Picture 74.
Old Tun Tavern Lodge

ORDO AB CHAOS

As we can conclude, the eighteenth century was, for Freemasonry, the century of expansion. There were few important moments in this progress. First- the revival of the Grand Lodge of 1717 in London; second - the publishing of the Anderson's <u>Constitutions,</u> which after 1723, universally became a set of basic principles, rules and regulations governing Freemasonry; third- the appearance and development of high degrees and foundation of different Rites; fourth- the establishment of the independent Grand Lodges in European countries and former American colonies; fifth - the beginnings of the organized reaction of the official Catholic Church to the growth of Freemasonry; and sixth- the involvement of women in Masonry through the appearance of the Rite of Adoption.

While the eighteenth century was a time of great expansion of Freemasonry, it was also a time of great chaos and confusion. In England itself, for most of the century, there were three, and for a while even five, Grand Lodges claiming authority over Freemasonry. They were all chartering and establishing Lodges and Provincial Grand Lodges in the Colonies and elsewhere. Irish and Scottish Jurisdictions had done the same. In the American colonies at the time, in the very same area, one could find Lodges empowered to work by five different authorities. The same thing was happening in the other parts of the world. In South America, often in the same areas, Lodges would be open by the Grand Orient of France, Spain, Portugal, as well as the Grand Lodge of England. In Australia and in New Zealand, English, Scottish, and Irish Masonic authorities warranted Lodges.

The situation in the continental Europe was even more complicated. With appearance of the high degrees and formation of the new Rites, various groups and individuals claimed sole authority over them. Different groups performed often identical degree work under different names, and sometimes, they would perform completely different degrees, under very same name. There were literally thousands of variations of hundreds of degrees floating around Europe. People of questionable qualifications were often conferring degrees for large fees. Certain individuals, aimed at gaining personal power and wealth, were pulling into schemes those desirous of "higher knowledge". The concept of the "Masonic authority" was interpreted very liberally. Lodges were chartering Lodges and individual Freemasons were establishing Lodges and Grand Lodges without any established Masonic organization empowering them to do so. Some Lodges would adopt the title "Grand Lodge" just to show their importance. By the end of the century, many Freemasons, resenting such development and tiring of ever-new higher degrees, decided to clean out and bring order to the house of Freemasonry.

1804

8

19th CENTURY
- INSTITUTIONALIZATION AND GROWTH

During the French Revolution and in the years leading to Napoleonic Wars, activities of all secret societies, including Freemasons, were suppressed in most of the European countries. With the Rule of Napoleon I, the end of the Holy Roman Empire, and French predominance in the central Europe, Masonic activities were revived, particularly through the efforts of French military Lodges. Most of the Latin American countries won their independence by 1825. Through the formation of the Grand Orients, Grand Lodges, and Scottish Rite Supreme Councils in Brazil (1822), Mexico (1825),Venezuela (1838), Argentina (1856), and Chile (1862), Freemasonry was firmly established. The Grand Orient of France established most of the South American Jurisdictions, and generally, they were working Scottish Rite Craft degrees.

The world in the nineteenth century was a scene of events that would forever change how people work, think and live. Britain abolished slavery in 1833.The Ottoman Empire was slowly collapsing with the number of nations gaining their independence, like Greece in 1830, and Serbia in 1864. The Industrial Revolution and the Romantic Movement in the Literature and Arts were in full swing. Political, economic, and social pressures of the new "Capitalist Age" were building up to explode with the Revolutions in France, Germany, and the Austro-Hungarian Empire in 1848. In the same year Carl Marx and Friedrich Engels wrote "The Communist Manifesto". By the middle of the century introduction of the "Free Trade" represented the beginning of the Golden Age of British capitalism. While Darwin, in 1856, wrote the <u>Origin of Species</u>, Pope Pius IX was preparing his third Bull against Freemasonry- "*Quanta Cura*". The American Civil War erupted in 1861 and finished in 1865 with the victory of the Union and abolition of slavery. A year later, the unification of Italy was completed as well. The last three decades of the nineteenth century were characterized with the rise of German Empire under Bismarck, who in 1878 introduced the "Anti Socialist Laws". In spite of it, in the next ten years, ninety Socialist Parties would be founded around the world. This was the time when Darwin wrote <u>Descent of Man</u>, Dostoevsky wrote <u>Anna Karenina</u> and <u>Brothers Karamazov</u>, Tchaikovsky composed "Swan Lake" and "Sleeping Beauty", and Albert Pike wrote <u>Morals and Dogma</u>. The end of the century brought Spanish American War. Sometime about the same time, a little known elementary school teacher in Russia named Lenin was arrested for his radical activities. While Chekhov published <u>Uncle Vanya</u>, Freud was writing his <u>Interpretation of Dreams</u>, to be published in 1900.

ENGLAND

After nearly sixty years of parallel existence, the Grand Lodge of "Moderns" and Grand Lodge of "Ancients" started, in 1809, negotiations about the possibility of union. After four years of discussions, in December of 1813, the two Grand Lodges merged into United Grand Lodge of England with the Duke of Sussex acting as Grand Master. Lodges outside of London were grouped into Provincial Grand Lodges with the Provincial Grand Master at its head, appointed by the Grand Master. The Royal Arch degree was accepted as a part of "pure Ancient Masonry" in the "Act of Union". It was also acknowledged that the Orders of Chivalry have rightful connection with the approved Masonic structure.

The nineteenth century was a period of enormous growth of the United Grand Lodge. After the unification, Lodges grew in number from 637 to 2850 by the end of the century. Promotion of Freemasonry in public by Albert Edward Prince of Wales (who was known as King Edward II and who was elected Grand Master in 1874), contributed a great deal to such success. In 1817, two Grand Chapters of the "Moderns" and "Ancients" united into Supreme Grand Chapter of R. A. M. of England. At the same time, the control of the Mark Master degree was given to the Grand Lodge of Mark Master Masons of England and Wales.

Picture 75.
Coat of Arms of the Grand Lodge of "Antients " and the Grand Lodge of "Moderns"

UNITED STATES OF AMERICA

After the American Revolution, in the new independent states, Freemasons established Grand Lodges, which had exclusive authority over the State in which particular Grand Lodge existed. The concept of territorial integrity of the Grand Lodge was new to Freemasonry. It, essentially, meant that only one Grand Lodge could exist and work on the certain territory.

By the beginning of the nineteenth century, Freemasons in the United States were well on the road of consolidating the degree systems and organizing the bodies that would control them. In 1783, the first separate Royal Arch Chapter, independent from the Lodge, was organized in New York City. The Grand Chapter of Pennsylvania was formed in 1795, which was followed by Grand Chapter of Massachusetts (1796), Maryland (1797), and New York (1798). The same year "The General Grand Chapter of Royal Arch Masons" was established. The first Cryptic Council was founded in New York in 1810. This led to the formation of the Grand Council of Royal and Select Masters of New York in 1828. Numerous other Grand Councils were established during the century. Controversy regarding cryptic degrees, which arose out of the understanding that they were side degrees of Ancient Accepted Scottish Rite, was overcome when the Supreme Council of the 33° AASR (Charleston, S.C.) issued an edict in 1853 giving up the right to any claim regarding the cryptic degrees. In 1890, The General Grand Council International was founded. The institutionalization did not skip Chivalric Orders as well. The Grand Encampments of Knights Templar were founded in Pennsylvania (1797), Massachusetts and Rhode Island (1805), and New York (1814). Two years later, General Grand Encampment of the United States of America was established.

As we already know, the first African-Americans to become initiated into Freemasonry in American Colonies were Prince Hall and fourteen other black men in 1775, in Boston. Nine years later (1784), they were granted charter by the Grand Lodge of England (Moderns) and with this, "The African Lodge" No. 459 was established. This Lodge gave warrants to other Lodges of African-American men (which was not unusual at the time), and soon there were Lodges established in Philadelphia (African Lodge No.459) and Providence (Hiram Lodge No.3). In 1815, members of the Lodge in Philadelphia decided to transform their Lodge into the Grand Lodge under name "*African Grand Lodge of the Free and Accepted Masons For And In the Jurisdiction of North America*".

After the union of 1813, United Grand Lodge of England (UGLE) dropped from its registry most of the Lodges warranted by the Grand Lodge of "Moderns" in American colonies, including African Lodge No. 459 from Boston. In 1827, after UGLE refused to issue them a new warrant, members of the Boston Lodge, proclaimed their independence and formed a Grand Lodge. In the same year, they issued a Charter to the "Boyer Lodge No. 1" in New York. In 1847, the African Grand Lodge changed its name into "Prince Hall Grand Lodge" in honor of its founder who died in 1807.

In 1801 The Supreme Council of 33° Ancient Accepted Scottish Rite for the Southern Masonic Jurisdiction of the United States was founded in Charleston, South Carolina. In 1804, Count de Grasse Tilly received a Patent from the Charleston Supreme Council giving him right to establish Supreme Council in France, which power he exercised the very same year. The Supreme Council for the Northern Masonic Jurisdictions of the United States, covering thirteen northeastern states was established in 1813. This Supreme Council issued a warrant in 1845 to the Supreme Council of England and Wales, which in turn authorized the foundation of the Supreme Council of Canada in 1874.

The nineteenth century brought the first taste of the anti-Masonic attacks to the American Masons. Many leaders of the Revolution and many leaders of the newly formed independent states including George Washington, were Freemasons. Throughout formative years of the American Republic, the membership of the Fraternity had grown enormously. According to some scholars, at the beginning of the century, there were 16.000 Freemasons in United States. Twenty years later, in 1820, the number of members was close to 80,000. Such rapid growth brought resentment among some groups and individuals, who saw in the Order a potentially dangerous concentration of power and influence in society.

In 1826, Captain William Morgan, a disgruntled member of the Masonic Lodge in Batavia, in upstate New York, decided to write a book, which would "reveal the secrets" of Freemasonry. He was arrested on trumped up charges, then released in the hands of his fellow Masons, who abducted and, apparently, killed him. After the suspects, all respected citizens, were tried and ended up with few minor jail terms, the public was outraged. The "Morgan Committee" was founded to establish the truth about the crime and Morgan's destiny, since his body was never positively identified. Soon the committee became a statewide movement and, subsequently, grew into an "Anti-Masonic Party", whose candidate was running for President in the elections of 1832. The Anti-Masonic hysteria influenced many Freemasons to leave and denounce their membership in the Order. In 1826, before the Morgan Affair, there were, in New York State, about five hundred Lodges with nearly 20,000 members. In 1830, at the climax of the fury, there were only eighty-two Lodges with about 3,000 members. Although the Anti-Masonic Party died out soon after elections of 1832 it would take next twenty years for the Fraternity to recover.

Picture 76.
Captain William Morgan

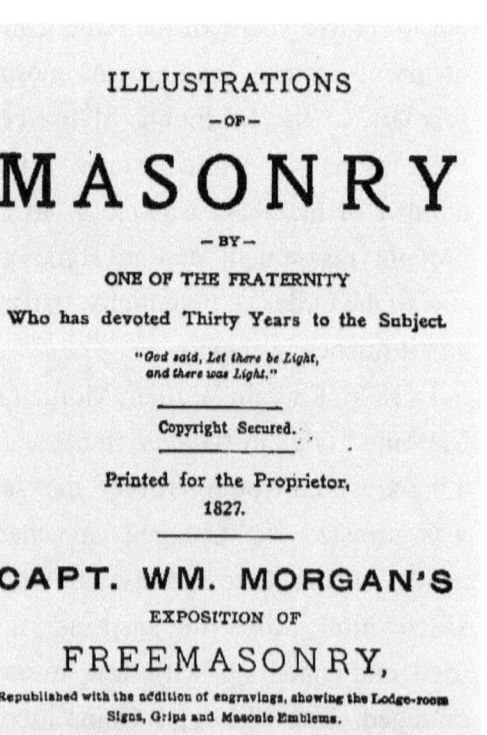

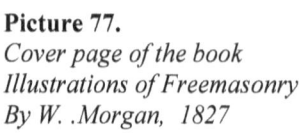

Picture 77.
Cover page of the book Illustrations of Freemasonry By W. .Morgan, 1827

CANADA

Members of the Provincial Grand Lodge of Canada, decided, in 1855, to secede from the United Grand Lodge of England and establish an independent Grand Lodge, which was done in the November of the same year. At that time, Canada consisted of Ontario and Quebec. In 1869, sixteen of the Lodges from the Grand Lodge of Canada withdrew and formed The Grand Lodge of Quebec. Within ten years, from 1866 to 1875, the Grand Lodges of Nova Scotia, New Brunswick, British Columbia, Manitoba, and Prince Edward Island, were formed, which brought the number of Grand Lodges in Canada to seven. The Grand Lodge of Canada, being in reality, a Jurisdiction with the authority only in Ontario, changed its name, in 1888, to the "Grand Lodge of Canada in the Province of Ontario".

SCOTLAND AND IRELAND

In the nineteenth century, the Grand Lodge of Scotland did not look with favor and sympathy at the practice of higher degrees. So much so, that when the Supreme Grand Chapter R.A.M. of Scotland was established in 1817, by the representatives of thirty four Chapters, the Grand Lodge ordered that *"no person holding an official position in any Masonic Body sanctioning higher degrees than those of St. John's Masonry, should be entitled to sit, act, or vote in the Grand Lodge"*. It was only in 1870, that the Grand Lodge accepted the degree of "Installed Master" and recognized the Mark Master degree as Masonic. The Supreme Council of Spain chartered the Supreme Council 33°

A.A.S.R. of Scotland in 1846. The Grand Lodge of Scotland was very active in forming Lodges in the British Colonies throughout the world.

It could be said the same for the Grand Lodge of Ireland with their Lodges established in New Zealand, Australia, India, West Indies, and the Far East. The Papal Bull of Leo XII *"Quo Graviora"*, issued in 1825, had much grater effect on Freemasonry in Ireland than the previous ones. Many Freemasons, who were Catholics, had to resign from the membership under the threat of being excommunicated from the Church. Nevertheless, Freemasonry in Ireland recovered. Certainly, the Third Duke of Leinster, who was Grand Master for sixty-one years, left the greatest mark on the development of Freemasonry in Ireland in the nineteenth century. The Supreme Council 33° A.A.S.R. of Ireland was founded in 1824.

AUSTRALIA

Upon the visit of the Pro Grand Master of England to Australia in 1888, the United Grand Lodge of New South Wales was founded out of eighty-two English, fifty- six Scottish, and fifty-one mostly Irish Lodges. A year later, The United Grand Lodge of Victoria was formed and had under its authority ninety-four English, sixteen Irish, thirteen Scottish, and fifteen other Lodges. Before the end of the century, the Grand Lodges of South Australia, Western Australia, Queensland, and New Zealand were established.

GERMANY

Out of many Grand Lodges founded in Germany, only eight made it through the nineteenth century. During this era, German Freemasons had to deal with two major issues. The first one concerned the return to the traditions of the Craft Freemasonry after half a century of domination of Strict Observance and various high degree esoteric systems. Schroeder's Rite of three Craft degrees gained in popularity. The second issue regarded the effect of the pure Christian character of German Freemasonry on Freemasons of other faiths.

The National Grand Lodge of Saxony, which was the heart of the Strict Observance, was reconstituted in 1811. By 1847, it amended its Constitution in order to be able to admit Jewish men into the membership. The Grand Lodge of Hamburg adopted Schroeder's Craft Ritual of three degrees in 1802. The Grand Lodge of the Eclectic Union from Frankfurt-on-Main broke its ties with the Grand Lodge of England in 1823, due to the conflicts regarding membership of Jews in the Masonic Lodges. Twenty-five years later, all restrictions regarding the initiation of Jews were removed from the Constitution. About the same time, The Grand Lodge of Sun at Bayreuth made the same corrections of their Constitution. By the end of the eighteenth century, the Grand Lodge "Three Globes" from Berlin had twenty Lodges with almost thousand members. By 1808, in spite of the break in their work during the French occupation, this number almost tripled. For most of the century, Grand Lodge Three Globes did not receive Jewish Freemasons as visitors. Three other Jurisdictions that made it into the 20th century, were the National Grand Lodge of All German Freemasons, founded by Count Zinnendorf, Grand Lodge "Royal York of Friendship" (an offshoot of the " Three Globes"), and Grand Lodge Concord from Darmstadt.

EASTERN EUROPE

The second part of the century brought further expansion of Freemasonry in Europe. The National Grand Lodge of Hungary was founded in 1870. There was a record of a Lodge in Belgrade in Serbia in 1852. The name of the Lodge was "Ali Koch". This Lodge had a mixed membership composed of Serbian, Turkish, Jewish, Italian, Polish, and French men. Some referred to this Lodge as a Grand Lodge with the subordinate Lodges across the Balkans. It seemed that this group died out after 1862. The Grand Orient of Italy chartered, two years later, the Lodge "Lights of Balkan" in Belgrade.

The first Lodge in Bulgaria existed around 1870, and the Grand Orient of France opened the very first Lodge in Romania in 1856. Fourteen years later the Grand Orient of Romania was founded with twenty Lodges. Constantine Moroiu was elected Grand Master. The following year, this ambitious Mason established the Supreme Grand Chapter of Royal Arch Masons, Supreme Council 33° A.A.S.R. and Rite of Memphis. The first Lodge known to exist in the Ottoman Empire was the "Iskenderun Lodge" in Aleppo, chartered by the Grand Lodge of Scotland in 1748. In the nineteenth century, there were three Lodges in Istanbul: "Ser" in 1861, "Prodos" and "Etoile du Bosphore" in 1867. Many prominent figures from the public life of the Empire were members of these Lodges. Some of them had significant influence in conversion of the dying medieval Empire into the Constitutional Monarchy.

Picture 78. *The very first Masonic Temple in Belgrade (Serbia) - Lodge Ali Koch, 1848*

Picture 79.
The Archbishop of the Diocese of Karlovci (the Province of Vojvodina) Stefan Stratimirovic was a member of the Lodge Vigilantia in 1785, working under the protection of the Grand Lodge of Draskovic Observance

FRANCE

The Grand Orient was assuming stronger and stronger control over the degree systems and different Masonic groups. By 1799, the Grand Orient and the Grand Lodge merged under the name the "Grand Orient of France".

As we already learned, the Supreme Council 33° A.A.S.R. was established in France in 1804. The Grand Orient was not impressed with such a development. Some kind of agreement was attempted where the Grand Orient would control the first eighteen degrees and the Supreme Council remaining fifteen, but that did not last for long. By the end of Napoleonic Era, in 1813, Rite of Mizraim appeared in Paris and got immediate attention from many prominent Freemasons. The Grand Orient was steadily expanding. From twenty Lodges at the end of the French Revolution, it grew to eight hundred Lodges and three hundred Chapters in fifteen years. By 1815, however, half of the Lodges became dormant. At the same time, Scottish Rite Supreme Council broke apart. The following five years were full of events. Grand Orient formed its own Scottish Rite Supreme Council, while the revived Supreme Council of 1804 split into two fractions. Numerous reconciliations were attempted, but they all failed. The key point of disagreement would always be who had the highest authority - the Grand Orient or the Supreme Council. For most of the century, the two organizations would co-exist, while constantly changing levels of mutual recognition and understanding. Very turbulent times in the history of France at the time, such as the Revolution of 1848, and establishment of the Second Republic, just further complicated their positions.

In 1867, Grand Orient recognized the Supreme Council 33° A.A.S.R. of Louisiana (from New Orleans). This body was founded in 1855, under questionable circumstances, but disappeared after Grand Lodge of Louisiana recognized Supreme Council from Charleston as the only Authority for the Scottish Rite degrees (from 4th –33rd) in the southern part of the United States. Many French-speaking Lodges in Louisiana, originally chartered by the Grand Orient of France, practiced Scottish Rite Craft degrees. This caused the reappearance of the closed Supreme Council from New Orleans in 1867, when the Grand Orient of France and two other Grand Orients immediately recognized it. The fact that this Supreme Council claimed authority over Craft Lodges in the territory where Grand Lodge already existed brought controversy among American Masons. Grand Lodge of Louisiana and some other Grand Lodges from United States broke their relations with the Grand Orient of France. This, however, was not the end of the story. In 1869, Grand Orient of France issued a statement that race, color or religion should not disqualify any candidate from Freemasonry. This caused other American Grand Lodges to severe their relations with Grand Orient of France. Although, this statement was completely in the spirit of Freemasonry, most of the American Grand Lodges at the time were very sensitive of the racial issue, since they did not receive men of color into membership nor recognized independent Masonic Jurisdictions of African-American men.

In 1877, Grand Orient of France amended its Constitution, so that reference to the "belief in God and immortality of the soul" was substituted by the "absolute liberty of conscience and solidarity of Humanity". Changes in the Ritual were made accordingly and the presence of the Bible in the Lodge room was left as an option for the individual Lodges to decide. It was generally accepted that this decision caused most of the Jurisdictions in the English-speaking world to break their ties with the Grand Orient of France. This, certainly, was just one of the conflicting points that led to the split of Freemasonry into two different understandings of the very same concept.

Many Scottish Rite Craft Lodges in France working under The Supreme Council had a problem with the autocratic manner in which the Supreme Council governed. In 1848, an attempt was made to form Grand Lodge, but the newly formed "National Grand Lodge" lasted only two years. In 1880, a new, more successful attempt was made and twelve Lodges organized themselves into the "Scottish Symbolic Grand Lodge". Other Lodges working under Supreme Council wanted to gain independence as well, which prompted the Supreme Council to establish independent "Grand Lodge of France" in 1894. This Grand Lodge and "Scottish Symbolic Grand Lodge" merged in 1897, in what is now known as "Grand Lodge of France".

Picture 80.
The Seal of the Grand Orient of France

CONSOLIDATION AND GROWTH

When in the first year of the nineteenth century, a group of Freemasons in Charleston, South Carolina, established the Supreme Council 33° A.A.S.R., they adopted as their motto "*Ordo ab chaos*" (Order from chaos). This motto best illustrates the difference between the nineteenth and eighteenth century Freemasonry. While the major characteristic of the speculative Freemasonry in eighteenth century was worldwide expansion and innovations with the introduction of the high degrees, the nineteenth century was the age of institutionalization of the Masonic organizations, consolidation of the degree systems, and strong membership growth. It was also a century that would witness the division of the Masonic community in two large groups according to and in reference to their understanding of the place of the belief in God, the immortality of the soul, and the Book of the Sacred Law in the Ritual, Regulations, and Philosophy of Freemasonry. It was also a time of the continuing attacks on Freemasonry from the Pope and official Catholic Church and from the political groups and individuals who perceived Freemasonry as a treat to their ideologies or political aims.

Large membership, consisting of respected and well-to-do citizens, with the Grand Masters often coming from the ruling class or Royal Families (in a case of Monarchies), made Fraternities of Freemasons important and powerful groups in societies of many countries. The material wealth accumulated over years through the dues and donations from the members was used to establish numerous trusts and charities aimed at helping, not only members and their families in need or distress, but also orphan children, disabled war veterans, elderly, blind, deaf or disadvantaged and poor individuals and families that could not afford food, lodging, or medical care. Orphanages, retirement homes, hospitals and schools were built and financed in many countries by the Masonic Fraternities. In the century of Liberal Capitalism, with the growth of urban living, the systems of Social Security in the rapidly developing industrial countries had not yet been established. The Masonic benevolence and practice of mutual aid and support further attracted men from all walks of life to join Fraternity of Freemasons. Masonic Authorities did not forget their own needs. Beautiful Masonic Halls and Temples were built throughout the world. Some of the most impressive are the Masonic Hall in London, Temple of Grand Orient in Paris, House of Temple in Washington, D.C., and Grand Lodge buildings in Philadelphia and New York.

Picture 81. *House of the Temple, Washington DC, A Headquarters of the AASR Southern Jurisdiction USA*

Picture 82.
Grand Lodge of Pennsylvania, Masonic Temple in Philadelphia

Picture 83.
Freemasons Hall In London United Grand Lodge of England

9

20th CENTURY—TURBULENT TIMES

The twentieth century probably brought more changes to the world than any previous period in history. In the first decade of the century, men finally realized their dream to fly. Watching silent movies became the new form of entertainment and Ford's Model-T was the new and most popular form of transportation. While Einstein was working on his Theory of Relativity, the world was coming closer to the one of the bloodiest conflicts in history - World War I.

During this time, Freemasonry was flourishing all over the world. In 1903, the very first international Masonic organization, the "International Bureau of Masonic Affairs", was opened in Switzerland under the sponsorship of Grand Lodge Alpina. The purpose of this institution was to facilitate contacts among Grand Lodges, help the development of Masonic ideas, and collect information about Freemasonry in the world. The Grand Lodge of Norway was established in 1905 and Grand Orient of Turkey in 1908. The following year, 1909, the first Conference of Grand Masters of North America was held in Philadelphia. This would become an annual event in the years to come and the "Conference of Grand Masters" as a coordinating body of the Grand Lodges would gain in importance. The year before the Great war, in 1913, a new Grand Lodge was founded in

France under the name "The National Independent and Regular Grand Lodge of France" (today "National Grand Lodge of France") and it was immediately recognized by the United Grand Lodge of England, and soon by other English-speaking Jurisdictions.

In 1914, World War I erupted, followed by the Russian Revolution in October of 1917. At the end of the war in 1918, the Symbolic Grand Lodge of Bulgaria came into existence. Under the Paris Peace Treaty, new independent states were created in Europe. Freemasons in those countries immediately proceeded to organize Grand Lodges. The Grand Lodge of Yugoslavia was founded in 1919 out of the Lodges from Serbia and Croatia. The same year Grand Lodges of Czechoslovakia and Austria were formed. The Grand Lodge of Finland started its work in 1924. The Masonic Service Association of the United States was established in 1919, to provide various services to member Grand Lodges in the fields of membership education and Masonic relief. At the Masonic Congress held in Geneva in 1921, the International Masonic Association was founded with similar aims, but ceased to exist along with the International Bureau of Masonic Affairs around 1925.

Political developments in Europe and the world (between the two World Wars) caused an increase in anti-Masonic propaganda and closure of many Jurisdictions throughout Europe. Russia's October Revolution brought Communists to power. In 1922, at the Fourth International Congress of Communist Parties, it was decided that Freemasonry and Communism were incompatible. All members of the Communist Parties in Europe, and particularly those in France, who were members of the

Masonic Fraternities, were ordered to resign their membership in Freemasonry. Although, Freemasonry was outlawed in Russia, there was evidence of underground Masonic activities until the Second World War.

After Mussolini came to power in Italy, he immediately started a process to ban Freemasonry. The Grand Orient did not give up and was using all legal tools to prevent the Fascists from closing them down, in spite of intimidation and assassination of prominent Masons. After the buildings and property of the Masonic Lodges had been seized by the state in 1926, the Grand Master dissolved the Lodges, but declared that the Grand Orient of Italy did not cease to exist. In Hungary, soon after Dictator Horthy took over the country in 1920, the scene of intimidation and pressure was similar to that in Italy. By 1937, Freemasons of Hungary had to stop their activities. In 1928, the Grand Orient of Spain was closed down and many Freemasons, including the Grand Master, were arrested and charged with conspiracy against the Government. Three years later, Salazar in Portugal outlawed Freemasonry, Lodges were closed and the Grand Master arrested. After strong pressure from the Italian and German Governments, the authorities in Yugoslavia banned all Masonic activities in the spring of 1940. In June of the same year, the Grand Master ordered all Lodges to go dormant.

In Germany, General Von Ludendorf, veteran of the First World War, was very active in spreading Anti-Masonic Propaganda. Enemies of Freemasonry often quoted claims from his two books, <u>Annihilation of Freemasonry through Revelation of its Secrets</u> and <u>Cause of the War</u>. After Hitler came to power in 1933, Grand Lodges were ordered to stop all Masonic activities.

A move was made to transform Masonic organizations into Christian patriotic, educational, and charitable societies with a Ritual compatible with Nazi ideology. Members were to be of "clean" Aryan descent. The Grand Lodge of Prussia changed its name to the "German Christian Order of Friendship", and the Grand Lodge of Three Globes became "National Christian Order of Frederick the Great". When this plan failed two years later, on August 8, 1935, Hitler ordered the final closure of all Masonic Lodges in Germany.

The Second World War and German occupation of most of Europe brought about the suspension of Masonic activities in occupied countries. Nazi activists and their collaborators looted Masonic Temples and organized Anti-Masonic exhibitions all over Europe. Prominent Masons were arrested and often charged as British Spies. The German Gestapo was particularly cruel with French Freemasons, many of whom were active members of the underground Resistance.

Picture 84. *The Masonic Service Association of the North America was established in 1919, and the first Conference of the Grand Masters of Masons of North America was held in 1909.*

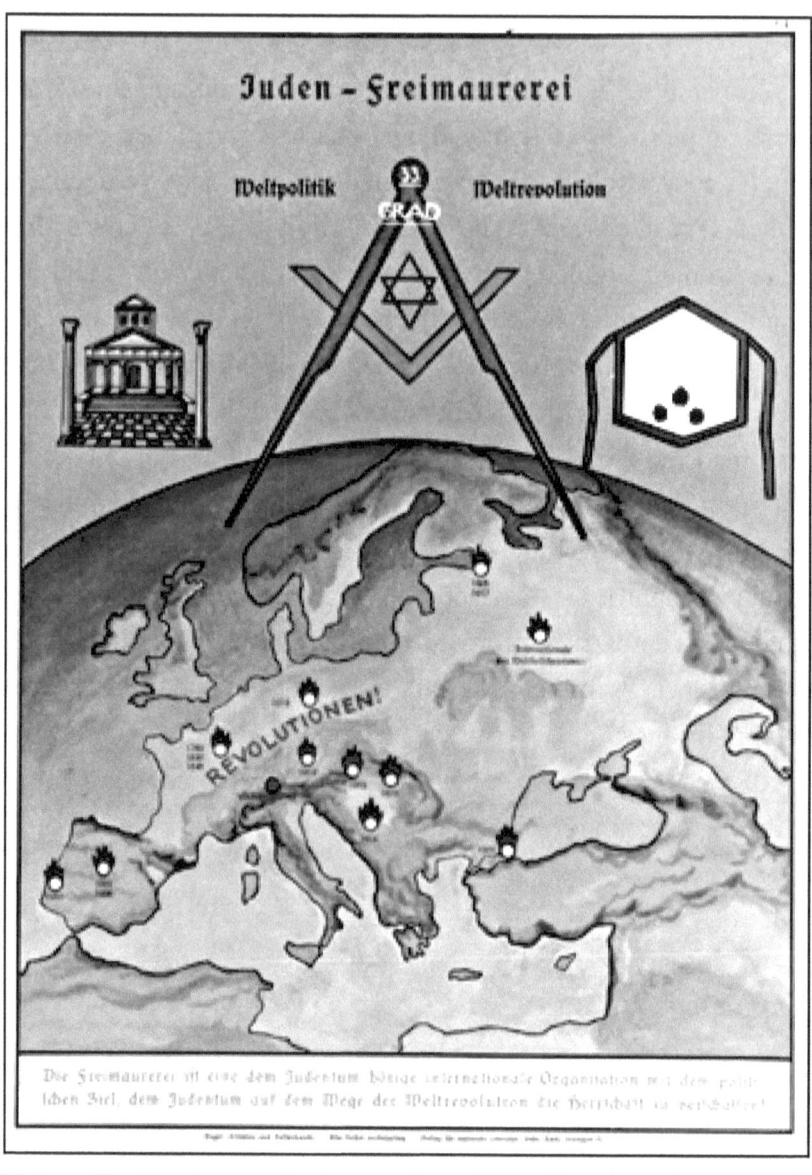

Picture 85. *The German Nazi poster from 1935—The text at the top reads: "World politics World revolution." The text at the bottom reads, "Freemasonry is an international organization beholden to Jewry with the political goal of establishing Jewish domination through world-wide revolution." The map, decorated with Masonic symbols (temple, square, and apron), shows where revolutions took place in Europe from the French Revolution in 1789 through the German Revolution in 1919.*

The end of the Second World War brought peace and economic progress to Western civilization, but the world, in total, was far from prosperous. Eastern Europe was under Communist dictatorships and there was the constant threat of Nuclear War. "The Iron Curtain" was in place and "The Cold War" was in progress. The Communists won in China and Communism was spreading to other countries of Asia. Former colonies were still fighting for their independence in Africa and Asia. The State of Israel was founded and conflicts started in the Middle East. Unresolved problems in the Arab world caused the birth of Radical Islam. While people were watching on their television sets the first man stepping on the Moon, the world was rapidly entering a new age of Technological Revolution, which was to bring about industrial automation, ecological concerns, widening of the gap between the rich and the poor, new fatal diseases, computers, and the Internet.

After the Second World War, Freemasonry was soon re-established in all free European countries. In those countries under Communist Rule, Masonic activities were still outlawed. The Grand Lodge of China was founded in 1949 on Taiwan, and in 1951, the Grand Lodge of Iceland was formed. This was followed by the establishment of Jurisdictions in Israel in 1953, in Japan in 1957, and in South Africa and India in 1961. At that time, according to most estimates, there were four million Freemasons worldwide, with half being in the United States. Then, for no apparent reason, membership numbers started going down, particularly in the United States.

This tendency has continued into this century. Many Grand Lodges lost up to eighty percent of their members, such as the

Grand Lodge of New York, which had around three hundred eight thousand members in 1958, and came to the end of the century with a little over sixty five thousand. Masonic scholars have tried to understand and explain this tendency. Many Grand Lodges were established institutions with large commitments towards maintenance of the property and established charities. Any loss of membership directly affected their ability to respond to such obligations. A number of individual Lodges, which had their own Temples and properties, were not able to keep up with the cost of taxes and maintenance and were forced to sell them and hold their meetings in rented spaces. Grand Lodges came out with a number of innovative programs to attract new members to join the Fraternity. The requirement that the candidate himself had to request to join and not be asked or solicited by a member of the Fraternity was dropped in many Jurisdictions. American Jurisdictions were shortening the required time needed to elapse between the successive degrees. Still, there was not a clear picture for the reasons behind the decline in membership. In contrast, membership in some European Jurisdictions was actually going up, especially after 1989.

In 1989, the Berlin Wall came down, which symbolically represented the beginning of the fall of the Communist regimes in Eastern European countries. The very same year the Symbolical Grand Lodge of Hungary was reestablished. Grand Lodges in Yugoslavia (Serbia and Montenegro), Romania, Bulgaria, Russia, Czech Republic, Croatia, Slovenia, Poland, and in other new countries soon followed. The United Grand Lodge of Germany, National Grand Lodge of France, Grand Lodge of Austria, and the United Grand Lodge of England sponsored most of these new Grand Lodges. At the same time, the Grand Orient of France sponsored the establishment of the Grand Orients on the same territories.

Therefore, by the end of twentieth century, in most of the Eastern European countries, there existed two parallel Jurisdictions. Higher degrees were soon introduced, followed by the formation of Scottish Rite Supreme Councils. It is interesting to note that many newly made Masons in Eastern Europe were not aware of the distinction between Regular and Liberal Masonry. They would join the Lodge, only to realize that the Regular Masonic Authorities did not recognize their Lodge. This caused a lot of confusion. A number of Lodges warranted by one Jurisdiction would as groups give up their Charters and *en masse* effectively become renegades by transferring their allegiance to another Jurisdiction on the same territory.

In the last decade of the twentieth century, long over- due recognition of the Prince Hall Jurisdictions by other American Grand Lodges became reality in number of American states. The first Grand Lodge to recognize Prince Hall Grand Lodge

Picture 86. *In 2010 Romanian Post Office issued stamps commemorating 130 years of the Freemasonry in Romania. Freemasonry was revived in Romania in 1989.*

on its territory as an equal was the Grand Lodge of Connecticut. This was followed by California, Massachusetts, and other states. This only happened after the United Grand Lodge of England, in 1994, resolved that the Prince Hall Grand Lodge of Massachusetts "should now be accepted as regular and recognized".

Picture 87. *The Annual Assembly of the Serbian Freemasons in 2010. Freemasonry in Serbia was revived in 1989.* Photo © UGLS

Picture 88.
A quarterly publication of the United Grand Lodges Of Serbia

Picture 89.
The Grand Seal of the UGLS founded in 2007

10

THREE TRADITIONS AND TWO CONCEPTS

For three centuries, large number of men and growing number of women around the world, trying to understand and improve themselves and possibly change their surroundings for the better, have practiced speculative Freemasonry. This certainly cannot leave Freemasonry unchanged. Although many point to the unchanging "Landmarks and Principles" of Freemasonry, few ever understood, successfully defined, or agreed about what they were. My opinion is that over period of time Freemasonry has evolved in three basic Masonic traditions with many variations of those three. It also split into two different concepts along the line of acceptance or non-acceptance of religious dogmas in Freemasonry. Three traditions are those of traditional English Craft Freemasonry, American York Rite Freemasonry, and Freemasonry in the Continental Europe based on various Rites. What are the characteristics of these traditions?

Picture 90. *Master Mason's Apron: American York Rite, English Emulation Rite, and European Ancient Accepted Scottish Rite*

ENGLISH CRAFT MASONRY

English Craft Freemasonry has not changed greatly since it was set up by the Act of Union of 1813. While it was, by large part, de-Christianized and defined as a secular fraternal society, it remained universally religious. Periodical changes that occurred in Ritual and Regulations over the years were more about form than substance. Masonic research of ritual, symbolism or philosophy of Freemasonry is less encouraged than examination of the history or traditions of the Craft and biographies of prominent Masons. Great attention has always been given to the quality and proficiency of the Ritual performance, and much less to the candidates understanding it, except within the limits of the prescribed Lectures. Form and Protocol are always to be observed and maintained to the last detail.

Ritual work and other practices are not to be rushed. From the conferral of degrees, advancement through the Offices in the Lodge and Grand Lodge, to the issuing warrants for new Lodges and recognition of the foreign Jurisdiction, everything must be done with measure and dignity. Minimum time required to elapse between successive degrees is four weeks. English Freemasons are always reminded that they are members of the Mother Grand Lodge in the world and that they should always act as such. After all, this is still the largest Jurisdiction in the world, with three hundred thousand members in over eight thousand Lodges in England and overseas.

Fraternalism and benevolence are a very important part of, and make a difference in the life of many Masons. On other hand, mentoring and instructing Brothers is limited to the subjects prescribed by Lectures and Catechesis of the three degrees during required Schools of Instruction. English Masons were never too impressed with high degrees, but those who practice them, do so for all the right reasons and with the sense of personal quest. It takes long time and serious commitment to "study of Freemasonry" to be invited to become a member of any of the Bodies practicing additional degrees and Orders.

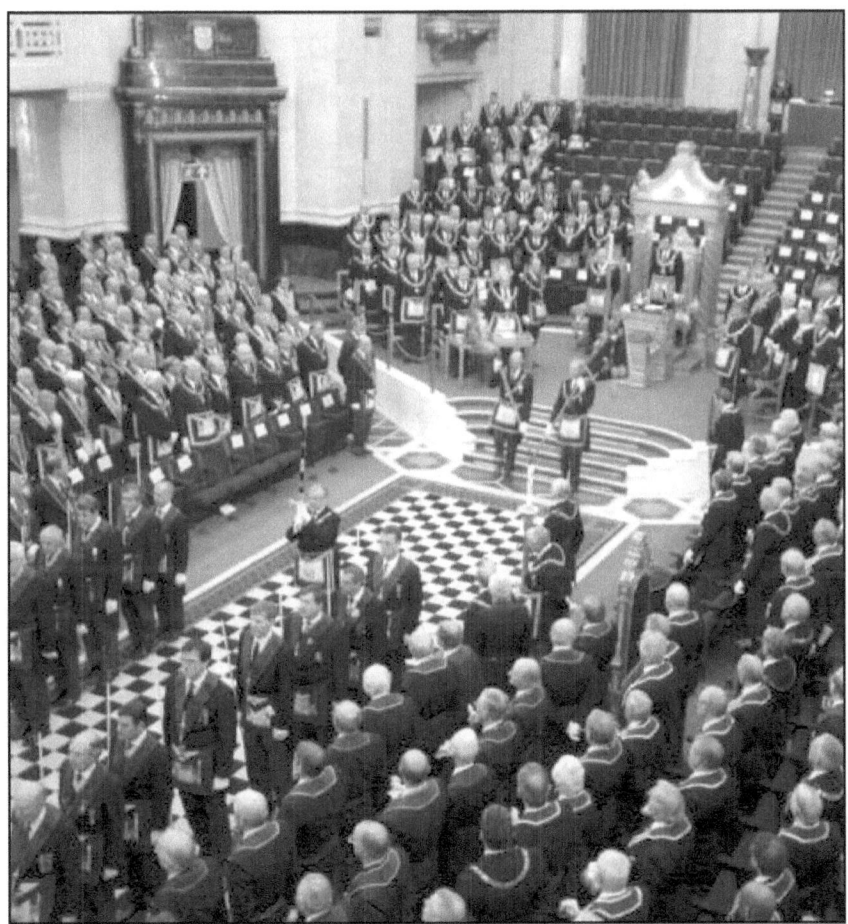

Picture 91. *United Grand Lodge of England Annual Assembly 2008*
Photo © UGLE

AMERICAN YORK RITE MASONRY

American York Rite Freemasonry is still in the process of trying to define itself. Social conditions in the formative years of American states made Freemasonry very attractive to men. Therefore, influx of the members was so strong and constant that Grand Lodges never had the need for serious study or reexamination of the concept of Freemasonry. The only major change that ever occurred was in the years following Morgan Affair, when most of the Grand Lodges in the United States made extra effort to enhance social, patriotic, and charitable character of their institutions. Since then, patriotism is the natural part of their existence as Masons, expressed by the presence of the national flag in the Lodge room, and reciting the "Pledge of Allegiance" after the Lodge is open. Fraternalism and conviviality are very important components of their associations, as well as charity work through the established non-for-profit charitable organizations.

American York Rite Ritual is generally older than English Emulation, coming out of the uncorrected versions of English Rituals of "Moderns" and "Antients". According to number of scholars, it has precious qualities of the early English Rituals, including unaltered Christian references. It is always to be delivered from memory. Unfortunately, many Jurisdictions shortened their official Rituals to accommodate easier memorization of the ritual, by administratively cutting out parts of the Lectures deemed too long. In most of the Jurisdictions, however, the tradition of Masonic education is almost non-existent or limited to required memorization of Catechesis or Ritual. Mentoring is not required and it is accidental, pending on the affinity of the Lodge or current Master. This is not to say that official, institutionalized, educational programs are not existent within Grand Lodges; but only that, for the most part, they are not implemented as mandatory and as such do not give desired results. Often, the obligatory duty of the Master of the Lodge "to deliver or caused to be delivered lecture or the portion of the Lecture during each meeting" is bluntly and routinely ignored. Sometimes, such practice is excused with the statement that the ritual of the opening and closing of the Lodge is the Lecture in itself, and that there is no need for other Lectures.

In the United States, quantity and speed are the major characteristic of the process through which candidates are put on their path through the degrees. Since the Lodge regularly works in the third degree, most of the candidates are taken through the three degrees in the matter of months. In twenty-five of the American Jurisdictions, there is no minimum time required to elapse between two degrees. Seven Grand Lodges require two weeks and the rest of the Jurisdictions require one month. New Master Masons are usually immediately solicited to proceed in higher degrees in the York or Ancient Accepted Scottish Rite, or both. One of the new and controversial practices, introduced by the American Jurisdictions, is the "One day degree", which enables candidates to go through all three degrees in oneday. The Supreme Council A.A.S.R. for the Northern Masonic Jurisdiction adopted similar practice for the conferral of the Scottish Rite degrees.

Masonic education is left to the personal initiative of members. Those desiring to learn will have to find each other for support and exchange of information. Individual and group efforts in the field of education within the numerous Masonic Research organizations are very developed, but limited only by those who show personal interest to join them and study. Form and Protocol are strictly observed and attractive to many who wish to satisfy their ego through the hierarchical advancement. In the face of large membership losses, many Jurisdictions are trying to come up with programs that will attract new members.

Picture 92. *At the One Day Masonic Journey on Oct. 30, 2010, a total of 1,937 men were raised to the Sublime Degree of Master Mason. Many went on to join the Scottish Rite and the Shrine.* (Grand Lodge of Pennsylvania)
Source: Freemason, Volume LVIII, Feb. 2011, No.1

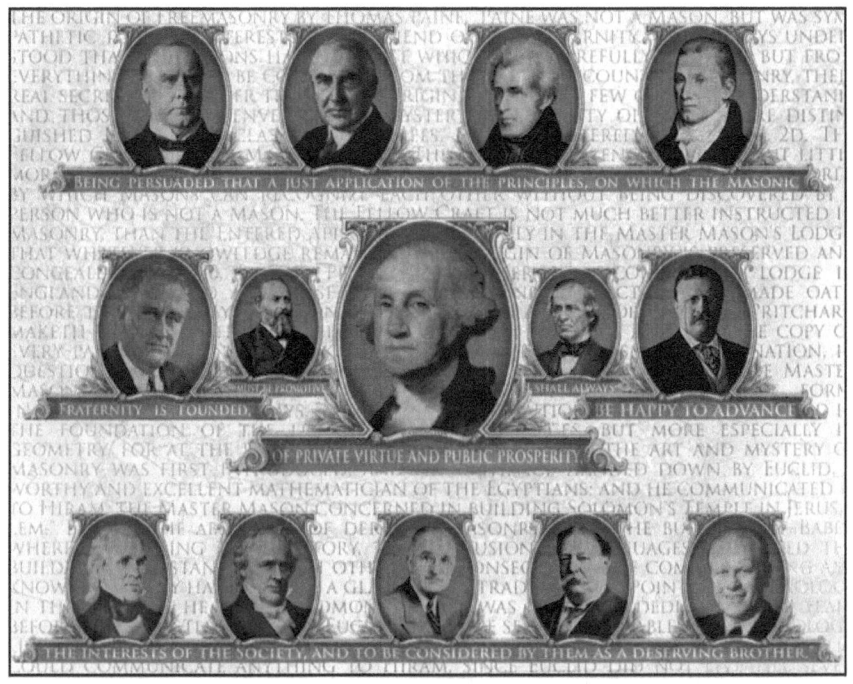

Picture 93. *American Freemasons are particularly proud of the fact that fourteen American Presidents were members of the Brotherhood of Freemasons*

Picture 94. *Masonic Charities are big part of the activities of the American Masonic Institutions*

EUROPEAN TRADITION

Freemasonry was, from the very beginning, received in Continental Europe as a philosophy of life and righteous living and, as such, was to be seriously studied and practiced. Membership is a privilege and opportunity. Therefore, the reason behind someone's desire to join is to be carefully investigated. Those worthy to be admitted are invited to the Lodge, brought in blindfolded and questioned by the members of the Lodge on any subject. The candidate is voted upon after that.

After an initiation, a newly made Apprentice is assigned a mentor to help him study lessons of the First degree. Usually, this mentor is for a life-time. The Apprentice has to write essays on symbolism of the First degree. He is also required to memorize certain information (Catechesis) in order to properly answer questions asked before he is admitted to be "passed" to the degree of Fellowcraft. The same process is repeated between the second and third degree with the increased amount of material to be studied over longer period and with more essays, this time covering Philosophy of Freemasonry. By the time a Freemason is "raised" to a degree of Master Mason, he accepts that practice of Freemasonry is closely connected with constant study and examination, which naturally leads to self-examination, so essentially necessary on the path of self-improvement. Conditions and requirements before one could be allowed to progress to the following degree vary in different traditions. While in some Masonic organizations it takes one to two years of study and work before becoming eligible to go further, in others there is as little as six months between two degrees.

Most of the European Jurisdictions allow the individual Lodges to choose the Rite that will be practiced. The most popular Rite is Ancient Accepted Scottish Rite, followed by the French Rite, Schroeder's Rite, and Rectified Scottish Rite. A number of Lodges is practicing English Emulation Rite. Ritual is normally read during the degree work and it is not required to be memorized. High degrees are very popular, but only the limited number of most qualified Freemasons is invited to proceed in the higher degrees of any of the Rites. Progression is slow, and filled with study and practice.

Membership in the Masonic Lodge is carefully kept private matter. In some Jurisdictions, if a Freemason reveals publicly someone else's identity as a member of the Fraternity, he is usually expelled from the membership. Often, Masonic affiliation can be revealed only after death, in accordance with the wish of either deceased Freemason, or his family. Charitable work is usually limited to fraternal benevolence, which is often provided anonymously.

There are various crossovers between these three traditions that usually come out of the affiliations and conditions in the specific Grand Lodges or individual Lodges. Most of the Jurisdictions in Australia, New Zealand, Canada, and South Africa are following English Tradition. West African, Central African, and South American Grand Lodges and the Grand Orients, practice the European model, with some Jurisdictions crossing over with English Tradition. Similar to the English Tradition, Scotland and Ireland have their own traditions. Interesting is an example of one Eastern European Jurisdiction, which is crossover between European and American Traditions.

What is the reason for such drastic differences in the practice and understanding of the meaning of Rites and Rituals, among various Masonic groups throughout the world? While for some, initiation is important first step into the period of apprenticeship where one is to remain until he is ready to progress, regardless how long it takes, for others initiation and Apprenticeship, or for that matter Ritual of any other degree, is just an expression of a trust put into the initiate that he will at his individual pace and according to his own abilities pass that road toward higher knowledge. In other words, in some Masonic organizations, one may go through all of three degrees and be called Master Mason, but still, for years, be far from that level of knowledge and spirituality essentially necessary to comprehend lessons of the third degree and to build oneself upon it. This approach may appear odd, but in many ways, it is a harder road to take. Lack of the assistance and directions force those taking this path to lean only on themselves and only those who are vigilant and persistent will endure. Like it is said in the old expression "Many are called, but few are chosen".

Picture 95. *The Headquarters of the Grand Orient of France in Paris*

TWO DIFFERENT CONCEPTS

Two major concepts that exist today came out of different socio-political conditions in which Freemasonry has been developing: in the Anglo-Saxon countries and dominions on the one side, and in the continental Europe - most particularly in France - on the other. It seems that an objective analysis of the differences was seldom attempted, and when it was it would usually be met with ignorance, misrepresentation, prejudice and even slander on both sides.

One model of speculative Freemasonry, which we know as Anglo-American or "regular" Freemasonry, came out of rather strict interpretations of the Anderson's <u>Constitutions</u>, Rules, and Regulations of 1723. According to this model, the most important principles and requirements are that a candidate for Freemasonry believes in the existence of a Supreme Being, that an open Volume of the Sacred Law – whichever the faith - is displayed on the Altar while the Lodge is at work, that political and religious subjects are not to be discussed in the Lodge room, and that women are not to be permitted into membership.

The sole object of Masonic work should be man himself and his inner being, in order to make good man better in accordance with highest moral principles, and in order to bring him to realization of the absolute truth regarding God and our existence. It is believed that such a man will, ultimately, be a better and more productive member of society and that the benefits of his moral upbringing will reach much further than his immediate surroundings. Freemasons always are to follow the three great principles of Brotherly Love, Relief, and Truth. Brotherly Love is defined as an expression of respect and tolerance for the opinions of others and as kindness to fellow human beings; Relief is a constant practice of charity; and Truth is the symbol of the eternal search for absolute Knowledge.

The second model, which we refer to as "liberal", officially appeared with the constitutional changes made by the Grand Orient of France in 1877, regarding the "belief in God" and the presence of a "Book of the Sacred Law" in the Lodge room. However, these changes were only a conclusion of the process started with the events in Europe during the Revolution of 1848. The Grand Orient of France was not unique in their actions - the Grand Orient of Belgium made similar changes even earlier. When French Masons stated, "Masonry has for its principles, mutual tolerance, respect for others and for itself, and absolute liberty of conscience", they understood this move as parting with religious dogma, not with Masonic principles. After centuries of Catholic Church involvement in every aspect of human existence, the Enlightenment and the Age of Reason brought the need for "total secularism" and absolute separation of Church and State. This was not perceived only as a political liberation, but also as liberation of the Spirit. The concept of *"Laïcité"* was born and accepted by French Freemasons. This was not an original or revolutionary concept. The idea of separation of church and state was already successfully implemented in the American Republic, albeit not in American Freemasonry.

This concept came out of two basic ideas: a complete freedom of moral conscience and a separation of Church and State. It gave to all men without distinction of class, race, color, origin, religious belief or non-belief, the "means to be themselves, to have freedom of choice, to be responsible for their own maturity and be Masters of their destiny". Freedom of moral conscience is aimed toward liberation of all dogmas, prejudices, preconceived ideas and all kinds of cultural, political, economic, or social pressures. Personal morality is based on the "principle of mutual tolerance and respect of others as well as oneself". The duty of Freemasons is not only to work towards their own improvement and perfection, but also towards the improvement of the societies in which they live, in hope that *"like living stones, they will build themselves in that Temple of a more enlightened world and universal peace, where the ideals of liberty, equality and love for each other will be fully realized"*. In that spirit, discussions on "social" subjects are permitted in the Lodge room and members are asked to discuss and take a stand on various social issues.

"Laïcité" as a concept is thus intended not only to make good men better, but also to enable them to be pro-active members of society, always part of good and positive forces of social, economic, and cultural progress. Building tools of Speculative Freemasonry are not only to be used for moral and spiritual self-improvement, but also for the improvement of society in which masons live and of which they are an inseparable part. Thus, the basic practical difference between the two concepts is in their understanding regarding the reference to a belief in God and the presence of the open Bible in the Lodge room. For the Grand Orient of France, such an insistence is a source of religious limitation rather than an inspiration for enlightenment.

These two concepts, in reference to their position on religious dogma, could be defined, in my view, as "religious" and "secular". The religious concept is originally referred to, by those who practice it, as "regular Freemasonry". The secular concept is one in which the belief in God and immortality of the soul is not required to be admitted into membership. This form of Freemasonry is referred to (by those who practice regular Masonry) as "irregular". Those who practice the latter form of Free Masonry call it "liberal" or "adogmatic".

However, this is not to say that those who chose to practice the secular form of Masonry are all atheists, not religious or not spiritual. It only means that they prefer this approach in practicing Freemasonry. Similarly, some "regular" Freemasons, who express belief in God and immortality of the soul, often do not practice any religion.

Regular and liberal Freemasonry existed in parallel for almost century and a half. It could be safe to say that in the entire non-English speaking world, wherever a regular Masonic Jurisdiction existed, there also existed one practicing, secular form of Freemasonry. Lodges chartered by the Grand Orient of France were founded (and still exist), in the United States, Canada, Australia, and England. It was generally accepted that departing from religious dogma prompted regular Grand Lodges to break their ties and de-recognized the Grand Orient of France and all those Jurisdictions following their model. Nevertheless, as we already mentioned, some of the American Jurisdictions made that break in 1867 and 1869, following recognition of the spurious Scottish Rite Supreme Council of Louisiana by the Grand Orient of France. This recognition was considered as a flagrant breach of the conduct and serious Masonic offence, according to the American standards, where notion of the "Exclusive territorial Jurisdiction" by only one Grand Lodge was firmly established and fully accepted by all in the United States. The Grand Orient of France, and for that matter, United Grand Lodge of England at that time, did not give importance to this idea. They were chartering Lodges all over the world, in various colonies. This practice is continued to this day. As we know, at the very same territories one could find Lodges and Jurisdictions that originated in England, Scotland, France, and Ireland etc.

Another bigger issue that contributed to the complete break between English Freemasons and the Grand Orient concerns high degrees. The British felt very uncomfortable with the number of Rites and Degrees practiced in Europe and with the superior position of the Grand Orient in administrating those Rites. There was a general feeling that they were "taking it too far", and when the final change in the Constitution of the Grand Orient of France came about, that was the "last straw". At that point, the United Grand Lodge of England, together with the Grand Lodge of Ireland, sent a letter to all other Jurisdictions informing them of their de-recognition of the Grand Orient of France and suggested that they do the same. From then on, any Jurisdiction practicing a secular form of Freemasonry would be called "irregular" and, as such, would not be recognized by the regular Grand Lodges as a Masonic organization. This stand was reinforced in 1929, with the adoption of the "Basic Principles of the Masonic recognition of the Grand Lodges".

After the "Conference of Grand Masters of Masons" of the United States established the "Commission on Information for Recognition" in 1952, standards of recognition of Jurisdictions were taken even further. It was accepted by the majority of regular Grand Lodges that any regular Grand Lodge, which has established relationship with the Grand Orient of France or any other Jurisdictions in amity with Grand Orient, could not be recognized. It was further decided that on any foreign territory where two regular Jurisdictions exist, only one could be recognized.

This brings us to two related terms, besides concepts of regular and irregular - "recognized" and "unrecognized". With the blessing of the U.G.L.E., this American tradition of exclusive territorial integrity of the Grand Lodge was quietly accepted by all regular Jurisdictions in amity with them. That caused a number of Jurisdictions, which were absolutely regular in all aspects of their work and origin, not to be recognized as such, for a simple fact that other regular Jurisdiction from the same territory was already recognized. Sometimes, such regular Jurisdictions would enter in amity with Grand Orient of France, which would just further distance them from the other regular Grand Lodges.

Many Freemasons around the world are starting to question the motives and sanity behind the divisions of Freemasonry on the basis of regular versus irregular, and recognized versus unrecognized. While it can be simply explained with the concerns regarding preservation of the original Masonic principles and Landmarks, one cannot, but ask a question: What happened with brotherly love and understanding?

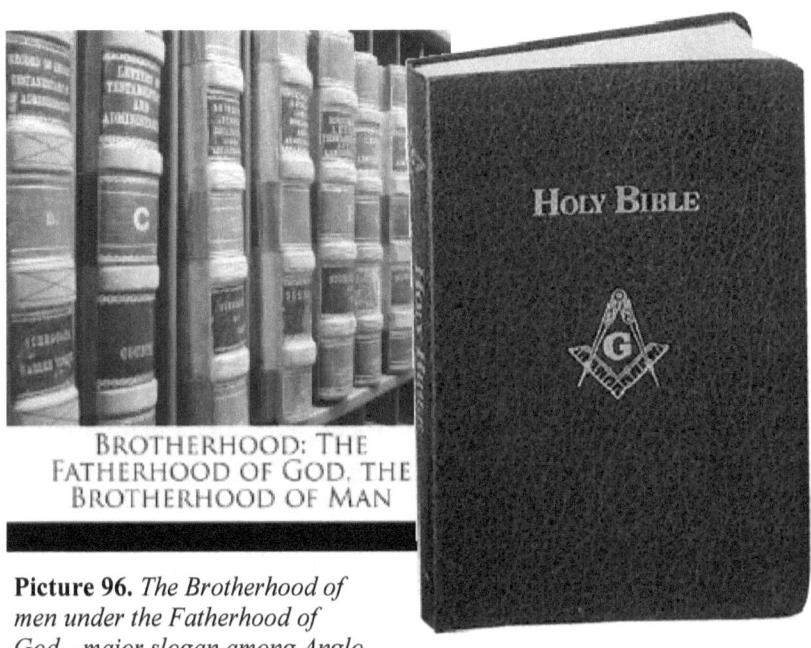

Picture 96. *The Brotherhood of men under the Fatherhood of God—major slogan among Anglo-American Masons*

Picture 97. *Laïcité - concept built into the structure of the adogmatic Masonic teachings in Europe*

11

MASONIC SECRETS

The motto of the United Grand Lodge of England for a very long time was *"Audi, Vidi, Tace"* (hear, see, and remain silent). Some individuals often used this motto in order to point out the secret nature of Masonic association.

Are the Masonic Institutions secret organizations? Certainly, in most of the countries, Masonic groups are legally formed and registered with the appropriate branch of government as private organizations of citizens with publicly (through Constitution and By-Laws) declared programs and aims. Freemasons like to point out that the privacy upon which Masonic groups insist is often confused with the secrecy. Nevertheless, the notion of Masonic secrecy has deeper origins than that.

At the time of the Rite of Strict Observance and during most of the eighteenth and the large part of the nineteenth century, Masonic meetings were secret events in the continental Europe. Members often used pseudonyms instead of their real names and the armed guards secured the access to the meeting place. There was nothing symbolic about their duties or about secret nature of the meetings, they were guarding. One can say that there is a distinct difference in observing privacy or (in some countries) straight-out secrecy, regarding Masonic activities, between English-speaking countries and the rest of the world.

In the United States, Masonic Temples are clearly marked with the appropriate symbols and their contact information and a schedule of work are often prominently displayed on the road signs approaching towns or printed in the phone books and other guides. Often, Masonic Temples are open to public, at the certain time, for guided tours. Members, proud of their association, are wearing clothes and jewelry with the Masonic symbols in public. On special occasions, they may publicly wear their aprons and regalia while marching in Parades.

In England, Masonic Temples are visible and Masonic charitable activities are public, but members stick to the tradition of not "showing off" their membership, keeping it private, except when men of certain professions are required to notify their superiors of their Masonic affiliation. Normally, Masonic symbols on jewelry or clothing are not worn except in the Lodge room.

Alternatively, in many other countries, Masonic temples are in unmarked buildings. Addresses and the phone numbers are available only through the Masonic network and Masonic jewelry is not worn in public. In the Masonic publications and correspondence, initials are used instead of full names and Masons keep their Masonic affiliation private. Access to some of the Masonic websites is limited to those with a password only. Such practices have their origin in strong anti-Masonic sentiments among public or by the governments in number of countries with the tradition of radical religious beliefs or political systems. Until the middle of the twentieth century, membership in the Masonic group for many Catholics meant a threat of intimidations from the community and excommunication from the official church. Still today, in some countries, Masonic membership potentially can lead to criminal charges and even death penalty.

Therefore, while Freemasons insist upon not being a secret society, but rather private or closed association of men or women with honorable aims, they insist on their tradition of having secret signs, secret passwords, and modes of recognition. This tradition, coming out of the practices of medieval operative stonemasons, is still observed, in spite of the fact that information regarding these signs, passwords, grips, and other modes of recognition is widely available to the public from the variety of sources.

From the very beginning of the speculative Freemasonry, there were individuals who were for different reasons trying to "expose" the secrets of Freemasonry. They published books containing complete Rituals of the Craft and high degrees with full explanation of work, signs, passwords, and grips. For this reason, in some Jurisdictions, in addition to passwords coming out of the Ritual of degrees, members are required to be in possession of the "semester" password when entering the Lodge room. This password is supplied by the Grand Lodges to the Lodges and changed every few months.

Beside the fact that, due to the perception of the public, in some societies Freemasons keep their affiliation private or even secret, one could logically ask the question: Why do Freemasons have a guard in front of the Lodge room, preventing all who are not entitled from entering, when most of their work is not such a big secret after all? The answer lays in private and intimate nature of the Masonic Ritual.

One entering the Lodge room is leaving outside, not only his everyday material life, but also his physical nature. To work on oneself, means that one has to reach to the deepest parts of his subconscious and his inner being and to enter upon uncharted levels of his existence. Rites performed during the Rituals are like "portals" to another dimensions and those going through, need, not only complete concentration, but also protection from disturbance in the time of intensive mental, emotional, and spiritual activities, when their psyche is extremely vulnerable. This need for privacy is not particular to Freemasonry. In many fields of their activities, human beings need a private setting in order to perform and feel the benefits of their acts.

The accusations of the existence of "secret knowledge" possessed by Freemasons are often mentioned in popular literature intended to mystify Freemasonry. Through most of their history, Masons never denied nor admitted the existence of such a body of knowledge. This tradition and policy of not answering accusations of any kind only broadened suspicions, and brought new biased claims, that would just inflame resentment and contribute to more and new accusations. Sometimes, Freemasons themselves, by responding with "pretentious ignorance" to the provocative questions directed to them, would further the mystification of this noble institution.

Is there any secret knowledge out there possessed by Freemasons? First, if there was, or is, knowledge of the existence of such a secret, it would be a secret itself, so we would not be in the position to discuss it. Most likely, notion of the "secret Masonic knowledge" arises from the inability of Freemasons to verbalize some of their spiritual and subconscious experiences, which they can feel but not transmit to another person in any known material form. One could often hear among Masons that the only way to understand and benefit from the certain ritualistic experiences is to actually go through them personally. Only those who sincerely seek through their hearts, truly ask with their minds, and knock through their faith in loving kindness, have a chance to obtain that valuable insight in the rich depths of their personalities.

Although today, some Freemasons like to simplify this issue by saying that the "biggest Masonic secret is that there are no secrets"; that is just an expression of either their poor Masonic education or unwillingness to discuss their very intimate experiences. One has to admit that the object of Masonic work – his inner being, his soul, his spiritual body, absolute truth and questions regarding life and death remain a secret for scientists and philosophers alike, and any potential insight in that field represents a great and valuable knowledge.

Picture 98.
Many try to profit from "exposing" Masonic secrets

Picture 99. *UGLE Library and Museum - Many Grand Lodges offer regular tours of their buildings, lodges, and museums to the general public.*

Picture 100. *Masonic Rituals are performed in the privacy of the Lodge rooms.*

12

ANTI-MASONRY

Anti-Masonry is as old as speculative Freemasonry. From one of the first anti-Masonic leaflets published in 1698, by M. Winter from Holbourn in England where Freemasons were associated with labels such as "Mischiefs and Evils", "Antichrist" and "Evildoers" to contemporary conspiracy theories, Freemasons and Freemasonry have been under constant attack from various groups and individuals. A generally accepted practice among Masonic organizations of not answering any accusations against them has made them an easy target for all kinds of claims.

Certainly, the most outspoken critic of Freemasonry was the official Roman Catholic Church. From Pope Clement XII in 1738 with his bull "*In Eminenti*", until Pope Leo XIII in 1902 with "*Annum ingressi*", there were eight Popes issuing seventeen Bulls and Encyclicals, criticizing Freemasons and their practices and ideas, and urging men of Catholic faith not to join or if they were members, to demit (resign) and confess. Threat of excommunication from the Church was used to press Freemasons of Catholic faith to leave the Order. The "Code of Canon Law", from 1917, clearly declares that joining Freemasonry is cause for automatic excommunication. The revised Code issued in 1983, does not explicitly name the Order of Freemasons among the condemned secret societies. Nevertheless, as one can read in the letter to the United States Bishops from the Office of the Sacred Congregation for the Doctrine of the Faith, in their interpretation, the prohibition against Catholics joining Freemasonry remains.

Catholic Theologians and Scholars tried very hard to prove incompatibility of the Christian teachings and Masonic philosophy. In spite of this, numerous Catholic Priests were Freemasons, particularly in the eighteenth century. The best documented example was Lodge "*Prudentia*"(1773) from Croatia ("Draskovich Observance"), where the majority of Lodge members were Catholic Priests and "*fraters*" of various Catholic monastic Orders, including the Archbishop of Zagreb Maximilian Vrhovac. Today, three Lodges, one in Zagreb (Grand Lodge of Croatia) and two in Belgrade (Regular Grand Lodge of Serbia and United Grand Lodges of Serbia) bear name of this prominent Mason.

Unfortunately, the Catholic Church was not the only religious institution against Masonry. Attacks were (and still are) coming from many Christian, Muslim and Jewish religious groups, sects and denominations. Among the most vocal groups against Freemasonry today are Southern Baptists and Born-Again Christians in the United States, some dignitaries of the Episcopal Church in England, the Russian Orthodox Church, most of the radical Muslim groups, and orthodox Jewish sects in the Middle East, and many more. There is a variety of claims that these groups make about Freemasons. From trying to prove that Freemasons are Deists to labeling them Gnostics and Cabalists, or even calling Freemasonry a "false religion". Other claims are that they are practitioners of necromancy, devil worshipers, stanch atheists, or just a secret society trying to establish a new world order and rule the world. One could ask what causes all these different groups to be so persistent in their often controversial claims. The notion that all men are equal regardless of their religious beliefs or non-beliefs, does not comply with most of the religious **dogmas** of different religions. To go even further and have, in the same room, men of different religions, calling one another a "Brother" and invoking the name of God, is unfortunately, still unthinkable in many parts of the world today. The existence of any privately organized group of citizens in any society, regardless of their aims, particularly if they are oath-bound, having closed meetings, and claiming possession of some secrets, makes most governments uncomfortable. Claims by the Catholic Church in France in the nineteenth century that Freemasonry, through the practice of Ritual, reference to God and presence of the Bible in the Lodge room, is in effect a "false religion', prompted Grand Orient of France, in 1877, to erase from its Constitution all religious references, including belief in God and to leave to the discretion of the Lodges use of the Bible and reference to God in their individual working.

As mentioned, Freemasonry has been repeatedly outlawed in different countries as a secret society, especially in the times of wars and social upheavals. Most notably, Masonic activities were forbidden in France and Central Europe during French Revolution; in most of the Europe during Revolutionary 1848; during the Second World War in all countries occupied by Nazis and Fascists; and after the Second World War in most of the Communist dictatorships and in countries ruled by radical Islamists. Membership in the Order by many important political, military and public personalities like George Washington, Simon Bolivar,

Giuseppe Garibaldi, Kemal Ataturk, Lajos Kosuth, Ismail Pasha, and Abd-El-Kader (who were all instrumental in significant political and social changes in their countries), brought to Freemasonry a label of being an organization of men with secret and subversive political agendas. On other hand, the fact that many Kings, Presidents, Generals, Judges, and prominent public figures all over the world were Freemasons, brought resentment for the "powerful associations" among different groups and individuals feeling underappreciated in their societies. The best example of that was the Morgan Affair in the United States in 1820s. Even today, in some countries, Judges, Military and Law Enforcement Officers, and Medical Doctors are required to report their membership in the Masonic Order to their superiors.

Often, the cooperation of religious and political anti-Masonic forces would bring out all sorts of fantastic claims of Masonic wrongdoings. A skillful mix of lies, half-truths, and truths in a credible story sometimes would cause confusion even among Freemasons themselves. When General Ludendorf fabricated a story in the late 1920s, linking Serbian Freemasons to the assassination of the Archduke Ferdinand in Sarajevo (the event that triggered the First World War), many western European Masonic Jurisdictions believed the claim. The fact was that the assassins were not of the legal age to be Freemasons and that membership of their organizer in any of the Serbian Lodges was never recognized. Even the official statement of Freemasons from Serbia did not receive too much attention in the following years. The policy adopted by some Freemasons in Europe, of active promotion of the universal principles of Freemasonry in their societies through personal and group efforts of building more humanistic political and social structures based on universal tolerance, brought reaction among anti-Masonic conspiracy theorists with a concept of "New World Order" as being a secret plan of Freemasons. According to conspiracy theory, the foundation of the European Union is a proof of the existence of such a plan. The Communist Propaganda Machine also readily used the concept of a "New World Order" in the time of the Cold War.

The popularity and reputation of Freemasonry in the United States was conveniently linked to foreign policy of the American Government in the Middle East. Out of it was born the theory of "American –Jewish- Freemasonic conspiracy" to rule the world. Number of radical Muslim groups throughout the world is still exploiting such a theory. A fairly fast expansion of Freemasonry in the Eastern European countries after the fall of Communism was highlighted by Anti-Masons as proof of Masonic involvement in the political changes in that part of the world. Political, financial, and criminal affairs involving members or former members of the Masonic Fraternity would immediately be connected to their Masonic affiliation, in effort to present their private or professional misdoings as a part of larger activities of the Order. An affair involving members of the Italian Lodge P-2 is well known and overexploited by journalists. The still unsolved case of a London serial killer "Jack the Ripper" inspired fiction writers into "claiming" his Masonic affiliation. Even freak accidents sometimes occurring in the buildings belonging to Masonic organizations are used to perpetuate rumors of the violent Masonic Rituals.

Their enemies often represent the policy generally accepted by most of the Masonic organizations, of never answering attacks or entering into ideological quarrels, as silent admission of guilt. They explain even the charitable activities of Masonic groups as the efforts of Freemasons to "buy" favorable opinion of the public or even "repay" for their wrongdoings.

Anti-Masonic forces skillfully use the division of Masonic regular and liberal organizations. They often come up with the claims about one of the sides that would be possibly accepted by the other as reliable, thereby further deepening the differences in the Masonic world. It is not rare to hear from an American Freemason to refer to members of the Grand Orient of France as "atheist political conspirators" or from the member of Grand Orient calling his American Brothers "ignorant religious fanatics". Such harsh positions are not a result of different Masonic concepts, but of the years of constant propaganda from those forces in the world that perceive great danger from Freemasonry being again truly universal.

Picture 101.
Anti-Masonic stamps issued by the Serbian Post Office in 1942. commemorating Anti-Masonic Exhibition organized in Belgrade under Nazi occupation by German forces in Winter of 1941.

Condemnatio Societatis, feù Conventiculiarum -- de Liberi Muratori -- aùt -- de Francs Maſſons -- ſub pœna Excommunicationis ipſo facto incurrendæ, ejus abſolutione excepto Mortis Articulo Summi Pontifici reſervata.

CLEMENS EPISCOPUS
SERVUS SERVORUM DEI.

Uniꞷerſis Chriſtifidelibus ſalutem, & Apoſtolicam Benedictionem.

N eminenti Apoſtolatus Specula, meritis licèt imparibus, Divina diſponente Clementia conſtituti iuxtà creditum NobisPaſtoralis providentiæ debitum jugi (quantum ex alto conceditur) ſolicitudinis ſtudio iis intendimus, per quæ erroribus, vitiiſque aditu intercluſo, Orthodoxæ Religionis potiſſimùm ſervetur integritas, atque ab univerſo Catholico Orbe difficillimis hiſce temporibus perturbationum pericula propellantur.

Picture 102. *In 1738 Pope Clement XII issued his bull "In Eminenti" condemning Freemasonry*

13

MORALS AND ETHICS

How often do Masons hear about a "peculiar system of morality veiled in allegory, and illustrated with symbols", or "lessons of morality", or "high ethical standards', when referring to Freemasonry? Indeed, there are many in the wide Masonic community who don't see anything else in Freemasonry but a school of morality. To make good men better is the ultimate goal. But the question comes to my mind immediately: What kind of morality are we talking about here? Whose morality? Or as Arthur Waite asks: *"under what pretence is it needful or even tolerable to veil ethical teaching under figurative vestures, whether of allegory or types?"* Unless we refer to some special type of morality, the moral law has no need of "allegorical two-part plays." From the Decalogue of Moses, to the Gothic Charges, to the Anderson Constitutions, to Masonic Obligations, everything was spelled out in clear and simple language. All it takes is a "good man and true" to live by it.

According to Anderson's Constitutions of 1723, Freemasons were required to obey the "moral law", to be good men and true, men of honor and honesty; to work honestly on working days that they may live creditably on holy days, to avoid ill language and behave courteously within and without the Lodge, not to envy a brother or supplant him, to avoid excess and offensive language, not to continue together too late or too long from home after lodge, and to avoid gluttony and drunkenness. Furthermore, if we add moral requirements from the obligations in three degrees: to help a brother and his family in distress, not to cheat or defraud a brother or Lodge, not to violate the chastity of a brother's wife, mother, sister or daughter; we have pretty much covered all of the moral rules in Freemasonry.

It is still difficult to see way any of these requirements should be veiled in allegory or illustrated with symbols. None of the Masonic moral rules are different from the general moral rules of the western European cultures in the past couple of centuries based on Judeo-Christian ethical teachings. More so, some may be offended or confused by the requirements: not to cheat a brother or lodge, to help brother of the lodge in distress, not to violate the chastity of the female members of brother's family. Particular attention to moral offence against a fellow Brother Mason and his family brings up a logical question: What about everyone else? Is it acceptable to act immorally with non-masons? Shouldn't these requirements apply to all our actions towards all human beings?

I remember reading Masonic stories from the American civil war. In one of those stories, the wife of a Mason who was off to war displayed his Masonic apron on the porch of the house. The enemy unit was advancing through the area, burning houses, killing livestock, raping women, and destroying everything on their way as the Armies usually do in wars. When the enemy unit came to this mason's house, the commanding officer, who happened to be a Mason, observed the Masonic apron on the porch. He ordered his soldiers not to touch this property, and they continued on their way without doing any harm to it. The commanding officer was holding to his Masonic obligation. This is really something to think about. Can we accept this officer as a good man and true, obeying the moral laws? Certainly not; he was obeying his Masonic obligation but not the moral laws. There is nothing moral about destruction, killing and raping.

In another Masonic story "The man that would be King" by Brother Radyard Kipling, two main characters, both of them Freemasons met in quite an unusual manner. One of them picked the pocket of the other on a train and stole his watch. Upon noticing Masonic symbols on the pocket watch, he ran to return it to its owner. Again, he was obeying to his Masonic obligation, but not the moral law of not stealing. This is very troubling, for one may conclude that the Masonic obligation has priority over moral obligations. Of course, in a world where religious moral norms have failed for thousands of years to bring men onto the true ethical path of loving kindness toward oneself, one's neighbor and the whole of Creation, it is not realistic to expect that the identical moral rules prescribed by the fraternity of Masons would do any better. And if Masons at least obey moral codes in respect to fellow members of the fraternity, every little helps in the global picture.

From all of this, one can conclude that there must be some different set of moral rules to which the Order refers, when describing Freemasonry as a "set of moral lessons, veiled in allegory, and illustrated by symbols." A clue to the answer may be found in Albert Mackey's Encyclopedia where he refers to "moral law" as the law of nature *"lex naturae"*.

What do we mean by "the law of nature"? In philosophy, it is described as a system of right or justice held to be common to all humans and derived from nature rather than from the rules of society. Generally, this phrase relates to a set of divine and unchanging rules that transcends the "here and now" to apply everywhere and at all times in the universe. What we are really talking about is a particular set of ideas that are remarkable in their simplicity, that appear to be universal and have been verified by experiment. In its strictly ethical meaning the natural law is the rule of conduct which is prescribed to us by the Creator (what ever or whoever he/she may be) in the constitution of nature with which He has endowed us. According to St. Thomas, the natural law is "nothing else than the rational creature's participation in the eternal law" (I-II, Q. xciv).

By the virtue of his intelligence, his reason, and free will, man is the only master of his conduct. In contrast to the other living beings, he can, by the use of reason, weigh his actions, act or not act as he chooses. His choice is not always right. But there is more than free choice for humans in the perfect order of the Universe. Deep within his inner being he has a law laid down for him. This law is nothing else but the reflection of the eternal order of the Universe of which man is an inseparable part. The natural law is universal. It applies to the whole human race. Every man, because he is a man, is bound, if he is to obey the rules of the universal cosmic order, to live in agreement with his own rational nature, and to be guided by reason.

So the morality that Masonry is referring to is not the set of moral laws coming out of the Scriptures, but the universal cosmic law coming out of the deepest parts of the human soul. As we already concluded, the only way to bring something out of the human subconscious is by the use of symbols, After all, reference to the "lessons of morality, veiled in allegory, and illustrated with symbols", makes sense if understood in correlation to the natural law. This is not to say that Masons should not comply with the traditional moral codes coming out of the Scriptures and other sacred books or established through the social contracts. It is just pointing to the particular method of approach to the question of morality in the Masonic philosophy.

The major flaw of all moral codes throughout the history of human kind is that they were given to men in the form of prescribed rules and laws. Do not steal. Do not commit adultery. Do not kill. If one kills, he is a killer, evil. He will be punished. If one does not kill, he is good. There were always only two choices to a solution; and there were many desires and passions. Man was motivated to obey moral laws out of the fear of punishment, and not by the reason of his conscience. Contrary to this, in Masonic methodology one will dive deep into his inner being to find a proof that man is predisposition to create, not to destroy, that his human nature is stronger than his animalistic carnal instincts; therefore he will not kill- he is good. So in this case the motivation to obey is not fear or social moral norms; obedience is conditioned and guaranteed by the positive state of conscience, by the rule of the soul over the body, by the absolute moral principles of the Universe.

Nevertheless, the absolute principles of the Universe exist as the unity of the opposites: Light and dark, good and bad, positive and negative, life and death, male and female. We can not know light without presence of darkness, nor distinguish good without the presence of bad. A positive loses its positives if negative is not present. Unity of opposites defines a situation in which the existence or identity of a thing depends on the co-existence of at least two conditions which are opposite to each other, yet dependent on each other and presupposing each other, within a field of tension. Natural Principles of polarity, wholeness, balance, pattern and harmony, were understood by philosophers much before they were discovered by scientists. This understanding did not come solely out of observation of their surroundings, but for the most part out of the inner experiences of the soul.

The principle of the unity of opposites as a philosophical concept is an ever present theme in the Masonic studies, particularly in relation to moral and ethical questions. To the Masons of Judeo –Christian background it gave a completely new perspective of the Biblical dilemma of God who is at the same time merciful creator and vengeful destroyer. It helps to realize fully the meaning of the salvation of the human race, coming out of the sacrifice of Man.

The Freemason's spiritual life follows the natural, both in order and method. To learn the way to immortality, he has to live a moral and righteous life, to be true to himself, to his neighbor and to the Great Architect of the Universe. He has to cherish human life, for only respect for life can bring one to immortality. To achieve all of this he has to use the tools of Freemasonry. After all, he is the Builder, in the true sense of that word. He has to live on the square, circumscribe his desires, cut out all the vices from his life, act by the plumb, and walk on the level *"to that undiscovered country from whose bourne no traveler returns"*.

The Palace
By Rudyard Kipling
1902

*When I was a **King** and a **Mason** -- a Master proven and skilled --*
I cleared me ground for a Palace such as a King should build.
I decreed and dug down to my levels. Presently, under the silt,
I came on the wreck of a Palace such as a King had built.

There was no worth in the fashion -- there was no wit in the plan --
Hither and thither, aimless, the ruined footings ran --
Masonry, brute, mishandled, but carven on every stone:
"After me cometh a Builder. Tell him, I too have known."

Swift to my use in my trenches, where my well-planned ground-works grew,
I tumbled his quoins and his ashlars, and cut and reset them anew.
Lime I milled of his marbles; burned it, slacked it, and spread;
Taking and leaving at pleasure the gifts of the humble dead.

Yet I despised not nor gloried; yet, as we wrenched them apart,
I read in the razed foundations the heart of that builder's heart.
As he had risen and pleaded, so did I understand
The form of the dream he had followed in the face of the thing he had planned.

* * * * *

*When I was a **King** and a **Mason** -- in the open noon of my pride,*
They sent me a Word from the Darkness. They whispered and called me aside.
They said -- "The end is forbidden." They said -- "Thy use is fulfilled.
"Thy Palace shall stand as that other's -- the spoil of a King who shall build."

I called my men from my trenches, my quarries, my wharves, and my sheers.
All I had wrought I abandoned to the faith of the faithless years.
Only I cut on the timber -- only I carved on the stone:
"AfterT me cometh a BuilderT. Tell him, I too have known!"

Picture 103. *One of the most famous Masonic poems - "The Palace"*
by Rudyard Kipling, a poet and a Freemason

14

CHARITY AND COMMUNITY INVOLVEMENT

Charity in the biblical meaning of the word means love and goodwill toward fellow human being. In modern language it generally means relief and assistance to the poor. In the language of Freemasonry we could say that charity, in addition to relief, also means tolerance, kindness, consideration and helpful attitude towards all. From the very beginning of organized Freemasonry in 1717, members of the Craft held Brotherly Love, Relief and Truth to be the most important tenets of the Order.

In Article VII of the "General Regulations" of the premier Grand Lodge of England (Moderns), adopted in 1723, it was stated: *"A new brother should deposit something for the relief of the indigent and decay'd Brethren, as the candidate shall think fit to bestow, over and above the small Allowance stated by the by-laws of that particular lodge; which Charity shall be lodg'd with the Master and Wardens, or the Cashier, if the members shall think fit to chose one."*

In 1727 the very first Charity Committee of the Grand Lodge was established for the purpose of the distribution of charitable funds to needy Brothers. Two years later, the first fixed fee was established for the new Lodge warrants, of which a portion was designated the Charity Fund.

This model was subsequently adopted by most of the Grand

Lodges throughout the world and further developed in its many aspects. There are two basic aspects of Masonic charity: one is the fraternal benevolence and relief which is concerned with help and assistance to the members of the fraternity and their families; the second one is general charity, which is concentrated on the needs of non-Masonic segments of the community, town, area, state and even internationally.

Organized Masonic Charity also exists on several levels. From the individual Mason helping Brother in need, to Lodge charity funds, to Grand Lodge Funds, to the specialized Masonic Charity organizations supported by the donations of the Masonic community at large.

A part of the obligation of each and every Freemason in the world is the requirement to contribute to the relief of every human being in need, particularly to a Brother. Charity is not understood here as simple monetary donations, but much more than that, as a general attitude towards all living beings without hope of reward. This is often overlooked by some Masons. As an example, I can mention a Brother who is very generous in supporting "The Knights Templar Eye Foundation" (A Masonic charity for help to the blind), and at the same time ignores the blind men in need of assistance at the street crossing or at the train station. Lodge charities probably existed within individual lodges long before the formation of the Grand Lodges. Collective help to the Brother in need was a natural part of the setting of any fraternal organization, particularly in the time when organized means of state or government relief to the citizens, like welfare and social services, didn't exist in most countries. In the early years of the American republic, fraternal relief was one of the main reasons for fast rise in membership. In the rough social conditions of liberal capitalism, the idea that there are men around you who will help you and your family by any available means, if necessary, was very attractive to most of the men and served as a kind of social security network.

Even today, many Lodges around the world have their fraternal benevolence funds, general charity funds and specialized charity funds. Money for all of these charities is collected through the donations of the members of the Lodge. Often, membership donations are very large, and in the case of some very old lodges, the charity funds are, through the large donations and wise long-term secured investments, extremely rich.

A very important characteristic of fraternal benevolence on the individual and Lodge level is that in many cases it is anonymous. I remember a story my grandmother told me. During the Second World War, my grandfather was a prisoner of war in the German prison. Once a month, my grand-mother would receive a package from Switzerland with canned and dry food and household items from an unknown sender. After the war, she learned that a Masonic lodge from Switzerland was sending relief packages to the families of the Serbian Freemasons who were imprisoned in Germany.

On the Grand Lodge level, charity funds are controlled and distributed by specialized Committees. Most of the Grand Lodges, depending on size, have separate fraternal benevolence funds and several specialized charity funds. For the purpose of fraternal benevolence, most of the Grand Lodges formed Masonic Boards of Relief. In 1885, at the informal meeting of several Masons from various Jurisdictions, The Masonic Relief Association of the United States and Canada was established. The Association serves as a clearing house to assist local lodges and Boards of Relief throughout the Continent with inter-jurisdictional communication and problems. It helps with hospital and nursing home visits upon the request of the brother's lodge; assists elderly brothers seeking admission to nursing homes and hospitals; provides food and looks after the welfare of widows of Freemasons; arranges for Masonic memorial services, and in some cases contributes funds towards funeral expenses of the Brother. Several Boards of Relief and some individual Lodges own cemetery lots for the interment of indigent Brothers. Some assist with blood donations and assist sojourning Brothers who were victims of crimes.

In many cases, Grand Lodge charity Committees became non-profit charity organizations with huge funds on their disposal, sometimes just nominally responsible to the Grand Lodge. Frequently, individual Masons were establishing independent Masonic clubs and groups with sole purpose of charity work. The most typical example is the case of the "Ancient Arabic Order of the Nobles of Mystic Shrine", better known as "Shriners". Founded in 1870 as a Masonic club by a group of New York Freemasons who wanted, besides serious lodge work, to have some fun, and in the process, do some charity work, it grew into the national non-profit organization "Shriners of North America". With over four hundred thousand members in the U.S.A., Mexico and Panama, Shriners today own and operate nationwide 22 children's' hospitals for the treatment of children with orthopedic conditions, burns and spinal cord injuries. All of the services in the Shriners Hospitals are completely free. Since the first Shriners Hospital was opened in 1922, over 855.000 children have been treated in them.

Originally, the only condition for becoming a Shriner was to be either a 32° Scottish Rite Mason or a York Rite Knight Templar. In the year 2000, this requirement was changed, so now every third degree Mason can become a Shriner. Also, originally, the biggest part of the funding was secured through the donations of the members. In the over one hundred and thirty years of their existence their investment portfolio and assets grew so much, that the membership donations today are only a small fraction of the income. Due to ambitious expenditure of their charitable services they started to look to non-Masonic sources of charitable support to their organization. It is realistic to expect that at some point, even the membership requirement that one is a Mason, will be dropped and the Masonic character of this valuable charity organization will completely disappear.

Masonic charity work, particularly work directed toward non-masons, became a very significant part of the community involvement of the Lodges and Grand Lodges. The purpose of charity is to help those in need. But for many Masonic organizations it became a way of introducing themselves to the general community, to show who Freemasons are and what they stand for. In some Masonic brochures one can read that Freemasons in the U.S.A. give over one million dollars for charities daily.

It is unfortunate that there are disagreements among Masons regarding their charity work. A certain number of Masons believe that this kind of advertising in the community is not appropriate; that Masonic giving should stay anonymous - "without hope of reward." Furthermore, some believe, that while individual Masons should be encouraged to contribute to non-Masonic charities, Masonic organized charity should be limited to fraternal benevolence. On the other side, there is not any definite proof that Masonic giving to the community helps to popularize Freemasonry in the community or influence the public view of the Craft. It is interesting to note that while the United Grand Lodge of England is one of the biggest donors to the charities of the Anglican Church, nevertheless, some leaders of the Anglican Church are very eloquent in their anti-Masonic statements, advising members of their churches not to join Freemasonry. Along the same lines, anti-Masonic groups in the U.S.A. came up with a statement explaining the charitable activities of Masonic organizations as an effort to "buy" the favorable opinion of the general public, or even "repay" society for their "wrongdoings".

Besides charity work, there are many other means of Masonic community involvement. Many Lodges and Grand Lodges have their scholarship programs open to applicants who are from both Masonic and non-Masonic families. Masonic Nursing Homes, originally designed as a service to elderly Masons and their spouses or widows are today open to non-masons as well. Scottish Rite Learning Centers help children with dyslexia and are open to all children free of charge. The Child-ID Program helps fast identification of lost children. Blood donor programs are regular in many Jurisdictions. Often individual Lodges are very inventive in finding ever new means of community involvement and voluntarism: Taking orphan children from the local orphanage on a one day fishing trip; taking a needy family Christmas shopping; painting or cleaning a local school or library. There are many ways for a willing and good Masons to show their appreciation of the community in which they live and to give their little part for the common good.

Many Freemasons have found their "reason d'être" in charity work and community involvement. They completely identify this aspect of Masonic activity with Freemasonry, totally denying any other purpose of the Order. Such an understanding was, in many cases, reflecting on the official policies of numerous Grand Lodges, particularly in the U.S.A. Philosophical education and ritual work became secondary issues, while great attention was given to Community involvement and Charities.

Picture 104. *"Shriners of North America" own and operate nationwide 22 children's' hospitals for the treatment of children with orthopedic conditions, burns and spinal cord injuries. All of the services in the Shriners hospitals are completely free. Since the first Shriners hospital was opened in 1922, over 855.000 children have been treated in them.*

15

SOCIAL ACTIVISM

Social Activism, as an aspect of community involvement, could be described as the effort of Freemasons, Masonic Lodges and Grand Lodges to take an active role in the society, both as individuals and as a group, to take a stand and voice their opinion on various social issues affecting society in general. This is done out of a belief that the duty of a Mason is not only to build his inner being and improve himself, but also to use the same symbolic tools and methods in building and improving the society of which he is an inseparable part.

Social Activism is a completely strange concept to most of the Regular Masonic Jurisdictions. Furthermore, since the border between involvement in politics and religion and being socially active is very thin and blurry, some regular Masons would claim that social activism is against Masonic principles and obligations. Contrary to this, liberal Grand Lodges give special attention to discussions on social questions. In some Jurisdictions these discussions are mandatory. There are many unsolved issues and controversial questions that the world faces today: poverty, global warming and pollution, religious radicalism, human rights abuses, aids, abortion, social security and health insurance, child labor, immigration, human trafficking and forced prostitution, global economy, islamization of Europe, ethnic genocides, and many more.

While regular Masons believe that Freemasonry should concentrate on making a man a better human being, and that this improved man will ultimately be a better part of the society and give his best for the betterment of the society in general, liberal Masons are of the opinion that they should use the tools of Masonry not only for self-improvement but also actively for the improvement of the societies in which they live. In the light of this understanding it is their duty to discuss social issues in the Lodge, come up with unified position, and give their best in promoting their understanding, thereby influencing their community in a positive solution to the given issue.

A member of the Grand Lodge of Italy, which is a liberal Jurisdiction, told me an interesting story from his Lodge in Northern Italy. Several years ago, during the municipal elections, they learned that one of the candidates for the town mayor was a member of the local neo-Nazi party. They discussed this problem in the Lodge room and agreed to write an open letter to the citizens of their town and publish it in the local newspaper. In the letter they voiced their concern and outrage with the possibility that a neo-Nazi could become Mayor and urged their fellow citizens to vote against him. They also campaigned openly against this candidate at their places of work and neighborhoods.

This approach to community involvement, in the eyes of many regular Freemasons, is quite unusual. The very first concern is that bringing discussion of social questions into the lodge room may cause disagreements between members and destroy the harmony of the Lodge. We can often find in the same Lodge men who are against and pro-abortion, against and pro free health care, against and pro illegal immigration.

On the other side, liberal Freemasons have arguments affirming social activism. If man is in search of light and of the ultimate truth; if he sincerely wants to subdue his passions and improve himself; if he learns Masonic lessons of morality and study its philosophy; if he tries to implement the builder's tools to his own life, if he uses reason and do his best for himself, his neighbor, and his God; if he really lives Freemasonry: then he will ultimately be of the same mind set as his Brother in the Lodge or any other true Mason around the world regardless of their religious or ethnic origin.

Let's look for a moment at this argument. What they are really saying is that to start with, men with radical views on any issue could not become members of the Lodge. Racists, bigots, chauvinists, nationalists, religious and political radicals, and in general people with prejudices of any kind, in the view of liberal Freemasons, are not fit to knock on the door of Freemasonry. Their beliefs prevent them from having an open mind and an open heart, which is the very first condition for entry. Such an understanding was common to many Freemasons in Europe, particularly in France, in the early times of organized Freemasonry. In 1869, Grand Orient of France issued a statement that race, color, or religion should not disqualify any candidate from Freemasonry. At the same time, in the U.S.A. a black man could not join a Regular Lodge, nor could a Jew in Germany become a Mason. Furthermore, it was only in the second part of the twentieth century that Grand Lodges in the U.S. started admitting into membership men of African-American origin, and the Prince

Hall Lodges were recognized by some regular American Jurisdictions only at the beginning of this century. I could never understand the problem of racism in American Freemasonry. In my mind, following Masonic teachings and being a racist or bigot of any kind is completely incompatible. Yet it happened in the American lodges. The reason for this is obvious. A requirement to join a Lodge in the regular Jurisdictions is to believe in God and in the immortality of the soul. Nobody asks a candidate if he is a racist, a bigot or prejudiced.

Arguments of the liberal Masons affirming social activism have merit, but only in the Lodge environment where constant Masonic education is a given; where a presence of strong and wise Master guaranties that members never deviate from true Masonic conduct. My research in the history of Freemasonry in Serbia, where Freemasons tried over and over again to be socially active and to take part in solving different social issues showed me that on several occasions, Lodges and Grand Lodges were divided, or they ceased their activity due to disagreements inside the Lodge on various social issues. The solution to the problem of social activism is in better selection of the candidate for Freemasonry and in better Masonic education.

Maybe it is time to update our Masonic obligation by bringing requirements for membership to the level of the time in which we live. The Masonic obligation of the third degree in the York Rite mentions all categories of people that should not be made Masons: an old man in declining years, an underage man, a woman, atheist, libertine, person of unsound mind or a Eunuch. I am particularly amused with the mention of Eunuchs. Not that it is of any importance that last Eunuch probably died in Turkey at the turn of the twentieth century, but I really don't understand reasons behind preventing a Eunuch from joining Freemasonry. Was he considered unmanly because a certain part of his body was missing, or was Eunuch a symbolic reference for a disabled man? What ever it is, in my mind, it does not belong in the Masonic obligation.

I am not going to comment on the rest of obligation, because the history of Freemasonry has thoroughly commented on it already. Women's Grand Lodges exist worldwide as well as Jurisdictions where a belief in God is not a requirement to become a Mason. Maybe it is time to edit our obligation and substitute Eunuch with the bigot, atheist with religious and political extremists, and woman with prejudice of any kind. Or we might at least consider the views of the potential candidates at their investigation and measure their compatibility with the Masonic teachings.

In doing so, we would bring into the Lodge men with a positive attitude toward themselves, their neighbors and the whole of Creation. As in the eighteenth century, Masons disqualified Atheists from joining because they did not believe in the existence of the Supreme Being, we can equally today disqualify those whose religious or other beliefs discriminate against individuals on the base of color, gender, race, sexual orientation, or ethnic origin.

The positive ethical experiences of Masonic teachings are true only if we put them to work. We cannot be hypocrites and obey one moral code in the Lodge and another when we are out in the world. It defeats the purpose of being a Freemason. It is our Masonic obligation to bring out into the world the best we have made within our hearts, minds and consciences in the Lodge room. We cannot be good men and true only in the Lodge room. If the benefits of our moral upbringing are not shared with our families, our neighbors, and every human being, than the work done in the Lodge was in vain.

It is obvious that the result of the making of a true mason should be of benefit for the society. In the light of that argument, social activism as a kind of community involvement makes sense as a natural continuation of the work done in the Lodge, or as the effect of the same. It is also obvious that in the regular Masonic Jurisdictions, it will take some time before they realize the importance and meaning of the social activism, if indeed they ever do.

In many ways, it is a question of two different approaches to the same point. Many roads lead to the Heavenly City and they are all right in the minds of those who choose them. However the logical question remains. If we believe that Freemasonry is a gate to the Heavenly City, where one can already feel the benefits of its citizenship, why do we not see each other as fellow seekers and treat each other with the due respect.

Picture 105. *Poster announcing the Public Conference organized by the GODF on the subject: "Citizenship, Republic and Freemasonry"*

Picture 106. *Masonic Code of Conduct (French)*

16

PRACTICAL PHILOSOPHY

Whenever someone raises questions about the nature of Freemasonry, I always feel most comfortable with the idea that Masonry is a specific philosophical concept. There are many definitions of philosophy. Its field of research has changed with historical circumstances and its relevance has varied with the times, but it is generally accepted that philosophy is a method, rather than a collection of theories, claims and propositions.

Philosophical work, in the modern sense, is based on rational thinking and reason and not on faith, simple analogy, or unproven assumptions. Most often philosophy is understood as an abstract discipline. Nevertheless there are many practical applications. The political and economic philosophies of Confucius, Sun Zi, Niccolò Machiavelli, Gottfried Leibniz, John Locke, Jean-Jacques Rousseau, Karl Marx, John Stuart Mill, Mahatma Gandhi, and many others – have been used to outline and justify actions of rulers and governments through the history. A contemporary example of applied philosophy is the political movement in the U.S.A. called "Neo-conservatism", which started as a philosophical concept based on Leo Strauss's interpretations of the works of Plato. This movement very much influenced policies of the presidency of George W. Bush.

A very developed field of applied philosophy is in the sphere of Ethics. Applied Ethics tries to employ basic ethical principles in the attempt to deal with practical moral dilemmas of the time. The field of applied Ethics is most prone to disagreements, due to the many possible practical understandings of theoretical ethical conclusions.

In respect of its lessons, Freemasonry is very close to applied Ethics. Nevertheless, there is one major difference between applied philosophy and Freemasonry. Applied philosophy speculates on the existing conditions and provides advice for the action to change given conditions. Freemasons in the Lodge room, by the application of various Rites during the ritual, artificially create various conditions in the attempt to understand those conditions and use their understanding in order to change conditions in real life. In many ways it is like a scientific experiment in the laboratory. But the Masonic laboratory does not deal with material things, but with abstract forms and concepts.

In order to do "experimental" work, Masons had to establish several ground rules or basic principles. Sure enough, if we look at the body of Masonic knowledge, we will notice several recurring ideas common to all Masons:

1. The Creator is one and universal
2. The name and the nature of the Creator are of no consequence
3. The Creation is universal and harmonious
4. Human life is in harmony with the life of the universe
5. Human life exists as a unity of the eternal spiritual body or soul and the temporal carnal body
6. The temporal nature of man makes his material side imperfect and prone to mistakes.

7. We should use the logic of the natural laws as well as the instincts of our unconscious to bring our material body back to the harmony with the soul and whole of creation.

These are seven basic principles on which the Masonic "philosophical laboratory" works. I want to warn the reader that these are not officially accepted principles of Freemasonry, approved as such by the Masonic authorities, but my own personal observations. I came to these seven principles by logical deduction and I will try now to explain them in the context of Masonic teachings.

The Creator is One and Universal. On joining Freemasonry, candidates have to express their belief in One God. This part is very simple. It gets complicated with some liberal Masons who claim to be Atheists. I belong to those who believe that Atheists are as much in relationship with God as those who say they believe in God. If everything was created by God, then everything and everybody carries a part of that Divine touch within. It is just that some fail to recognize it. Atheists often claim that God does not exist because one cannot prove it empirically. Following the same logic, one cannot prove empirically that he does not. The only question in respect to Masonry is whether we can accept as Brothers those who claim that God does not exist. My answer to that dilemma is affirmative. If we are on the path to enlightenment and my fellow journeyman does not believe that at the end of the path he will meet God, it does not make him less worthy. If I know that we will meet God, I can be confident that once we both come to the end of the path, he will change his mind. The fact that he took the path of enlightenment means that he is a good man and desirous of learning the truth. Why deny him a chance to meet God? People frequently forget the Gospel story of Jesus at the dinner in tax collector's house, and his parable of the lost sheep.

The name and the nature of the Creator are of no consequence. As Freemasons, we use a nonsectarian name for God – The Great Architect of the Universe. This was done so Brothers of every religion can relate to Him and can pray together. We also do not go further than that regarding his image or condition. If we are made in his image or He is the Universal Principle, it is of no consequence to Masonry. It is the private matter of each Mason how he will relate to Him.

The Creation is universal and harmonious. Everything in the universe is connected and works together. By simply observing the nature around us we can realize how everything in creation is harmonious. There is a certain order in the life of the universe. Human life is in harmony with the life of the universe. Like all other living beings, we are a part of the big and eternal circle of life. Our bodies are mirror images of the whole of creation.

Human life exists as a unity of the eternal spiritual body or soul and the temporal carnal body. Freemasons believe in the existence of the inner nature of man as well as his external physical body. Our inner nature is in its original state good and harmonious with the rest of the Universe.

The temporal nature of man makes his material side imperfect and prone to mistakes. Passions, desires, fears, confusion, ignorance – they are all the result of the carnal instincts of our temporal bodies. According to the natural laws, through reason and rational thought, and by use of the symbolic tools of Freemasonry, we can work on our material nature, bring it in balance with our soul and in harmony with all of creation, or as Freemasons say, "build the Temple within".

To achieve this, we have to be able to get to our inner bodies, to reach within, to our spiritual or higher state, to find the models of our true – good nature – to find "Self". Carl Gustav Jung tells us: *"(Self) is the organizing, guiding and uniting principle which gives the personality direction and meaning in life....The self is the "homo totus", the timeless man that not only expresses his unique individuality and wholeness, but is symbol of man's divinity, when he touches the cosmos: the microcosm reflecting the macrocosm."*

The only way to reach within is by the use of symbols. All Great Teachers and philosophers agree with this. Jesus tells us in the Gospel of Peace: *"The Truth never comes into world naked".* When the initiate enters the Lodge room, the first thing he was told is: Here, everything is symbol. In other words, only if one learns to look into the symbolic nature of everything, does one have a chance to comprehend the full meaning of our constantly changing reality on many different levels, and in doing so enlighten one self and learn the ultimate truth. In the words of the Masonic ritual we are trying to "gather that which was scattered" and "find that which was lost".

Now it is easier to understand why Masonic moral lessons are "veiled in allegory and illustrated with symbols". The moral norms we are after are not of this material corrupt world, but of cosmic, divine origin, the expressions of the absolute Order of the whole of existence.

We are not talking here about "out of body" experiences of the "New Age" type. We are talking about the practical philosophical method, no more or less empiric than any other philosophical method. Through the symbolic use of the working tools of Masonry, we are implementing rational thought and reason through Logic; to find whether something is good or bad, just or unjust through Ethics; to realize the beauty and harmony of the Creation by the design of our Temples through Esthetics; to learn the nature of things in our rituals – thereby imitating the "great circle of life" we are entering upon the field of Metaphysics and Psychology; to find absolute knowledge and the meaning of truth through Epistemology.

Some may be misled after reading this and conclude that Freemasonry is rational. It is rational, as any other abstract science, to the level of human comprehension. But our "Self", our inner body, our soul, or whatever you want to call it, is, in many ways, beyond our material comprehension. Our "Self" is aware of its material invisibility, so it dresses itself in symbols in order to interact with our external body.

It is very much like with the signs on the road. If we drive towards an intersection, usually there is a stop sign, warning us to stop, look left and right for the possible vehicles, and if none, we can proceed. If we don't stop and look, we may collide with the other vehicle, damage our car, and cause injuries to ourselves and others. Here the stop sign was a warning of the possible danger on the road. It was a symbol of danger. Danger on the road expressed itself through the symbol of the stop sign. The stop sign itself is not a danger; it is a painted round piece of aluminum affixed to the pole on the side of the road. There is nothing dangerous about that. But its symbolism at that place is that of danger. Likewise, if we take the very same sign off the pole (as many youngsters do) and hang it in room on the wall as a piece of design art, it will lose its symbolism; it will be a simple stop sign on the wall. At the same time, Danger will remain on the intersection for all vehicles driving through, but there won't be any symbols to warn them.

Here we come back to Freemasonry. To read symbols and understand them one needs to be trained. As it is case with the stop sign – one has to go to driving school where he learns that a stop sign is a symbol of danger. If he doesn't learn that, then the stop sign is just a piece of round aluminum sheet affixed on the pole next to the intersection.

As human beings, we are predisposition to react to the symbols of our inner beings, to the true self. That's exactly why we reacted to the "look" in somebody's eyes. It is unmistakably a symbol that provoked our reaction. The problem is in understanding the symbols. It is necessary to have training. The results of the training will not necessarily lead to the conscience understanding, but to the development of unconscious' instincts. For example, when I was a young Mason, I asked a senior Brother how I can recognize a Brother Mason out in the world. Of course, there are secret signs, handshakes, and words, but suppose, somebody should learn them on the internet (today everything can be found on Internet); how to recognize a Brother from the foe? My Brother just smiled and said:"You will know." Many years passed until it got to me. Now, whenever I meet a man, one look in his eyes will be enough to realize if that man is a Mason or not. Can I explain it? I can not, but it works almost all the time. It is the instinct of my inner being, trained to react to certain symbols on the subconscious level.

It doesn't work only with Freemasonry. Sometimes, this training to recognize symbols is an unintentional result of one's life circumstances. The experienced policeman would recognize a thief in the crowd, and in the same way the experienced thief would feel the presence of the undercover policeman.

By the use of Freemasonry and its philosophical methods, one is enabled to learn to subdue his passions, come into balance with the mysteries of life, and ultimately become better man for himself, for his family and neighbors, and for the whole Universe. All that is needed is good will and sincerity. Challenges are many and responsibilities great. As Carl Jung said: *"The images of the unconscious place a great responsibility upon a man. Failure to understand them, or a shrinking of ethical responsibility, deprives him of his wholeness and imposes a painful fragmentariness on his life"*.

Picture 107. *Temperance, Prudence, Fortitude, and Justice - Four Cardinal Virtues of Freemasonry*

Picture 108. *Masonic Principles - Faith, Hope, and Charity*

17

WOMEN IN FREEMASONRY

In most of the Craft Rituals in use today by the "regular" Masonic Lodges throughout the world, women are mentioned in several prominent places. One can say that women in their different stations in life as mothers, sisters, daughters, wives, or widows of Master Masons have direct and unconditional claim to Mason's relief and protection equal to that given a "worthy Brother" (if not more).

Freemasons are also reminded in the Ritual, as well as by the third of the "Old Charges", as it was written in Anderson's <u>Constitutions</u> of 1723, that woman could not be made a Mason. They were further instructed neither to participate in the initiation, passing, or raising of a woman, nor to have any Masonic relationship with woman claiming to be a Mason, or with such a Lodge. One would assume that these regulations came out of the tradition and regulations of the medieval stonemasons. After all, even today, it is somewhat unusual, although not unheard of, to see a woman as a building engineer, stonemason or carpenter.

Knowing all this, it is very hard to make sense of the curious passage in the York MS No 4 from the 1693, which relates how, when an Apprentice is admitted "the *one of the elders takeing* *the Booke, and that **hee** or **shee** that is to bee made mason shall lay their hands theron and the charge shall be given"*. Some Masonic scholars try to explain "**shee**" as a copyist's mistake for "they", but many who have examined the document are skeptical of such an explanation. There are even older records still in existence mentioning membership of women in the Companies of operative Masons. Regardless, one of the very first qualifications to become a speculative Freemason, according to Anderson's Constitution, is to be a man.

In spite of this strict rule, many women of the eighteenth century, particularly those of "advanced mind and of wealth", showed strong interest in the speculative Masonic teachings. This resulted in the creation of the so-called "Adoptive Masonry" in the 1740s in France, to "allow the fair sex to take part in charity and philosophy". These "Adoptive" Lodges consisted of both men and women and in 1774 were recognized and placed under direct control of the Grand Orient of France. By that time, a system of degrees known as a "French Rite of Adoption" was already fully established. This opened up the door for the further development of female Freemasonry in continental Europe, in England, and in the Americas.

Adoptive Masonry developed over the period of some two hundred years in three distinct directions. The first was the original direction of the Adoptive Orders continued in numerous organizations of which the largest and best known is "The Order of the Eastern Star". The second was of so-called "Co-Masonry" or mixed Masonic groups of men and women and third was a pure "female Freemasonry" where Masonic Lodges consisted only of women.

ADOPTIVE FREEMASONRY

"Adoptive" in Freemasonry means sponsored, recognized or approved by the regular competent Masonic Body. A major characteristic of this organization is that it is a fraternal group not claiming to be Masonic, but practicing its own Ritual and subscribing to its own teachings, with the only requirement that the male members of the Order are Master Masons "in good standing". For a very long time one of the conditions for the women to become a member of the Order was to be related to a Freemason.

The first Lodge of Adoption in the United States was founded in Philadelphia in 1778. Albert Pike wrote one of the very first versions of Rite of Adoption in English, based on the French originals. Nonetheless, as it is a case with many other questions regarding Freemasonry, the origins of the Order of the Eastern Star are not that clear as it is officially accepted and generally assumed. One can read in Coil's Masonic Encyclopedia that the degrees and Ritual of the Order of the Eastern Star were "conceived and arranged" by the Rob Morris of Kentucky in 1850. Morris stated at the time that his ritual was based on a French ritual *"La Vraie Maconnerie D'Adoption"* which appeared in Paris in 1780s in numerous editions. His ritual was first printed in 1855 under the name The Mo-saic Book, as a part of his efforts to form "The Supreme Constellation of the American Adoptive Rite". Later, he simplified this very complex Ritual, and published it in 1860, under the title Manual of the Eastern Star Degrees. In 1865, he published the third version of the Ritual under the title The Rosary of the Eastern Star. In the same year, Robert Macoy, a publisher from New York, using Rob Morris's last edition of the Ritual as a base, published a <u>Manual of the Order of the Eastern Star</u>. In December of 1868, Macoy organized a Supreme Grand Chapter of the Order of the Eastern Star in New York and with this, the Chapter system was established, as we have it today.

The very first Chapter to be founded was Alpha Chapter No. 1 in 1868. There are now over seventy Grand Chapters all over the world, the oldest one being The Grand Chapter of the state of New York, founded in 1870. The Order of the Eastern Star is still one of the largest and oldest fraternal organizations in existence worldwide. There are some doubts, however, regarding Rob Morris as originator of the system of Eastern Star degrees. Some scholars mention the publication from 1793 entitled <u>Thesauros of the Ancient and Honorable Order of the Eastern Star</u>, which shows that the Order already existed at that time in New Haven, Connecticut. To make things even more uncertain, there is a record of Morris saying that he has been "initiated into ladies Masonry in 1847." All of this points to the direction that the Adoptive Rite existed on the American continent long before Morris, since he obviously could not be initiated in 1847 into something that he founded in 1850. Additionally, there is a possibility that the Order died out in 1840s just to be revived in 1868.

The Order of the Eastern Star has five degrees conferred on the candidates in one ceremony of initiation. The degrees are based upon the female characters from the Holy Scriptures of the <u>Bible</u>. By portraying these worthy women through the stories, which display their many virtues, the initiates are taught moral lessons and encouraged to apply them in their lives. In going through the degrees, candidates have to pass five stations and, at each, receive lessons particular to the Biblical Heroines represented there. In doing so, while walking through the Chapter room, candidates would symbolically draw on the floor of the room, a five pointed star or pentagram, where the five stations represent the five points of the star.

The first point is Adah, Jephthah's daughter, which illustrates unconditional devotion, integrity, and truth. The color of her banner is blue and the emblems are sword and veil. The second point is Ruth, a widow who gleaned the fields of Boaz, illustrating loyalty, constancy, and industry. The color of her banner is yellow and the emblem is sheaf of wheat. The third point is Esther, the wife of Ahasuerus the King, which illustrates justice, courage, and fidelity. The color of her banner is white and the emblem crown and scepter united. The fourth point is Martha, the sister of Lazarus, which illustrates abiding faith. The color of her banner is green and the emblem is a broken column. The fifth point is Electa, the mother. She represents the elect Lady from the story in the Second Epistle of St. John, and illustrates beneficence, fortitude, and steadfastness. The color of her banner is red and the emblem is the Cup. At the completion of their voyage, candidates are instructed in the secret signs and words of the Order.

After examining the Ritual of the Order, one notices two major characteristics. In its outer form it has all of the required points of the Initiatory Rites: the Obligation of the Candidate, symbolic Journey to learn valuable lessons of morality, symbolism of the floor work, as well as secret words and signs. In this, it is not different from the Masonic ritual. In its inner form, the content of the teachings and symbolism are remarkably complementary to the teachings of Freemasonry. Any Freemason could relate to the symbolism behind stories of Jephthah, sheaf of wheat, or Boaz. Blue is the color of Craft Masonry and white is the color of a Masonic apron. The Pentagram and the Broken Column are important Masonic symbols. Martha is sister of Lazarus, who is "raised" from his grave by Jesus. Red is the color of the Mystic Rose of which one learns in the Scottish Rite Rose Croix Degree. The Cup as a symbol reminds one of that which is lost and what one seeks to find on his path as a Freemason. Heroines of the five stories are a daughter, sister, mother, wife and widow to whose relief and protection all Masons are obligated.

It seems that Lessons of the Eastern Star Degrees were originally designed for dual purpose. On one side to enhance and widened the experience and understanding of the Masonic Teachings for Master Masons who go through the Eastern Star Degrees. And on the other hand, the lessons give their female relatives, not only the set of moral teachings through the symbolism of five points of the Star, but also a way to understand, accept and join Freemasons on the path toward further Light or towards the Star in the East.

Picture 109.
Order of the Eastern Star Emblem

Picture 110.
Front Page of the Ritual of Adoption 18th Century, France

Picture 111.
The Ritual Book Of the Order of the Eastern Star

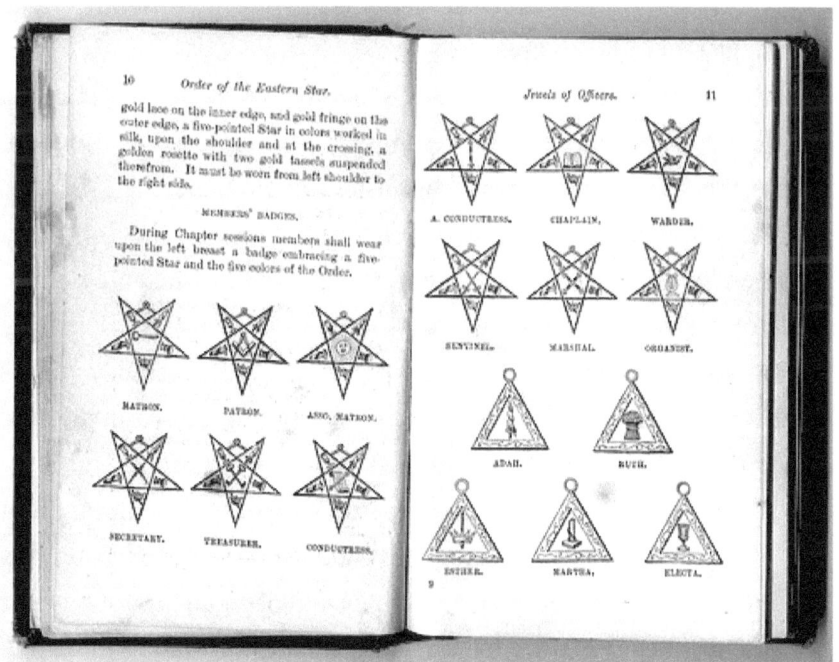

CO-MASONRY (MIXED FREEMASONRY)

In 1892, Maria Derasmes, writer and well-known activist for women's rights, was initiated in the Lodge *"Les Libres Penseurs"* in Le Pecq in France. This initiation was done against the rules of the Grand Orient to which this Lodge belonged. The Master of the Lodge was suspended and the Lodge closed down. This did not stop this very strong woman from pursuing her Masonic interest. In 1893 with the help of her Masonic friends and a few women, she founded a Grand Lodge under the name *"La Grande Loge Symbolique Ecossaise"*. Name of the (only) founding Lodge was *"Le Droit Humain"* (Human Duty). This Grand Lodge, open to both men and women was the very first co-Masonic organization, subsequently renamed *"Le Droit Humain"*. In 1900, they adopted the Ancient Accepted Scottish Rite for the use in their Lodges.

Two years later, Annie Besant, a member of the Droit Humain Lodge in Paris, opened the "Human Duty" Lodge in London. With this, co-Masonry was established in England. In 1925, the "Order of Ancient, Free and Accepted Masons for Men and Women" was founded in London. The first co-Masonic Lodge was open in the United States in 1903 in Charleroi, Pennsylvania. A few years later, members of the co-Masonic groups registered their Grand Lodge in the Washington, D.C. under the name "The American Federation of Human Rights". The system and ideas of Droit Humain spread very fast throughout the world and today co-Masonry is active in over sixty countries as a loose federation of the Masonic organizations under the name *"Ordre Maconnique Mixte International – Le Droit*

Humain" (International order of Mixed Masonry- Human Duty). The only significant difference between Le Droit Humain and any other regular Masonic group is in their acceptance of both men and women into membership.

Picture 112. *Le Droit Humain Emblem*

Picture 113. *Maria Derasmes*

Picture 114. *Le Droit Humain building in Paris (France)*

FEMALE FREEMASONRY

Many women felt a need to practice speculative Masonry separate from men. Considering that the same need for exclusivity existed among the majority of male Freemasons for the last three hundred years, it was easy to understand it. One of the very first female lodges appeared in Boston around 1790 under the name St. Ann's Lodge. The Mistress of this Lodge was Hannah Mather Crocker (1763-1829). Her letters, mentioning Freemasonry, were published in Boston in 1815. In 1908, a few female members of the "Human Duty" Lodge from London formed the "Honourable Fraternity of Antient Masonry", which in 1958 changed name to the "Order of Women Free Masons". To this day, membership is exclusively female and they practice Emulation Craft Ritual. In 1913, another female Grand Lodge was established in England under the name "The Honourable Fraternity of Antient Free-Masons".

After many years of working within Adoptive Lodges, at first under the auspices of the Grand Orient of France and then under the sponsorship of the Grande Lodge of France, women in France felt a need to make radical change in the way they practice Masonry. The emancipation of the women in the European societies in the nineteenth and first part of the twentieth century affected their position towards Freemasonry as well. Grand Lodge of France gave complete autonomy to the female Adoptive Lodges in 1935. This was followed by the period of non-activity due to the socio-political situation in Europe before and during the Second World War. On September 17, 1945, with the help of the Grande Lodge of France, *Union Maconnique Feminine de*

Picture 115.
Seton Challen, Grand Master of the Honourable Fraternity of Antient Freemasons, and her Grand Officers, 1938

Picture 116.
Women's Grand Lodge of France announcing a public conference about the purpose and aims of their Grand Lodge

France" (The Women's Masonic Union of France) was founded. In 1952, they changed name to the *"Grande Loge Feminine de France"* (Women's Grand Lodge of France). In 1959, they discontinued use of the Adoptive Rite Rituals and started using the Craft Ritual of the Ancient Accepted Scottish Rite. Subsequently, some of the Lodges introduced the practice of modern and traditional versions of French Rite, as well as Scottish Rectified Rite. In 1977, with the affiliation of the Lodge "Cosmos", which was still practicing Adoptive Rite, this Rite was reintroduced, as one of the Rites worked in the Women's Grand Lodge of France.

Today, women's Masonic Lodges exist in most of the European Countries, in Americas, and on other continents. Grand Lodges were established in England, France, Italy, Switzerland, Belgium, Portugal, Greece, Turkey, Chile, Argentina, and Brazil, with the number of Jurisdictions in making. Some female Grand Lodges are very active in sponsoring and chartering Lodges in other countries. One of the strongest Jurisdictions emerging in 1981 is the Women's Grand Lodge of Belgium with thirty-five Lodges, three of which are in the USA. As it is a case with male Freemasonry, various women's groups practice different Rites and have different understandings of the Masonic philosophy and practice. Nonetheless, there is no lack of women interested in Masonry; there is only a lack of male Freemasons willing to recognize women's ability to practice the same Rituals and study the same teachings in order to achieve positive goals. According to some estimates, at the present time, there are over two hundred thousand women, worldwide, practicing Freemasonry and co-Masonry, with an additional three hundred thousand involved in Adoptive Rites (mainly the Order of the Eastern Star).

18

AT THE DAWN OF THE THIRD MILLENNIUM

Technologically, today everything is different from three hundred or three thousand years ago. Mentally, human mind did not change much. Our Gods and our ideas are still in the service of our egos. History is repeating itself over and over again.

Humans have failed to learn from their mistakes. We are experiencing a crisis of morality on the global scale. Material greed, religious and ethnic hatred, thirst for power and domination, senseless wars, diseases, hunger – they are still part of who we are and what we do on the planet Earth.

However, the hope that we can be better and do better is as present as ever in the ideals of Freemasonry. By our nature, as many other living creatures, we are social beings. We feel stronger and more secure in ourselves when we are in a pack. Of course, the biggest enemies of our social character are our individual egos. It seems that the consumer culture of modern society is excellent nourishment for the growth of our egos, which on other hand, results in the slow - but steady - diminishment of the basic human group – the family.

To repair the world, man need to repair himself first. Need for the "good and true man" in the world today is as essential as ever. The purpose of Freemasonry is to enable man to improve himself and understand his place in the complex realities of his everyday life. The existence of Freemasonry for centuries is the best proof that the tools of speculative Masonry work. At present, there are almost three million Freemasons world-wide grouped in about five hundred Grand Lodges. Nonetheless, there are many issues that Masonic Institutions must address in order to successfully cater to the needs of the Freemasons of twenty first century. Those issues are:

1. discrepancy between the institutional codes and the philosophical concept of Freemasonry
2. lack of Masonic education and training
3. lack and a meltdown of leadership vision
4. a fragmentation of the universal Brotherhood
5. the curse of the material wealth

The very first issue of the discrepancy between institutional codes - actions and the philosophical concept of Freemasonry existed from the moment Reverend Anderson wrote his <u>Constitutions</u>. As is the case with any other abstract philosophical concept, there are aspects of it that are very hard to put into words. Verbalization leads to potential limitations and misunderstandings.

Let me use a parable: a racing horse can be a champion only if he is running in the race. If one puts a champion racing horse in the stable with a big sign on the door "champion horse" in order to attract people to come and see him in person, after a while, he will become just a stable horse that once was a racing champion. Furthermore, some people, who don't know too much about horses, may come to see him and assume that a condition of being a champion racing horse is to be permanently in the stable. As a proof they would use the sign that the original owner has put on the door of the stable saying "champion horse". Some may even think, since the horse is in the stable, that it would not be a bad idea to use him once in a while to pull the carriage. Accordingly, those who don't know horses could assume that a champion racing horse is the one which lives in the stable and pulls the carriage.

The same situation is true with Freemasonry. Even the first condition to become a Freemason, as it is stated in the Anderson Constitutions, is still a case of various interpretations. Anderson says: *"that religion in which all men agree, leaving other particular opinions to themselves; that is, to be good man and true, or man of honor and honesty"* There are several understandings of this statement. Some think that the "religion" to which Anderson refers is: to be a good man and true. Others think that it means to believe in the Supreme Being. The requirement to be "a good man and true" doesn't necessarily mean that one has to believe in the existence of the Supreme Being.

But this is just the beginning of the discrepancies between written Masonic codes and actions, and the concept itself. Further development of the institutional rules, regulations, and ritual alterations caused more discrepancies. The concern regarding the religious aspect of Freemasonry at the time of the Unification of 1813, resulted in a change of the original rituals by which most of the Christian references were deleted. After the Second World War, the American flag and the recitation of the Pledge of Allegiance became a required part of the Masonic decorum of the Lodges in the U.S.A. In 1871, Grand Orient of France, amid accusation from the Catholic church that it constituted a false religion, deleted from its Constitution "belief in God". The concept of "territorial exclusivity" means that two regular Masons on the same territory cannot regard each other as such, for pure political and administrative reasons which have nothing to do with the tenets of Freemasonry. The decision by the United Grand Lodge of England and the Grand Lodge of Ireland, followed by the majority of regular Jurisdictions, to derecognize Grand Orient of France, brought a big divide in the world of Freemasonry. The lack of membership in the American Jurisdictions resulted in the appearance of the "one day degrees", even "one day Scottish Rite degrees". This ludicrous idea practically means that a Master Mason can receive 4° to 32° in one single day. These actions were nothing else but expressions of a deep misunderstanding of the Masonic concept and its philosophy.

The reason for these discrepancies, of course, lies in the lack of Masonic education and training. To be a Freemason, one has constantly to learn and train. The lodge room is a "school", and the lectures are contained in the Rituals and Rites of Freemasonry. To attend school and not study is nothing more than a waste of time and energy. The history of regular Freemasonry shows that this very important fact about Freemasonry was disregarded by generations and generations of Masons.

We will go back to parable. If a man is concerned with his physical health he might join the local Gym and go there regularly. Of course, whenever he is in the Gym, he would work out, swim, or participate in some kind of physical TRAINING. He would also have to LEARN how to use different workout machines, so he does not hurt himself. If somebody regularly goes to Gym, sits on the side and observe other people working out, it would not make him stronger and healthier. He may be a very good member of the Gym, by paying regularly his annual dues, popularizing the Gym in the neighborhood, raising money for its activities, helping in cleaning and maintaining its facility, but still…it would not make him healthier and stronger unless he – himself does not learn and train.

In Freemasonry, things are about the same. We are not talking here about physical health and strength only. We are talking about mental and spiritual health, which is often the major source of our physical health. A Mason has to LEARN the language of symbols. In order to penetrate deep into his inner being and apply the archetypal qualities of his higher Self to his present experience, he has to go through rigorous TRAINING. There are no time limitations. A true Mason never graduates from the school of Freemasonry. It is a system of perpetual education.

If somebody joins Freemasonry and goes through initiation and all of the degrees without learning and training, he does not do more for himself than the guy in the Gym who sits on the side. Certainly, he may be a good man and a useful member of the Fraternity, participating in all activities of the Jurisdiction, donating to charities, attending regularly and paying his dues. Due to his fraternal activism he may become a distinguished member of the Order, he may get a 33° in the Scottish Rite, and even become a Grand Master. But he will never truly improve himself; he will never be a true Freemason.

Some live in the misconception that initiation, passing and raising, by themselves, represent the path toward understanding of the absolute truth and self-improvement. But Rites and rituals are not blank passports into a higher existence without mental (learning) and spiritual (training) efforts. In the same way, some may claim that circumcision makes a Jew or Muslim, or that Baptism makes a Christian. In some sense it does, but what if these Jews, Muslims, and Christians are not practicing their religion at all? They will never be true to their faiths. In the same way a non-practicing Freemason will never be true to himself.

This lack of education and training, particularly in American Freemasonry, over a long period of time, caused the meltdown of leadership vision. Generations of non-educated members of the Fraternity, by the natural process of going through the ranks in the Order, achieved positions of institutional leadership. Not knowing the true aims and aspirations of the Order, they could not give positive instructions to the membership. They simply didn't have a vision. How far this meltdown of the vision went, one can see from the example of one of the recent Conferences of the Grand Masters of North America. This gathering of the highest Masonic authorities in the country invited a professional marketing consultant, who is not a Freemason, to tell them what to do in order to improve their membership. All of those present at the Conference were, probably, 33° Freemasons, Grand Masters with long experience in the Craft, and presumably, with the knowledge of what Freemasonry is. Imagine the coach of the football team asking a marketing consultant for help how to bring the public to the stadium. Advertising won't help much. The team has to be winning the games and the coach has to train his players, and give them right directions. But the players have to learn and work hard in order to win – and public will come by itself. It is the same way with Freemasonry. The body of knowledge of Freemasonry is a precious and ancient heritage whose implementation can bring enormous benefits to the individual and to the society in general. But the institutional forms of Freemasonry, as they are now, do not motivate true leadership to come out and take initiative.

Instead, Freemasonry broke down along political and institutional boundaries. It was scattered and it will take a lot of effort to gather it back together. The lack of leadership vision in the regular Freemasonry resulted in more fragmentations. New independent Jurisdictions in England, United States, and Europe, subscribing to the "ancient charges", call for the practice of Freemasonry as it was before foundation of the premier Grand Lodge of 1717. New regular Jurisdictions in the Eastern Europe push for the social activism as a regular part of their Masonic work. Regular Freemasons are secretly joining mystical Masonic orders open both to women and men. Some members of the American Jurisdictions are calling for elimination of Rites and Rituals and for consolidation of the social and charitable aspects of the Fraternity. Liberal Freemasonry was not immune to all of these problems. But in most cases the requirement to learn constantly the symbolism and philosophy of Freemasonry limited membership only to those who were willing to learn and advance. Although, liberal Grand Lodges take their time in acceptance and in advancement of the Freemason through the degrees, the retention rate of the members is much higher than in the regular Jurisdictions.

Over the three hundred years of their existence, through membership donations and dues, and through skilled financial management, many Grand Lodges accumulated great material wealth. Grand Lodge and lodge buildings, Nursing Homes, Hospitals,

Orphanages, learning Centers, Countryside properties, magnificent Scottish Rite temples, non-profit Masonic charitable organizations, Masonic sponsored science and medical research institutions, all of this is maintained and financed from the purses of the Masonic Jurisdictions. Further expenses go to the financial support of countless non-Masonic charitable organizations. Of course, somebody has to manage all of this on daily basis and has to make strategic decisions. If we claim that Freemasonry is practical philosophy that one has to study all his life, it is hard to imagine that any student of true Freemasonry would like to get involved in the management of these material assets. And this is exactly what is happening in many Jurisdictions. Over hundreds of years, Masons imposed on themselves many institutional responsibilities of managing assets and supporting charities, that they neglected the main purpose of their Fraternity – Freemasonry itself. Masters, Grand Masters, Grand Secretaries, Treasurers, Trustees of the Funds, Chairmen of various Committees, - they are all so involved in the institutional issues of who is going to be in charge of what, and where the money will go, that they forget that our gentle Craft is not about money and honors, but about learning and moral advancement.

In connection with the universality of Freemasonry, a longstanding question regarding the place of the women in the Masonic communities today waits to be answered. It was more than hundred years ago when women realized that they could benefit from the teachings of Freemasonry and they started organizing themselves. In addition to all the same problems that male Freemasonry had in their development, these women had constantly to deal with complete ignorance from men Freemasons.

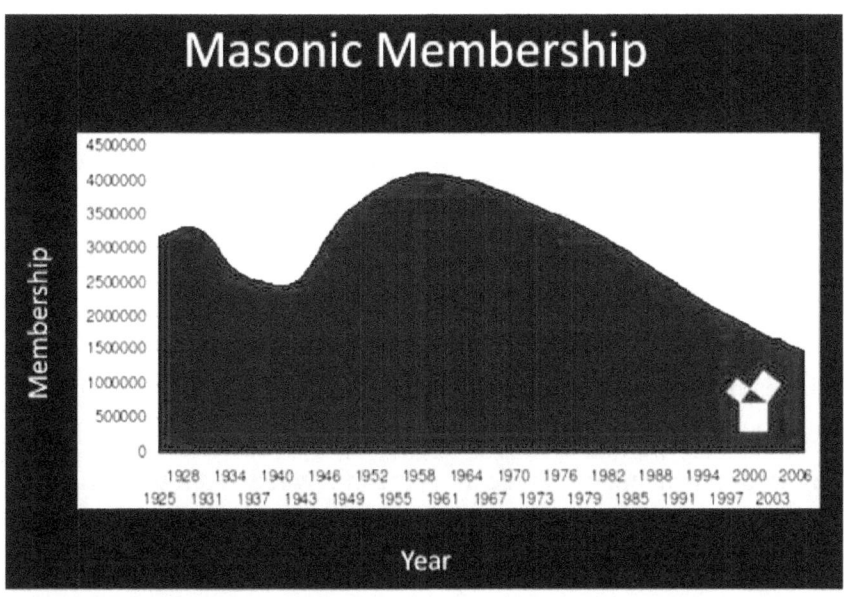

Picture 117–118. *Membership numbers from 1925 to 2006 in the USA and the rate of membership decline in past 50 years according to the Masonic Service Association. (Source: Masonic Business Review)*

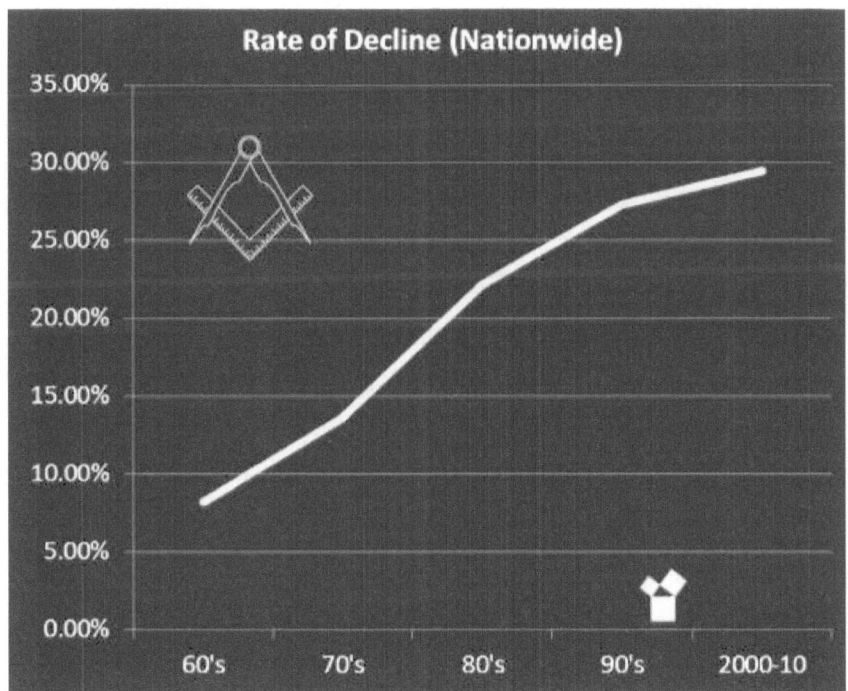

In the process, and in spite all of the obstacles, they managed to form a number of Grand Lodges. Today, still ignored by majority of male Jurisdictions, they are one of the fastest growing segments of the Masonic community, with over a hundred thousand members. Today, in France, out of total number of Freemasons, over twenty percent are women.

Of course, if the institution, that claims to be universal, excludes half of the Earth's adult population from membership, one would expect some very strong arguments. The fact that it is just an arbitrary decision made at the time when such thinking was acceptable, does not justify the perpetuation of the same. Is anyone among the Masons who dare to claim (and who can prove it) that women are incapable of comprehending lessons of our Craft or unable to make the transition and progress towards true Masonic Light?

This is not to suggest that women should sit in the male Lodges or that men should sit in the female Lodges (which most of the women Freemasons would not appreciate anyway). It is just to underline the universality of Masonic teachings and philosophy, and the benefits that they could have for both men and women. The experience of those Masonic Jurisdictions that have recognized the existence of female Freemasonry is that nothing basic has changed. Women and men are practicing Freemasonry separately as before, but the benefits of our Royal Art are reaching further then ever before. For those who desire to sit in the mixed Lodges, co-Masonry has existed for over a hundred years under the umbrella of the International Order of Mixed Masonry "*Le Droit Humain*", and is developing at its own pace. Maybe, sometimes in the future, regular Freemasons will have enough courage and confidence in their great Art and themselves, to accept the fact that Freemasonry is universal and powerful concept that can sustain all different kinds of approaches to its teachings, and remain a pure and unsoiled path of enlightenment for the benefit of all humankind.

Many in the Masonic Fraternity believe that as a social, charitable and community-oriented organization, Freemasonry cannot survive. In today's world, with so many opportunities to "belong to a group", be socially active, get tax credits through charitable donations to various non-profit organizations with worthy causes, Freemasonry is just one of many groups competing for the attention of young men (and women).

It seems to me, that the most precious parts of the Masonic heritage, its esoteric teachings, symbolism and philosophy, are left out and neglected by the majority of the regular Masons. Numerous Freemasons believe that esoteric teachings are the valid argument for any new initiate to proceed on the path of Masonry. I would go even further to claim, that to be the most valid argument. One could find proof for such a claim by examining the work of the original eighteenth century Lodges, and by looking at the experiences of the Masonic groups today that practice rigorous study of the symbolism and philosophy.

From the research done by a number of Masonic and non-Masonic scholars, we learn that one of the most important parts of the Lodge meeting in the eighteenth century, was the "oration", given by a Brother, followed by the discussion of assembled members. These speeches were on wide range of subjects, including natural sciences, art, history, economy, and philosophy (for the most part, ethics and metaphysic). Participation in the conversation that followed was a very important part, where those involved were, through the rhetoric and the intellectual exchange, sharpening their perception and clearing their minds, thereby ultimately perfecting themselves. It was a kind of the "intellectual gym", which attracted into membership gentlemen, merchants, professional men, erudite, and anybody well off and influential in the society. However, Masonic Lodge was not only "new form of sociability or leisure revolution" entertaining "utopian ideals", as some historians would like to see it, but a workshop of a "better man" and of a hope in better tomorrow.

Many Lodges today, particularly those following European tradition, give special attention to the general study and constant acquirement of knowledge, which could be beneficial on the path of the self-perfection, spiritual, and intellectual advancement of their members. It is somewhat ironic, that in the age of mass media, with the instant availability of the abundance of information on any subject, human beings are still in search of answers on basic questions regarding their origins, identity, and destiny. The purpose of the Masonic Lodge is not to be, yet another source of information, but a place to develop tools and methods for self-improvement, perfection, respect of oneself and another, and mutual tolerance. It is believed by many in the Masonic community, that this could be achieved through the constant study of symbolism and philosophy.

By examining membership roasters of various Lodges in different Masonic Jurisdictions, one can perceive that membership retention and growth, as well as the character of members, is in direct correlation to the content of the work done in the Lodge. Those Lodges, which require from their members commitment to study and education are more selective in the choice of new members, and their growth is steady and the retention percentage very high. Contrary to this, Lodges, whose main purpose is "making a Mason", by taking initiate through the three degrees, without meaningful follow-up, keep loosing members. This is most evident in some American Jurisdictions, where, in spite constantly new methods of attracting men into joining, through the mass-initiations, "one-day degrees", and public advertising, retention is low and membership numbers are in decline.

We often hear comments about prominent men who were, in their times, members of the Craft. This was usually followed by a question, why prominent men of today do not join Freemasonry. Both this comment and question, however, should be put in reverse. In other words, many famous men were Freemasons, before they achieved great things in different fields of human activities. It could be even said that practicing the Royal Art helped them in becoming who they were, by strengthening their character and maintaining positive attitude. The lack of the prominent men in Lodges today applies mostly to regular Freemasonry, following the American tradition, and is in direct connection with the lack of meaningful content of the Masonic work. In the rest of the world, following European and English traditions of Freemasonry, many members of the Craft today are prominent personalities from all fields of life. Roasters of the European, African, Asian and South American Grand Lodges read like a "who is who" in politics, economy, culture etc. None of these very busy and responsible men and women joined Freemasonry to have one more line in their professional career resumes, but because through the practice of the Royal Art, their lives have benefited.

A call to return to the basics - to the original practice of Craft - is often heard in the Anglo-American Masonic world. In spite of the individual efforts, it is still just a call. Established Masonic Institutions, with complicated hierarchical structure of Grand Lodges, Grand Chapters, Grand Councils, Grand Commanderies, General Grand Chapter International, Grand Encampment, Supreme Councils, Conference of Grand Masters, and many additional bodies, are so involved into day-to-day perpetuation of their institutions, that everything else, even the practice of Masonry, seems secondary. Grand Lodges are more interested in making capable managers and leaders to manage their vast "Empires", then making true Freemasons. Today in the United States, any Freemason desiring to climb the ladder of the hierarchical advancement has an opportunity to fill 165 offices on the different levels in various Masonic institutions.

This is not to say that Freemasonry is going to disappear in some parts of the English-speaking world due to the melting of the membership base. (Jurisdictions in the United States still number over 1,5 million members). It just means that established Masonic Institutions would have to drastically change their approach in practice of the Freemasonry. One of the ways to do this would be through implementation of the European experience. That does not mean the printing of yet another educational program, which will be sent to the Lodges with an impressive letter of recommendation. It means a real change of the attitude, in which a continuous study of the symbolism and philosophy of Freemasonry will be a mandatory part of Masonic work, mentoring and instructions will be a rule, not the exception, and where degrees and grades will be earned and not given.

The principles and teachings of Freemasonry are as valid today as they ever were. In many ways, the world is in crisis today – economically, politically and environmentally. True and good men and women are needed more than ever before. Tools of the Royal Art of Freemasonry are here and available to all who seek to learn, understand, and improve themselves and society. "Ask, and it shall be given to you, seek and ye shall find, knock and it will be open unto you."

Picture 119. *According to the Masonic Press Agency (APMR), on November 27th 2012 in the European Union's capital was held the traditional meeting of EU's leaders and Freemasonry's representatives of the Member States. On behalf of the EU participated José Manuel Durão Barroso (President of the European Commission), Herman van Rompuy (President of the European Council) and László SURJÁN (Vice-president of the European Parliament) and on behalf of the Craft attended: Grand Orient of Belgium, the United Grand Lodges of Germany, the Grand Orient of France, Droit Humain (Belgium, France and Spain), International Masonic Order DELPHI (Greece), Women's Grand Lodge of Belgium, Women's Grand Lodge of France, the Grand Orient of Hungary, the Grand Orient Lusitano (Portugal) and the Grand Lodge of Italy. _Freemasons of Europe discussed with EU's leaders on the establishment of parameters for the society of tomorrow in Europe.*

An Example of the social activism of the European Liberal Jurisdictions

From: **brusselsjournal.com**

The French Federation of Le Droit Humain represented by its president, Michel Payen, met on April 8, 2008 with the president of the European Commission, José-Manuel Barroso, [...] This meeting constitutes a major event regarding the place of Freemasonry in the construction of Europe; this place was underscored not only by the interest and attentiveness that President Barroso showed to the delegation and the time he accorded them, but also by the commitments he made to the values espoused by liberal and adogmatic Freemasonry, its positions and its opinions on subjects of concern. It was the first time that Freemasonry, as such, was able to express itself to such a high level European institution.

The delegation received assurances from President Barroso of his attachment to the spirit of "laïcité" and to the principle of separation of religion from the State. The delegation stressed the importance of the Enlightenment in the history of Europe, a dimension to be taken into account at least equally with its religious roots, and certainly more closely tied to the roots of antiquity.

Finally, a principle of communication between the liberal and adogmatic Masonic Orders and the services of the European Commission, to be used whenever needed, was decided upon. Thus the French Federation of Le Droit Humain will propose, in the near future, a recommendation concerning the principle of emancipation that ought to form the basis of all European education systems, in direct relation to a recognition of the contribution of the Enlightenment to the common culture of the peoples that compose Europe, and in accordance with the principles of the Charter of Fundamental Rights.

19

INSTEAD OF A CONCLUSION

How to conclude a story that does not have an end? After centuries of Masonic scholarship, the feeling that the last Chapter is yet to be written is as present as ever. We are still "in search of that which is lost". In the old Greek story, Aesop told his sons, before his death, that he had buried a great treasure in his vineyard. They did not find gold, but because they dug and stirred the ground around the roots of their vines, they had a rich vintage the following year. The story of Freemasonry is somewhat parallel to Aesop's Fable. Thousands of books were written and numerous Lectures were given, all in hope of finding that which has been lost. It is yet to be found, but because of the search for it, much knowledge in all branches of learning has been uncovered and accumulated.

Some Freemasons believe that our Royal Art appeared with the birth of the first man and that it will be around until the end of human kind. To be born a human being means having unalienable right to be "Human"- to act and to be treated as such. To practice Masonry means to strive constantly towards the highest ideals of humanity. Freemasons often disagree among themselves what the end result of their quest "for that which is lost" represents. For some it is the return from the fall to the original Divine state of the First Man. For others, it is the achievement of the inner perfection and happiness and improvement on all fields of human existence. Whatever it is, the quest is still one and the same: to enlighten our hearts and minds, search for absolute truth, believe in the inherited goodness of man, and maintain human dignity, practice virtues, and always, always endeavor to be in harmony with the whole of Creation.

Picture 120. *" Beyond Glory" , acrylic on wood by Tamara Nikolic*

It is not an easy task. It requires wisdom and strength of the Master Builders of ancient pyramids and Gothic cathedrals. It requires love for harmony and beauty. It requires measuring and weighing our thoughts and actions and being on the square with others and ourselves. It requires use of the best stone. The hardest stone to cut and carve is one within us.

It is heavy with passions and prejudice, it is rough with bad habits, and it is brittle with fears and confusions and often is invisible. Most of the people go through life without ever realizing their ability and right to create and improve. Nevertheless, those who dare to take the mallet and the chisel and strike that stone are rewarded with nourishment of learning, refreshment of achieving and joy of discovery. To make a perfect stone is the ultimate ideal of all the Master Builders. The responsibility is serious and consequences far-reaching. Stones cut centuries ago by Great Initiates like Socrates, Plato, Moses, Pythagoras, Jesus, Confucius, and Mohamed are still standing as the foundation stones of edifices they started. Each individual's life starts with a new rough stone waiting to be discovered by a willing Apprentice. Every Apprentice has a chance to be better than his Master, and every Master is obligated to contribute his part to that edifice called Humanity.

The sounds of each Builder's working tools are like Symphony of Creation that brings us closer to the Great Architect of the Universe. This Divinely inspired music lifts our bodies, expands our souls, touches our spirits, and...

APPENDIX

MASONIC ABBREVIATIONS

Abbreviations are frequently used in Freemasonry for two reasons. One relates to the simplification of the Masonic Protocol and Etiquette, where long titles of different degrees and Offices are attached to the names of the persons holding those titles; and where even longer names of the Rites and symbols are required to be repeated over and over again. The second reason lays in the practice of privacy (and secrecy), among Freemasons, where often, only initials, or the first letters of the words, are used in reference to various Masonic subjects or names.

The use of abbreviations is particularly widespread amongst French-speaking Masons, so much so, that a number of abbreviations of various words (as it appears in the French language) are often used in other languages, when referring to the same thing.

When writing Masonic abbreviations, it is common to place, between and after the letters of an abbreviation, three dots in the form of an equilateral triangle, instead of a period. These three dots are symbolic, and refer to the three distinct phases in the development of a Freemason: The Initiation (Apprentice), Education (Fellowcraft), and the Work (Master Mason). It could be also understood as the "Discovery", "Acceptance", and "Dispersal" of Masonic Light. Some Masons like to see it as the three pillars of Freemasonry, where pillars of Apprentice and of a Fellowcraft are supporting the pillar of Master Mason. The deeper, or esoteric, meaning of three dots was beautifully summarized by the French Masonic scholar René Guénon, who compared it with three enigmatic questions of the Sphinx. Where do we come from? Who are we? Where are we going?

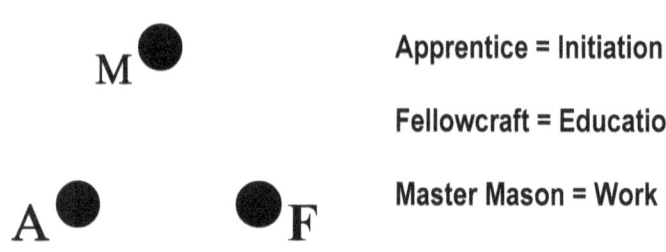

Apprentice = Initiation

Fellowcraft = Education

Master Mason = Work

Most commonly used Masonic Abbreviations:

English	French	
Bro.	F∴	Brother (Freemason of any degree)
S.	S∴	Sister (a woman Freemason)
E.A.	A∴	Apprentice
F.C.	C∴	Fellowcraft
M.M.	M∴	Master Mason
W∴M∴	W∴M∴	Worshipful Master
S.W.	1er Surv∴	Senior Warden
J.W.	2e Surv∴	Junior Warden
V∴W∴	T∴C∴F∴ (T∴C∴S∴)	Very Worshipful (Brother or Sister)
R∴W∴	T∴R∴F∴ (T∴R∴S∴)	Right Worshipful (Brother or Sister)
M∴W∴		Most Worshipful (Grand Master)
G.M.	G∴M∴	Grand Master
G.L.	G∴L∴	Grand Lodge
G.A.O.T.U.	G∴A∴D∴L'U∴	Grand (Great) Architect of the Universe
A.A.S.R.	R∴E∴A∴A∴	Ancient Accepted Scottish Rite
F.R.	R∴F∴	French Rite
R.S.R.	R∴E∴R∴	Rectified Scottish Rite
A.F.&A.M.		Ancient Free and Accepted Masons
A.Y.M.		Ancient York Masons

Appendix

English	French	
U.G.L.E.		United Grand Lodge of England
	G∴O∴D∴F∴	Grand Orient of France
	D∴H∴	Droit Humain (Co-Masonry)
L∴	L∴	Lodge
	O∴	Orient
A.L.	A∴V∴L∴	In the year of Light (*Anno Lucis*)

T.T.G.O.T.G.A.O.T.U(*English*)
A∴L∴G∴D∴G∴A∴D∴L'U∴ (*French*)
To The Glory Of The Great Architect Of The Universe

G.	G∴	Geometry (or "God")
Ill.	Ill∴	Illustrious (Brother or Sister)

MASONIC CALENDAR

Great Britain was one of the last countries to adopt the Gregorian calendar, which by the eighteenth century was in broad use in most of the Europe and colonies. Reason for this lay in the fact that Gregorian calendar (adopted by Pope Gregory XIII in 1582) was the calendar devised by the official Roman Catholic Church, and ignored by Protestant England. It was only in 1752, that necessary adjustments were made by dropping eleven days between September 3 and 14.

Before that time, most of the English were using calendar computed by Anglican Bishop James Usher in 1611. According to Usher's reading of the Bible, 4004 B.C. was the year of the Creation. This was called "the Year of Light" (Anno *Lucis*). Anderson in his <u>Constitutions</u> used this calendar, and subsequently, it was adopted as the official Calendar by most of the Masonic Authorities. The Masonic Year of the Light date could be calculated, by adding four thousand years to the current year. According to it 2013 A.D. (year of the Lord), becomes 6013 A.L. (year of the Light). Some of the Jurisdictions take March 1st as a beginning of the Masonic year of the Light.

With the appearance of the high degrees and different Rites, Masons devised several calendars based on the events from a variety of degrees. Royal Arch Masons calculate dates from the time of the "Second Temple" 530 B.C. This is called the "Year of Discovery" (*Anno Inventionis*). According to such calculation, the year 2013 A.D. becomes 2543 A.I.

Royal and Select Masters start their calendar with the date of the completion of the King Solomon's Temple, 1000 B.C. This is called the "Year of Deposit" (*Anno Depositionis*), so the 2013 A.D. becomes 3013 A.Dep.

The Rites based on the traditions of Knights Templar take as the beginning of the calendar the date of the foundation of the original Order in 1118 A.D. This was called *Anno Ordinis* (A.O.). Accordingly, 2013 A.D. is 895 A.O.

In the Ancient Accepted Scottish Rite, the calendar starts with the year of Creation according to Jewish chronology, which was mid-September in 3760 B.C. This is called *Anno Mundi* (or *Anno Hebraico*). In this calendar, 2013 A.D. becomes 5773 A.M.

To capture the essence of "time" one has to start with the words of a Poet: "The Time is a river without banks". Most of the Masonic calendars have a symbolic value, and they are generally used during the Ritual work, to help Freemasons in comprehending the true meaning of the time and the space. The only calendar that is today more regularly used by Freemasons, in official documents and correspondence, is *Anno Lucis*, often accompanied by the regular (Gregorian) date.

SHORT OVERVIEW OF THE RITES, DEGREES AND ORDERS

York Rite

1. Entered Apprentice 2. Fellowcraft 3. Master Mason	Symbolic Or Craft Degrees conferred in the Lodge of Free and Accepted Freemasons Under control of the Grand Lodge
4. Mark Master 5. Past Master 6. Most Excellent Master 7. Royal Arch Mason	Capitular Degrees conferred in the Chapter of Royal Arch Masons, under control of the Grand Chapter
8. Royal Master 9. Select Master 10. Super Excellent Master	Cryptic Degrees conferred in the Council of Royal and Select Masters, under control of the Grand Council
11. Order of the Red Cross 12. Order of Malta 13. Order of the Temple	Chivalric Orders conferred in the Commandery of the Knights Templar, under control of the Grand Commandery

Structure of the York Rite of Freemasonry
(as practiced in the American Jurisdictions)

CAPITULAR DEGREES

Many Freemasons understand Royal Arch Masonry as the completion of the third degree and the "Capstone of the Ancient Craft Masonry" (the top or the cap of the whole wall). This is the base of the term "Capitular" for the degrees conferred in the Chapters of Royal Arch Masons. In England and in some other countries following English Royal Arch tradition, Royal Arch is the only degree conferred within the Royal Arch Chapters. Every Royal Arch Chapter has to be attached to the Craft Lodge and take the same number as the Lodge (and often the same name). Three "Principal" officers elected for a year rule Chapters collectively. All of the Chapters are under control of a Supreme Grand Chapter. In the American tradition, four degrees conferred within the Chapters of Royal Arch Masons are Mark Master, Past Master, Most excellent Master and Royal Arch Mason. The presiding officer of the Chapter is called "High Priest". Chapters are subordinate to the Grand Chapters. The "Grand Royal Arch Chapter for the Northern States of America", which later became The General Grand Chapter of Royal Arch Masons International, was founded, in 1798, as an umbrella organization coordinating and overseeing the work of the Grand Chapters in the United States and overseas countries following American tradition.

Mark Master degree:- is one of the oldest additional degrees in any of the Masonic Rites. It is understood as a continuation of the Fellowcraft degree and most likely, it originated out of the ceremony where craftsmen were choosing their "Mark". It was an ancient custom among medieval stonemasons that each

Master builder has a personal mark which he would carve in the stone so everyone could recognize the authorship of the stonework or building, very much like signature of an artist. This degree first appeared in Scotland and normally it was conferred on Fellowcrafts. In England, this degree is conferred within the Lodges of Mark Masters that are subordinate to the Grand Lodge of Mark Master Masons. In most of the United States, Ireland, and Scotland, this is considered the 4th degree of the York Rite and it is conferred in the Chapters of Royal Arch Masons as the first of the four degrees following craft degrees. Teachings of this degree are inspired by the famous biblical story about the "head of the corner stone, rejected by the Builders, which has become the central Master piece of working" or the "key stone". (Psalms 118:22, Mathew 21:42, Mark 12:10, Luke 20:17).

Past Master Degree: There are really two types of the Past Master degree in Freemasonry. Before somebody is installed as a Master of the Lodge he is "invested" with the secrets of the Chair. This is called "Installed Master "degree. In other words, one could be Past Master only if he was previously Master of the Lodge. When the Royal Arch degree appeared one of the conditions for somebody to receive it, was to be a Past Master. Since many desiring to receive this degree never sat as Masters, occasionally, Grand Master would grant permission to a Brothers to formally "pass the Chair" in order to receive Holy Royal Arch degree. This exemption became regular practice and with that, the degree of Past Master was established. This degree is conferred in the Chapters and one going through it is called "virtual" Past Master. This title does not have any merit outside the Chapters.

Picture 121.
The Symbols of the Royal Arch Degrees –Keystone on the top of the arch and the Ark of the Covenant

Picture 122.
Royal Arch Apron (English)

Picture 123.
Royal Arch Apron (American)

Most Excellent Master Degree: In the American version of the York Rite, Most Excellent Master is the 6ᵗh degree or the third one to be conferred in the Royal Arch Chapters. It was originally part of the early Scottish Rite degrees and there are degrees with the similar name worked in Scotland today. This degree was based on the story of the completion and dedication of the King Solomon's Temple. In most of the Royal Arch systems, it is a required degree before receiving Holy Royal Arch.

Holy Royal Arch Degree: First references to Royal Arch degree appear in England in late 1730s. The Ancient Grand Lodge, founded in 1752, in England, was conferring this degree in its Craft Lodges as the fourth degree. It was understood as a completion of the third degree. Later, when the United Grand Lodge of England was founded in 1813, it was declared in the <u>Act of Union</u> that the *"pure Antient Masonry consists of three degrees and no more, viz, those of Entered Apprentice, the Fellowcraft and Master Mason, including the Supreme Order of the Holy Royal Arch"*. In the story of the Holy Royal Arch, a group of Jewish captives returns to Jerusalem from their captivity in Babylon and, led by Zarubabel starts the rebuilding of the King Solomon Temple. During the progress of rebuilding, they came across the secret vault under the Sanctum Sanctorum of the Temple, containing sacred artifacts from the First Temple. Further investigation results in the discovery of the secret word. There are slight variations in the story as presented in the American, Irish, and English version of the degree. In this allegory, a candidate is inspired to meditate upon the nature of God. The most important symbol of this degree is Triple Tau within Triangle within Circle.

CRYPTIC DEGREES

Eight, ninth and tenth degree of the York Rite are the Royal Master, the Select Master and the Super Excellent Master. They are called "cryptic" degrees. This name comes out of the setting for the stories used in Royal and Select Master degrees, which is underground crypt beneath the King Solomon's Temple. Originally, Royal and Select Master Degrees were side degrees of the Rite of Perfection that was brought by Stephen Morin to West Indies and then to America in the middle of eighteen century. The first Council was formed in New York in 1810 (Colombian Council No.1) by Thomas Lownds and a group of his Masonic friends. In 1817 they started conferring the "Super Excellent Master" degree on qualified candidates. Later, in 1821, they added the Select Master Degree.

Today these degrees are worked within the Councils of Royal and Select Masters under control of the Grand Councils whose work is coordinated, in turn, by the General Grand Council International founded in 1881. There are forty-nine Grand Councils in USA and one in each, Canada, France, and Germany. In Scotland, Cryptic degrees are under control of the Supreme Grand Royal Arch Chapter. In England, Cryptic Councils function under General Council of Cryptic Degrees. The story behind the cryptic symbolism was taken from the biblical legend of Enoch, who excavated nine vaults, one below the other, on the Mount Moriah. In the lowest, ninths vault, he placed a white cubical stone, known as a "Stone of Foundation". On the top of it he placed triangular gold plate with the Tetragammaton (Ineffable Name of God) inscribed upon it. Upon the construction of the

King Solomon's Temple, craftsmen discovered these vaults. King Solomon ordered that the secret vault be built under the Sanctum Sanctorum where these valuable relics were placed. This is where the stories of the Royal and Select degrees start. Most of the symbols of these degrees relate to understanding God's nature and man's search for the true purpose of life.

Royal Master Degree presents a story of a craftsman Adonhiram, in search of more knowledge. His efforts were finally awarded and he became a member of group entrusted with "Cryptic secrets", available only to few among the builders of the Temple. However, the search for a Divine Truth was not over. Fellowcraft, now called Royal Master must continue until the Temple is completed. The story of this degree was placed between discovery of the Hiram Abif's grave and his proper re-burial.

Select Master Degree: Chronologically, events described in the story of the Select Master degree predate those from the scenario of the Royal Master. Many think that it would make sense to confer it prior to Royal Master. In this degree, Hiram Abif is still alive and he is in charge of "select" group of Fellowcrafts constructing the vault in which secret and sacred artifacts are to be deposited. Besides moral lessons contained in both Royal and Select Master degrees, candidates also receive information regarding the manner in which the secrets discovered in the legend of the Royal Arch degree were deposited and preserved.

Super Excellent Master Degree is not a degree of the crypt. For a long time there were controversies regarding placement of this degree within the Cryptic system. Today most of the Councils are conferring this degree as an optional, side degree.

The story used in this degree concerns the period following the destruction of the first Temple. In this beautiful degree moral lessons regarding fidelity, friendship, and faith in the Almighty were presented in very strong manner. It is quite useful as a historical preparatory degree for the "Order of the Red Cross".

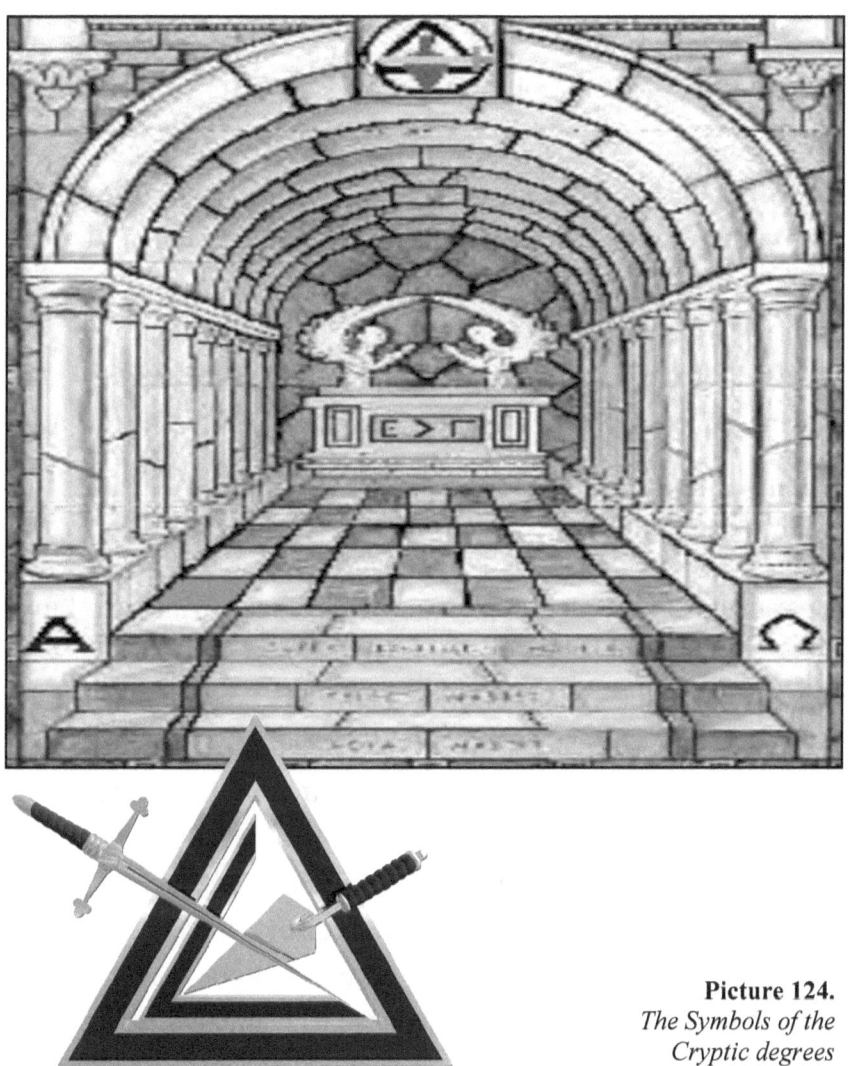

Picture 124.
The Symbols of the Cryptic degrees

CHIVALRIC ORDERS

Three last degrees of the York Rite are the Order of the Red Cross, the Order of Malta and the Order of the Temple. They are called "Orders" because candidate going through these degrees symbolically receives rank of a "Knight". Order of Malta and Order of the Temple were established upon the traditions of the medieval Christian Chivalric Orders. Since they were based on the moral values that are purely Christian in their character and teachings, one of the requirements for membership is to be of a Christian faith. The earliest documented references to the conferral of these degrees were the By-laws of the Stirling Kilwinning Lodge from Scotland dated 1745 (where the fee for the conferral of the Knight of Malta degree was listed) and the conferring of the Order of Temple in the St. Andrews Royal Arch Chapter in Boston in 1769. Today, the governing body for the Chivalric Orders in England is "The United Religious, Military and Masonic Order of the Temple and of St. John of Jerusalem, Palestine, Rhodes, and Malta in England and Wales and Provinces Overseas". They are divided into Provincial Priories who have direct supervision of the subordinate Preceptories. In the United States and on the Philippines, degrees are conferred in the Commanderies, which are under control of the Grand Commanderies. The Grand Commanderies are, in turn, subordinate to the Grand Encampment of Knights Templar USA. Great Priories were also organized in Canada, Scotland, Ireland, and Switzerland. There is a large number of non-Masonic organizations following the traditions of the medieval Chivalric Orders throughout the world. In some cases, they are direct descendants from

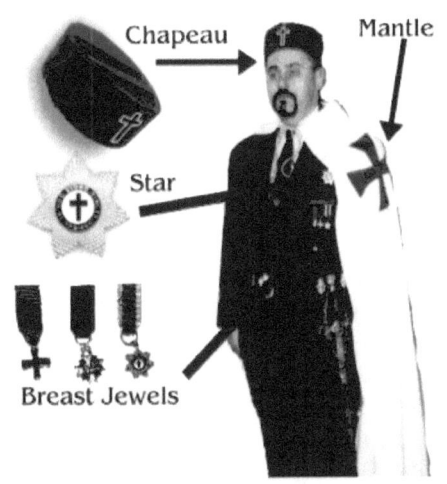

Picture 125 - 128.

Knight Templar - American regalia (top left)

Knight Templar - English regalia (top right)

Breast Jewels of the Orders—Knight of Malta, Knight of the Red Cross, and Knight Templar (left)

The Emblem of the Order of the Temple (below)

the original Orders. Although, they are fraternal organizations, their practices are much different from the Rituals of the Masonic Orders.

The Order of the Red Cross is the eleventh degree of the York Rite. The story of this degree was based on the writings of Josephus and the Book of Esdras. It teaches about the importance of truth, liberty, and justice. While there are no Christian references in the story, its message establishes important connection between teachings of the Old and New Testament.

The Order of Malta degree deals with the destiny of this chivalric order from the time they left Jerusalem until they established new home on the Island of Malta. Strong Christian symbolism is major characteristic of this degree. Motto of the Order is: *"Rex Rexum and Dominus Dominum"*.

The Order of the Temple: The last degree of the York Rite is the most impressive degree of the whole system. Teachings of this degree relate to the symbolism of the "Cross" in many forms, to Christ Crucifixion, Passion, Death and Resurrection, and to the story of many trials and temptations of the Order of "Poor Fellow-soldiers of Jesus Christ" (Knights Templar). Particular symbolism could be found in the banner of the Order- black and white *"Beauseant"*, symbolizing constant battle of the forces of good and evil. The motto of the Order is: " *In hoc Signo Vinces*" (By this sign I will conquer).

ANCIENT AND ACCEPTED SCOTTISH RITE (A.A.S.R.)

Symbolic or Craft Lodge under control Of the Grand Lodge	1. Entered Apprentice 2. Fellowcraft 3. Master Mason
Lodge of Perfection	4. Secret Master 5. Perfect Master 6. Confidential Secretary 7. Provost or Judge 8. Intendant of the Building 9. Elu of the Nine 10. Elu of the Fifteen 11. Elu of the Twelve 12. Master Architect 13. Royal Arch of Solomon 14. Perfect Elu
Chapter of the Rose Croix	15. Knight of the East of Sword or Eagle 16. Prince of Jerusamem 17. Knight of the East and West 18. Knight Rose Croix
Council of Kadosh	19. Grand Pontif 20. Master of the Symbolic Lodge 21. Noachite or Prussian Knight 22. Knight of the Royal Axe 23. Chief of the Tabernacle 24. Prince of the Tabernacle 25. Knight of the Brazen Serpent 26. Prince of Mercy 27. Knight of the Sun 28. Knight Commander of the Temple 29. Knight of Saint Andrew 30. Knight Kadosh
Consistory	31. Inspector General 32. Master of Royal Secret
Conferred by the Supreme Council	33. Inspector General Honorary

Structure of the Ancient Accepted Scottish Rite
(As it is practiced by the Southern Jurisdiction A.A.S.R. for U.S.A.)

LODGE OF PERFECTION

Degrees conferred in the Lodge of Perfection, 4th through 14th, are called "Ineffable" degrees because their major concern and purpose is man's contemplation of the nature of God and his search for the ineffable name of Creator. Ritual and drama of these degrees are inspired with the stories from the Old Testament and legends from the pre-Christian era.

Secret Master: the fourth degree, reflects upon the idea of our duty to God, family, country and Masonry. The lessons taught in this degree are about silence, secrecy, duty, and fidelity.

Perfect Master: the fifth degree deems honesty and trustworthiness as the cornerstone of the foundation of that edifice called "Masonic honor". The lessons of the degree are Good Faith, Honesty, and Sincerity.

Intimate Secretary is the name of the sixth degree and it teaches us faithfulness, self-control, and zealousness.

Provost and Judge is the Seventh degree, and there one learns that person, his property, happiness, and honor are only protected by impartial justice.

Intendant of the Building: In the eight degree perfection is our goal. The Lessons of this degree are about charity, morality, and kindness.

Elu of the Nine: the ninth degree, also called "Elected Knight of Nine" or "Master Elect of Nine" is about importance of guiding our life and conduct with the virtues of truth, generosity, and candor.

Elu of the Fifteen: the tenth degree is also called "Illustrious

Elect of the Fifteen" or "Master Elect of Fifteen". This degree teaches political, spiritual, and religious tolerance.

Elu of Twelve: the eleventh degree is also called Sublime Knight Elect of the Twelve or Sublime Master Elected. Lessons of this degree are about honesty, sympathy, and sincerity. The motto of the degree is *"Vincere aut Mori"* referring to the pledge that "one would rather die than betray the cause of the people, or be overcome through his own fear or fault".

Master Architect or Grand Master Architect is the twelve degree. Lessons of this degree point out that moral virtues are as necessary as the knowledge of liberal arts and sciences, and that the faith and hope of man could turn "a trial into a blessing".

Royal Arch of Solomon (Knight of Ninth Arch or "Master of Ninth Arch) is the thirteenth degree. In this degree one is taught liberty of thoughts and feelings, motivated by honor and duty.

Perfect Elu: the fourteenth degree is the last in the Lodge of Perfection. It is also known as "Grand Elect" or "Perfect and Sublime Mason". This is the ultimate degree of Ancient Freemasonry, because it is the last one to be based on the stories referring to the First Temple. The content of the thirteen and fourteen degrees is almost identical to that of the degree of the Holy Royal Arch. The Ineffable Name of God was found in the secret vault under the Sanctum Sanctorum. The secret word of Master Mason is found. It is time to reflect and look into oneself; the only way to achieve the "Completion of the Temple" is to learn to be true to oneself and to God. Each "Perfect and Sublime" Mason after the conferral of the degree receives the fourteen-degree Ring. It is a flat, plain gold band with the inscribed Hebrew letter *"yod"* within an equilateral triangle. Inside the ring is inscribed the Scottish Rite Motto *"Virtus Junxit, Mors Non Separabit"* (Virtue has united and death shall not separate).

PERFECT ELU

Picture 129. *Regalia of the Fourteen Degree—Perfect Elu*

CHAPTER OF ROSE CROIX

Knight of the East, of the Sword or of the Eagle is the fifteen degree, and the first one of the historical degrees (drama based on legends from 538 BC to 516 BC).

Prince of Jerusalem is the sixteenth degree. Same as the fifteen degree it teaches "loyalty to conviction in the face of temptation, fidelity to duty in spite of hardship and devotion to truth, which ultimately must prevail."

Knight of the East and West: the seventeenth and eighteenth are both historical and philosophical degrees, and represent the "spiritual heart" of the Scottish Rite Masonry. They are full of complex intellectual challenges and require serious study on many different levels. In the seventeenth degree "Knight of the East and West" one learns about man's inherited inability to learn from the past. "The Book of Life" is sealed to await a "New Law" which will direct man in the future.

Knight of the Rose Croix of Heredom: In the eighteenth degree, one learns that by the aid of three guiding virtues - Faith, Hope, and Charity, one may discover a "New Law of Love". The closed book was open and the Word was found. The events from the life of Jesus of Nazareth were used to present the lessons of the degree and the Cross becomes the symbol of self-sacrifice for all men. In this deeply religious degree, the Rose on the Cross, besides its many mystical meanings, typifies the "Beauty and the Glory of the New Law." Rose Croix degree is one of the oldest degrees in Masonry and in various forms can be found in all of the Masonic Rites. For a long time it was considered as the highest lesson one could receive in Speculative

Masonry. On the certificates of this degree issued prior to 1851, it was often written "*No Plus Ultra*" (no higher).

KNIGHT ROSE CROIX

Picture 130. *Regalia of the Eighteen Degree - Knight Rose Croix*

COUNCIL OF KADOSH

The Council of Kadosh degrees are called "Chivalric" but their content is very much philosophical and mystical as well.

Grand Pontiff: In the nineteenth degree, we learn that the "thoughts of the past are the Laws of the present and of the future". We should always try to improve our surrounding and ourselves. In doing so our good works should outlive ourselves. In their continuation, we could become part of the future.

Master of the Symbolic Lodge: the twentieth degree teaches about Liberty, Fraternity, and Equality. For one to be a teacher, he first has to earn. Learning Masonry means profound understanding of the morality, religion, and philosophy, as well as of the concepts of God, Nature and the Universe.

Noachite: the twenty first degrees is also called "Prussian Knight" or "Patriarch Noachite". Lessons of this degree are that the virtues of the true man and Mason are humility, modesty, and courtesy and that one should avoid arrogance, lies, and cowardice in his conduct.

Knight of the Royal Axe (or "Prince of Libanus"): the twenty second degree is about the values of work. Doing a good work and properly usingworking tools of speculative Freemasonry will enable one to build an inner Temple, improve, and through the good works contribute to the common good.

Chief of the Tabernacle is the twenty-third degree. In this degree, one learns that commitment to the "Service of God "and welfare of the whole human kind is essentially necessary in order to become an Adept of the Mysteries of Masonry. Practice of seven virtues and constant study of the inner meaning of things will lead one on the path of enlightenment.

Prince of the Tabernacle: in the twenty-fourth degree, to receive more light, a Mason must exhibit moral qualities of compassion, piety, and justice.

Knight of the Brazen Serpent is the twenty-fifth degree where one deals with the concept of the immortality of the soul. The Serpent (*Ouroboros*) is an ancient symbol of the circle of our existence, and comprehension of the mystical life, death and resurrection.

Prince of Mercy: the twenty-sixth degree is also called "Scottish Trinitarian". Wisdom, Strength, and Beauty are three Divine attributes and one as a Mason is in constant quest for their rewards. Freemasonry is universal and does not promote or belong to one religion, one epoch or one nation. The truth of all is the only truth.

Knight of the Sun (or "Prince Adept"): In the twenty-seventh degree one learns that one's love of Truth, love of Justice, and "Nobility of the Soul" is nothing else but the expression of one's love for God.

Knight Commander of the Temple is the twenty-eight degree. It teaches that one should not be selfish and greedy. Knight and Mason should practice virtues of charity, truth, and honor, and always strive to help poor, helpless, unhappy, and sick.

Knight of Saint Andrew ("Scottish Knight of Saint Andrew"), is the twenty-ninth degree. To love God, keep promises, be loyal, and not judge unfairly are most desired qualities of the character of a Mason. Here the Cross of Saint Andrew is a symbol of humility, patience, and self-denial.

Knight Kadosh: The Thirtieth and last degree in the Council of Kadosh is also called the "Knight of the White and Black Eagle". To be true to oneself and to stand for the just and right cause is the lesson of this degree, which is inspired with the legend of the Teutonic Knights and Knights Templar. One should always have faith in God, his country, mankind, and ultimately himself.

KNIGHT KADOSH

Picture 131. *Regalia of the Thirtieth Degree - Knight Kadosh*

CONSISTORY

Inspector Inquisitor is the thirty-first degree. It is, in many ways, self-examination in view of all of the knowledge that one has had acquired in all the preceding degrees.

Master of Royal Secret: Here we come to the philosophical culmination of the Scottish Rite. One realizes that he is but a link in the chain of universal Brotherhood in quest for the ultimate Truth and Divine Light. The motto of this degree is "Spes mea in Deo est" (My hope is in God).

Picture 132.
Regalia of the Thirty Second Degree - Master of the Royal Secret

SUPREME COUNCIL A.A.S.R.

Inspector General is the thirty third degree. This is an honorary degree conferred by the Supreme Council upon Scottish Rite Masons in recognition of their exceptional work and achievements in Masonry and in public life. Members receiving "Inspector General" degree become honorary members of the Supreme Council. The active members of the Supreme Council are chosen from among them.

Picture 133. *The Emblem of the Thirty Third Degree-Inspector General*

STRUCTURE OF THE RECTIFIED SCOTTISH RITE

Lodge of St. John (Under the control of the Grand Lodge)	1. Apprentice 2. Companion (Fellowcraft) 3. Master
Lodge of St. Andrew (Under the control of the Great Priory)	4. Scottish Master
Prefecture (Inner Order) (Under the control of the Great Priory)	5. Ecuyer Novice 6. C∴B∴C∴S∴ (Knight Beneficent of the Holy City)
Secret Order (Under the control of the Great Priory)	7. Professed Knight 8. Grand Professed Knight

STRUCTURE OF THE FRENCH RITE

Craft (Blue) Lodge (Under the control of the Grand Lodge)	1. Apprentice 2. Companion (Fellowcraft) 3. Master
The First Order of the Rose Croix (Conferred in the Chapter of Rose Croix)	4. Master Elect
The Second Order of the Rose Croix (Conferred in the Chapter of Rose Croix)	5. Scottish Master
The Third Order of the Rose Croix (Conferred in the Chapter of Rose Croix)	6. Knight of the East (Rose Croix)
Chapter of Rose Croix	7. Knight Prince of the Rose Croix

STRUCTURE OF THE SWEDISH RITE

Lodge of St. John	1. Apprentice 2. Fellowcraft 3. Master
Lodge of St. Andrew	4. Apprentice of St. Andrew 5. Companion of St. Andrew 6. Master of St. Andrew
Capitular (Provincial) Lodge	7. V∴Ill∴ Knight of the East 8. M∴Ill∴ Knight of the West 9. E∴ Bro. Of St. John's Lodge 10. V∴E∴Bro. Of St. Andrew's Lodge
Degree conferred by the Grand Lodge	11. M∴E∴Bro. Knight Commander of the Red Cross

Picture 134. *Swedish Rite Regalia*

MASONIC ORDERS WORKED IN ENGLAND AND WALES

ORDER	QUALIFICATIONS	DEGREES
Royal Arch (Under the control of the Supreme Grand Chapter)	Master Mason for a minimum of four weeks	Holy Royal Arch
Mark Master (Under the control of the Grand Lodge of Mark Masters)	Master Mason	1. Mark Man 2. Mark Master
Royal Ark Mariner (Conferred in the Mark Master Lodge)	Mark Master	Royal Ark Mariner
Order of the Secret Monitor (Under the control of the Grand Council of the Order of Secret Monitor)	Master Mason	1. Secret Monitor 2. Prince 3. Supreme Ruler
Royal and Select Master (Under the control of the Grand Council of the Order of Royal and Select Masters)	Mark Master Mason and Royal Arch Mason	1. Select Master 2. Royal Master 3. Most Excellent Master 4. Super Excellent Master
The Ancient and Accepted Rite for England and Wales -Rose Croix (Under the control of the Supreme Council A.A.R.)	Master Mason for a minimum of one year and must be of the Christian faith	4th-17th degree are communicated, 18th Rose Croix degree is conferred in the Chapter of Rose Croix, 19th –33rd are received by merit only

ORDER	QUALIFICATIONS	DEGREES
Allied Masonic Degrees (Under the control of the Grand Council of A.M.D.)	Mark Master Mason and Royal Arch Mason	1. St. Lawrence the Martyr 2. Knight of Constantinople 3. Grand Tilers of Solomon 4. Red Cross of Babylon 5. Holy Order of the Grand High Priest
Red Cross of Constantine	Royal Arch Mason	Red Cross of Constantine
Knights Templar (conferred in the Preceptory)	Royal Arch Mason of the Christian faith	Knight of the Temple
Knights of Malta (conferred in the Priory attached to the Preceptory of the Knights Templar	A Knight of the Order of the Temple	1. Knight of St. Paul or Mediterranean Pass 2. Knight of Malta
Holy Royal Arch Knights Templar Priests	Installed Master of the Lodge, Royal Arch Mason and Knight Templar	Holy Royal Arch Knights Templar Priest
Royal Order of Scotland	Master Mason for a minimum of five years	1. Heredom of Kilwinning 2. Rosy Cross

STRUCTURE OF THE ANCIENT AND PRIMITIVE RITE OF MEMPHIS-MIZRAIM

Craft (Blue) Lodge:
1. Apprentice
2. Companion (Fellowcraft)
3. Master
(One of the specific characteristics of the Master's Degree in A.P.R.M.M. is that is conferred as an esoteric installation of the Worshipful Master)

Lodge of Perfection:
4. Secret Master
5. Perfect Master
6. Intimate secretary
7. Provost and Judge
8. Intendant of the Building
9. Master Elect
10. Ill∴ Elu of the Fifteen
11. Sublime Knight Elect
12. Grand Master Architect
13. Royal Arch
14. Knight of the Sacred Vault

Chapter:
15. Knight of the East or the Sword
16. Knight Prince of Jerusalem
17. Knight of the East and West
18. Knight Prince Rose Croix

Council (Senate):
19. Grand Pontiff of Jerusalem
20. Knight of the Temple
21. Noachite or Prussian Knight
22. Knight of Royal Arch or Prince of Lebanon
23. Chief of the Tabernacle
24. Prince of the Tabernacle
25. Knight of the Brazen Serpent
26. Scottish Trinitarian or Prince of Mercy

27. Grand Commander of the Temple
28. Knight of the Sun or Prince Adept
29. Knight of St. Andrew of Scotland

Areopagus and Tribunal:
30. Knight Kadosh
31. Grand Inspector Inquisitor
32. Sublime Prince of the Royal Secret
33. Sovereign Grand Inspector General

Grand Consistory:
34. Knight of Scandinavia
35. Sublime Commander of the Temple
36. Sublime Negotiates
37. Knight of Shota (follower of Truth)
38. Sublime Elu of Truth
39. Grand Elu of Eons
40. Wise Sivaist (Perfect Sage)
41. Knight of the Arch-in-Sky
42. Prince of the Light
43. Sublime Hermetic Philosopher
44. Prince of the Zodiac
45. Sublime Sage of the Mysteries
46. Sublime Shepherd of the Hutz
47. Knight of Seven Stars
48. Sublime Prince of the Sacred Mount
49. Sublime Sage of the Pyramids
50. Sublime Philosopher of Samothrace
51. Sublime Titan of Caucacus
52. Wise of the Labyrint
53. Knight of the Phoenix
54. Sublime Scald (Poet)
55. Sublime Orphic Doctor
56. Pontiff of Cadmus
57. Sublime Magi
58. Prince Bramin
59. Grand Pontiff of Ogygia
60. Sublime Guardian of Three Fires

61. Sublime Unknown Philosopher
62. Sublime Sage of Eleusis
63. Sublime Kavi
64. Wise of Mithra
65. Patriarch Grand Installer
66. Patriarch Grand Consecrator
67. Patriarch Grand Eulogist
68. Patriarch of the Truth
69. Knight of the Gold Branch of Eleusis
70. Patriarch of the Planispheres
71. Patriarch of the Sacred Vedas

The Grand Council:
72. Sublime Master of Wisdom
73. Doctor of the Sacred Fire
74. Sublime Master of Sloaka
75. Knight of the Lybique Chain
76. Patriarch of Isis
77. Sublime Knight Theosophist
78. Grand Pontiff of Thebaide
79. Knight of the Redoubtable Sadah
80. Sublime Elu of the Sanctuary
81. Patriarch of Memphis
82. Grand Elect of the Temple of Midgard
83. Sublime Knight of the Valley of Oddy
84. Doctor of Izeds
85. Sublime Master of the Luminous Ring
86. Pontiff of Serapis
87. Sublime Prince of Masonry
88. Grand Elect of the Sacred Vault
89. Patriarch of the Mystical City
90. Sublime Patriarch of the Secret Philosophers Stone
(87th – 90th degree constitute the Mode of Naples or *Arcana Arcanorum*)

Grand Tribunal:
91. Sublime Patriarch Grand Defender of the Order
Grand Mystical Temple:

92. Sublime Cathechrist
93. Grand Regulator General of the Order
94. Sublime Patriarch of Memphis
Sovereign Sanctuary:
95. Sublime Grand Patriarch of the Order
96. Deputy Grand Master (Vice-President of the national Sovereign Sanctuary)
97. Grand Master
(President of the national Sovereign Sanctuary)
98. Deputy Grand Master International (Vice-President of the Sovereign Sanctuary International)
99. Grand Hierophant
(President of the Sovereign Sanctuary International)

OTHER RITES AND DEGREES

There is a great number of independent Masonic Organizations practicing so-called "side Rites or Degrees". Generally, they are invitational bodies with particular requirements for membership. Teachings and symbolism of their degrees are usually connected to very specific part of Masonic philosophy or tradition.

The Royal Order of Scotland is certainly the most prominent one. This Order has two degrees: "Heredom of Kilwinning" and the "Rosy Cross". Originally practiced in France in early 1740s by Scottish refugees, it was taken first to England and then to Scotland where in 1750, the Grand Lodge of the Royal Order of Scotland was founded. According to the legend of origin, King Robert the Bruce established this Order at Kilwinning. In the " Heredom of Kilwinning " degree lectures refer to a symbolism of the three Craft degrees and further explain their teachings. The "Rosy Cross" degree is based on the story of sixty three Knights Templar who, in 1314, after escaping from France, came to Scotland and helped King Robert the Bruce to win at the Battle at Bannockburn. Honor of receiving this degree was, for a long time, limited to Scotsmen and then only on sixty-three members. Over the time, Provincial Grand Lodges were founded in different parts of the world with the membership of various nationalities and the limitation on the number of members was relaxed. Still, membership in this Order is considered one of the highest honors in Freemasonry. In the United States, qualification for a Mason to become a member is to be thirty-second degree Scottish Rite Mason and the Freemason for at least five years.

Royal Ark Mariner is another interesting degree. This degree is practiced in England in the Royal Ark Mariners Lodges, attached to the Mark Masters Lodges, and subordinate to the Grand Lodge of Mark Master Masons. In the United States degree is conferred within the Councils of Allied Masonic degrees. It is often underrated, but very beautiful degree based on the story of Flood and Noah's Ark.

Order of the Secret Monitor is a degree open to Master Masons. It is conferred in the England within an independent body, and the United States as one of the A.M.D. degrees.

Societas Rosicruciana was founded in Edinburgh in 1866. Members of this Order have to be a Freemasons of the Christian faith. They consider themselves to be an educational research society meeting in " Colleges". The aim of the society is to facilitate study of the teachings of the "original" Rosicrucian Order (1450AD), and of other Hermetic, Platonic and Kabalistic teachings. It is organized in nine grades, each with appropriate ritual. Members are encouraged to write and present original papers. The Society Headquarters is in London with over fifty-six Colleges in England, Australia, Canada, and Holland. There are similar organizations existing in USA and elsewhere around the world.

The Allied Masonic Degrees of the USA: There is a number of honorary and invitational bodies related to the York Rite. "The Allied Masonic Degrees of the USA" is an invitational organization where requirement for a membership is to be a Royal Arch Mason. AMD Council is a research Masonic group particularly interested in research of Rituals of dormant degrees. Membership in the Council is limited to 27 and Councils are subordinate to the Grand Council AMD of the USA.

Knight Masons of the USA is another invitational organization where the requirement for a membership is to be Royal Arch Mason. Councils of Knight Masons confer so called "green degrees" which were originally worked in the Knights Templar Priories in Ireland.

Knights of the York Cross of Honor is an honorary organization where condition for membership is that candidate was presiding officer of the Lodge, Royal Arch Chapter, Cryptic Council and Commandery before he could be considered for a membership.

The Red Cross of Constantine is considered the highest honor in the York Rite Masonry and the membership in the Order is awarded to the eminent York Rite Masons for their lifelong achievements.

The Holy Royal Arch Knights Templar Priests is another honorary invitational organization, where the condition for the membership is to be Past Master of the Lodge, Royal Arch Mason, and Knight Templar.

Picture 135—136. *Royal Order of Scotland Regalia (top) and Royal Order of Scotland Seal (bottom)*

FAMOUS FREEMASONS

The speculative Freemasonry, in the three hundred years of its existence, was, and still is, very attractive to a men and women from all walks of life. Many of them made great achievements in different fields of human endeavor, and became eminently distinguished. The presidents and kings, military officers and politicians, scientists and artists, industrialists and bankers, the adventurers and explorers, they all had one thing in common – love for the Royal Art. Their dedication to the principles, and practice of the teachings of the Freemasonry, inspired and helped them in their life and work. We will mention just few of many thousands of prominent Masons, who left their mark in the history of last three centuries.

Col. Edwin "Buzz" Aldrin (born 1930)
-American astronaut, who in 1969, landed on the
Moon in the Appolo 11 lunar module.
He was a member of the Montclair Lodge No.144
(Grand Lodge of New Jersey)

Salvador Allende (1908-1973)
-President of Chile from 1970 to 1973, when he
was killed during the military coup.
He was a member of the Lodge "Progresso" No.4
(Grand Lodge of Chile)

Louis Armstrong – "Satchmo"(1900-1971)
-The Trumpet player and Singer, he was "the
legend" of the American jazz music.
He was a member of the Montgomery Lodge
No.18 (Prince Hall Grand Lodge of New York)

Mustapha Kemal Ataturk (1881-1938)
-The father of the modern Turkish state and the
President of Turkey from 1923 to 1938.
He was a member of the "Macedonia Resorta e
Veritas" Lodge (Grand Lodge of Italy)
Eduard Benes (1884-1946)
-President of Czechoslovakia from 1935 to 1938.
Member of the Lodge "Pravda Vitezi" (Grand
Lodge of Czechoslovakia)
Josephine Baker (1906-1975)
-Famous dancer and entertainer, she was well
known for her activism on the field of civil liberties
and racial equality. She was a member of
the "La Nouvelle Jerusalem" Lodge
(Women's Grand Lodge of France)
Irving Berlin (1888-1989)
-American composer and songwriter ("White
Christmas"-1942), member of the Munn Lodge
No.190 (Grand Lodge of New York)
Frederic August Bertholdi (1834-1904)
-French sculptor, best known as the author of
the Masonically inspired statue of "Liberty illuminating
the world" in the New York Harbor. He
was a member of the Lodge Alsace Lorraine in Paris.
Annie Besant (1847-1933)
-An English Theosophist, passionate advocate of
birth-control and Socialism, and active supporter
of the India's independence movement. She was
a member of the Droit Humain Lodge in France,

and the founder of the first co-Masonic Lodge in England.

Simon Bolivar (1783-1830)
- The revolutionary and the liberator of the South American countries from the Spanish rule. He became Mason in Spain, and in 1807 received his Scottish Rite degrees in Paris. He was The founder of the "Order and Liberty" Lodge No.2 (Grand Lodge of Peru)

Edith Clark Boiteux (1906-1937)
-French pilot and passionate skydiver, famous for her risky skydiving experiments (one of which was cause of her tragic death). She became member of the Lodge of Adoption "General Peigne" in 1926. (Grand Lodge of France)

Robert Burns (1759-1796)
-The most famous Scottish Poet (*"Auld Lang Syne"*). He was a member of the Canongate-Killwinning Lodge No.2 (Grand Lodge of Scotland)

Giovanni Jacopo Casanova De Seingalt (1725-1798)
- Italian adventurer and writer, known more for his controversial relationships with prominent women of the time, than for his writing. He was made Freemason around 1750, in France

Marc Chagall (1887-1985)
-Famous artist, born in Russia and lived in France. He was well known for his unique style in painting, often influenced by Biblical themes. He was made a Freemason in 1912, in Vitebsk, Belorussia.

Sir Winston Churchill (1874-1965)
-English statesman, the Prime Minister of Great Britain during World War Two, and the recipient of the Nobel Prize for literature in 1953. He was a member of the Rosemary's Lodge No.2851 (U.G.L.E.)

André Citroen (1878-1935)
-French engineer and car manufacturer, who in 1919, built the first mass-produced automobile in Europe. He was a member of the Lodge "La Philosophie Positive" (G.O.F.)

Harvey Corbett (1874-1954)
-Architect who designed the Rockefeller Center Complex in New York City. He was a member of the Sangamore Lodge in New York.

Edith Cowan (1866-1932)
-The first women to became member of the Australian Parliament. She was a member of the Droit Humain of Australia.

Cecil B. De Mille (1881-1959)
-American film director and producer, one of the Hollywood pioneers. He was a member of the Prince of Orange Lodge No.16 (Grand Lodge of New York)

Maria Deraismes (1828-1894)
-French journalist and activist for women's rights. She was initiated in the Lodge "Les Libres Penseurs" in 1882. In 1893 she founded co-Masonic order "Le Driot Humain".

Sir Arthur Conan Doyle (1859-1930)
-English writer novelist, best known as a creator of the "Sherlock Holmes". He was a member of a

Phoenix Lodge No.257 (U.G.L.E.)

Jean Henri Dunant (1828-1910)
-Founder of the Red Cross in 1864, and the recipient of the Nobel Prize for Peace in 1901.

Sir Alexander Fleming (1881-1955)
-Scottish scientist – bacteriologist, who in 1928, discovered the antibiotic properties of the penicilium mold, and was awarded Nobel Prize for medicine in 1945. He was a member of the United Grand Lodge of England, where he attained Grand Rank.

Henry Ford (1863-1947)
-The founder of the Ford Motor Company, developer of the "assembly-line" method, and many other innovations in the industrial production. He was also well known philanthropist.
He was a member of the Palestine Lodge No.357 (Grand Lodge of Michigen)

Benjamin Franklin (1706-1790)
- American statesman, scientist and philosopher. In 1731, was initiated in the St. John's Lodge in Philadelphia. While in Paris he was a Master of the Lodge "Les Neuf Soeurs" (G.O.F.)

Giuseppe Garibaldi (1807-1882)
-Italian patriot and the leader of the movement for the liberation and unification of Italy.
He was initiated in Lodge "L'Ami de la Vertu" in Montevideo, in 1644 (G.O.F.). Later he became Grand Master of the Grand Orient of Palerma (Italy).

Johann Wolfgang Von Goethe (1749-1832)
-Celebrated German writer-poet, most prominent representative of the Romantic School.
He was a member of the Amalia Lodge in Weimar.

Prince Hall (1748-1807)
-Methodist Minister from Cambridge, (Massachusets), he was the first black American Freemason. In 1775 he was made a Mason in an Irish military Lodge, and in 1784 he was the founding Master of the African Lodge No.459 (Grand Lodge of England).

Franz Josef Haydn (1732-1809)
-Austrian composer, famous for his symphonies, masses, and chamber music. He was a friend of Mozart, who introduced him to Freemasonry. He was a member of the Lodge "Zur Wahren Eintracht" in Vienna.

Claude Adrien Helvetius (1715-1771)
-French Philosopher, well known for his work on Encyclopedia; his most prominent work was on Ethics- "De L'Esprit", in 1758. He was a member of the Lodge "Les Neuf Soeurs" (G.O.F.).

Heinrich Heine (1799-1856)
-German Romantic poet, famous for his passionate ideas of political freedom and justice.He was made a Mason in Paris in the Lodge "Les Trinosophes" in 1844. (G.O.F.)

Harry Houdini (1874-1926)
-American entertainer and an escape artist. He was a member of the St Cecile Lodge No.568 in New York.

Ismail Pasha (1830-1895)
-Well-known Khedive (Governor) of Egypt, who promoted the building of the Suez Canal. In 1879, he presented an obelisk to the United States, which was erected in the Central Park, in New York. He was Grand Master of the Grand Lodge of Egypt.

Rudyard Kipling (1865-1936)
-Famous English writer, author of The Jungle Books, and The Man Who Would Be King, recipient of the Nobel Prize for literature in 1907. His most popular poems among Masons are, "The Palace", "If" and "The Mother Lodge". He was made a Mason in Lahore, India, in 1887, in the Lodge "Hope and Esperance" No.782. (U.G.L.E.)

Lajos Kossuth (1802-1894)
-Hungarian patriot and revolutionary. He fought for Hungarian independence from Austria in 1848, and helped Garibaldi in Italy. He was made a Mason in the Cincinnati Lodge No.133, in Ohio, in 1852.

Pierre Simon, Marquis De Laplace (1749-1827)
- French Astronomer and Mathematician, famous for his theory of the origin of the solar system. As a Freemason, he held a Grand Rank in the Grand Orient of France.

Charles Lindbergh (1902-1974)
-American pilot, famous for his solo non-stop flight from America to Europe in 1927. He was a member of the Keystone Lodge No.243 in Saint Louis. (Grand Lodge of Missouri)

Franz Von Liszt (1811-1886)
-Hungarian Composer and pianist, the most popular for his pieces composed for piano. He was initiated in 1841, in German Lodge "Zur Einigkeit", in Frankfurt.

George C. Marshall (1880-1959)
-American General, Diplomat and statesman. As a Secretary of State, he was author of the Plan for European Economic Recovery (Marshall Plan) after the Second World War, for which he received Nobel Peace Prize in 1953. He was a member of the Grand Lodge of the District of Colombia.

Wolfgang Amadeus Mozart (1756-1791)
-Austrian composer, famous for his concerts, symphonies and operas. Inspired with the Masonic teachings, he wrote opera "The Magic Flute", and composed several cantatas, specifically for the use during the ritual work in the Lodge. He was a member of the Lodge "Zur Wohltatigkeit" in Vienna.

Marianne Monnestier (born 1908)
-Prominent French journalist, she was a member of the Lodge "La Nouvelle Jerusalem" (Women's Grand Lodge of France)

Albert Pike (1809-1891)
- After serving as a Confederate General in the Civil War, he committed his life to Masonry, and particularly to the Scottish Rite. He was Sovereign Grand Commander of the Supreme Council

A.A.S.R. (Southern Jurisdiction U.S.A.) from 1859 until his death, but he was best known as a prolific Masonic writer. His book "Morals and Dogma" is considered one of the classics of Masonic literature.

Aleksander Pushkin (1799-1837)
- Famous Russian poet, author of the "*Eugene Onegin*" and "*Boris Godunov*".
He was initiated in the Lodge "Ovid" in Kischinev (Russia).

Charles Robert Richet (1850-1935)
-French psychologist, well known for his work on an immune serum and for the discovery of the phenomenon of anaphylaxis. In 1913 he received the Nobel Prize for medicine.
He was a member of the Lodge "Cosmos" (Grand Lodge of France)

The Ringling Brothers (Albert, Alfred, August, Charles, Henry, John, and William)
-Showmen and owners of the famous "Ringling Brothers Circus" founded by their father August Ringling in 1884. All seven brothers and their father were members of the Baraboo Lodge No.34 (Grand Lodge of Wisconsin).

Sir Walter Scott (1771-1832)
-Famous Scottish novelist and poet, author of the novels "Ivanhoe", "Quentin Durward", and poems "The Lady of the Lake" and "The Lay of the Last Minstrel". He was a member of the St. David Lodge No.36 (Grand Lodge of Scotland).

Peter Sellers (1925-1980)
-English stage and screen actor, famous for his role in "The Pink Panther". He was a member of the Chelsea Lodge No.3098 in London (U.G.L.E.)

Jan Sibelius (1865-1957)
-Prominent Finish composer. He was made a Mason in the Suomi Lodge No.1, the very same day when the Grand Lodge of Finland was founded in 1922. He composed numerous works on Masonic themes and for the use in the Lodge rooms.

François Marie Arouet Voltaire (1694-1778)
-French philosopher and writer, known for his progressive ideas of religious tolerance. He was made a Mason in the Lodge *Les Neuf Soeurs* in Paris two months before his death.

Arthur Edward Waite (1857-1942)
-English Masonic writer, well known for his esoteric approach to the study of Freemasonry.
He was a member of the Runymede Lodge No.2430 (U.G.L.E.)

Oscar Wilde (1854-1900)
-Anglo-Irish dramatist, author of popular plays, such as "Lady Windermere's Fun" and "The importance of being Earnest". In 1875, he was made a Mason in Apollo Lodge No.357, Oxford (U.G.L.E.).

Presidents of the U.S.A. who were Freemasons:

George Washington (1732-1799)
James Monroe (1758-1831)
Andrew Jackson (1767-1845)
James Knox Polk (1795-1849)
James Buchanan (1791-1868)
Andrew Johnson (1808-1875)
James Abram Garfield (1831-1881)
William McKinley (1843-1901)
Theodore Roosevelt (1858-1919)
William Taft (1857-1930)
Warren G. Harding (1865-1923)
Franklin Delano Roosevelt (1885-1945)
Harry S. Truman (1884-1972)
Lyndon B. Johnson (1908-1973)
Gerald Ford (born 1913)

Presidents of the French Republic who were Freemasons:

Francois Grevy (1807-1891)
Felix Faure (1841-1899)
Alexandre Millerand (1859-1943)
Gaston Doumergue (1863-1937)
Paul Doumer (1857-1932)

LIST OF THE GRAND LODGES

EUROPE:

Andorra
- Grand Lodge of Andorra
- Droit Humain

Austria
- Grand Lodge of Austria
- Grand Orient of Austria
- Grand Lodge Humanitas
- Droit Humain

Belgium
- Regular Grand Lodge of Belgium
- Grand Orient of Belgium
- Grand Lodge of Belgium
- Women's Grand Lodge of Belgium
- Droit Humain

Bosnia
- Grand Lodge of Bosnia

Bulgaria
- United Grand Lodge of Bulgaria
- Droit Humain

Croatia
- Grand Lodge of Croatia

Czech Republic
- Grand Lodge of the Czech Republic F.A.M.
- Grand Orient Czech
- Grand Lodge of the Czech Lands
- Humanitas Bohemia (Co-Masonic)

Denmark
- Danish Order of Freemasons- Grand Lodge of Denmark
- Danish Guild of Freemasons
- Droit Humain

England
- United Grand Lodge of England
- The Honourable Fraternity of Ancient Freemasons (for women)
- The Order of Women Freemasons
- Droit Humain
- Regular Grand Lodge of England

Estonia
- Grand Lodge of Estonia
- Droit Humain

Finland
- Grand Lodge of Finland
- Droit Humain

France
- Grand Orient of France
- Grand Lodge of France
- National Grand Lodge of France
- Women's Grand Lodge of France
- Droit Humain
- Traditional and Symbolic Grand Lodge "Opera"
- Mixed Grand Lodge of France
- Mixed Grand Lodge Universal
- Grand Lodge Memphis-Mizraim
- Women's Grand Lodge Memphis-Mizraim
- Grand Lodge of F.A.M. of France

Germany
- United Grand Lodges of Germany- Brotherhood of Freemasons
- Grand Orient of Germany
- Universal Freemasonic Order Humanitas Germany
(mixed men and women)
- Women's Grand Lodge of Germany
- Droit Humain

Greece
-Grand Lodge of Greece
- National Grand Lodge of Greece
- Serenissime Grand Orient of Greece
- Kalipatira (Women's Grand Lodge)
- Droit Humain

Hungary
- Symbolic Grand Lodge of Hungary
- Grand Orient of Hungary
- Droit Humain

Iceland
- The Icelandic Order of Freemasons- Grand Lodge of Iceland
- Droit Humain

Ireland
- Grand Lodge of Ireland
- Droit Humain

Italy
- Grand Orient of Italy
- Regular Grand Lodge of Italy
- Grand Lodge of Italy (Clipsas and Catena)
- Women's Masonic Grand Lodge of Italy
- Droit Humain

Latvia
- Grand Lodge of Latvia

Lithuania
- Grand Lodge of Lithuania A.F.&A.M.
- Droit Humain

Luxembourg
- Grand Lodge of Luxembourg
- Grand Orient of Luxembourg
- Droit Humain

Netherlands
- Grand East of the Netherlands
- Netherlands Grand Lodge of Co-Masonry
- Droit Humain

Norway
- The Norwegian Order of Freemasons
- Droit Humain

Macedonia
- Grand Lodge of Macedonia

Malta
- Sovereign Grand Lodge of Malta

Montenegro
- Grand Lodge of Montenegro

Poland
- National Grand Lodge of Poland
- Grand Orient of Poland
- Droit Humain

Portugal
- Regular Grand Lodge of Portugal
- Grand Orient Lusitano
- Droit Humain
- Women's Grand Lodge of Portugal
- National Grand Lodge of Portugal

Romania
- National Grand Lodge of Romania
- Confederation of the Grand Lodges of Romania

Russia
- Grand Lodge of Russia
- Russian Regular Grand Lodge

San Marino
- Grand Lodge of San Marino

Scotland
- Grand Lodge of Scotland
- Droit Humain

Serbia
- Regular Grand Lodge of Serbia
- United Grand Lodges of Serbia
- National Grand Lodge of Serbia

Slovenia
- Grand Lodge of Sovenia

Spain
- Grand Lodge of Spain
- Symbolic Grand Lodge of Spain (men and women)
- Spanish Federal Grand Lodge
- Grand Orient of Spain
- Droit Humain

Sweden
- Swedish Order of Freemasons- Grand Lodge of Sweden
- Droit Humain

Switzerland
- Grand Lodge Alpina
- Grand Orient
- Droit Humain
- Symbolic Grand Lodge Helvetia
- Mixed Grand Lodge of Switzerland
- L.U.F. Swiss National Group

Turkey
- Grand Lodge of Turkey
- Grand Lodge of Turkish Freemasons
- Women's Grand Lodge of Turkey
- F.&A. Grand Lodge of Turkey

ASIA

Armenia
- Grand Lodge of Armenia

India
- Grand Lodge of India
- Grand Lodge of Upper India
- Grand Lodge of South India
- Droit Humain

Indonesia
- Droit Humain
Israel
- Grand Lodge of the State of Israel
- Droit Humain
Japan
- Grand Lodge of Japan
New Zealand
- Grand Lodge of New Zealand
- Droit Humain
Pakistan
- Droit Humain
Philippines
- Grand Lodge of the Philippines
- The Deputy Sovereign Grand lodge of the Philippine Archipelago in America
Taiwan
- Grand Lodge of China F.&A.M.
Sri Lanka
- Droit Humain

AUSTRALIA

- Droit Humain (Australian Federation)
New South Wales
- United Grand Lodge of New South Wales A.F.&A.M.
- Grand Lodge Symbolic of Memphis-Misraim
Queensland
- United Grand Lodge of Queensland
South Australia & Northern Territory
- Grand Lodge of South Australia and the Northern Teritory
Tasmania
- Grand Lodge of Tasmania A.F.&A.M.
Victoria
- United Grand Lodge of Victoria
Western Australia
- Grand Lodge of Western Australia

AFRICA

Benin
- Grand Lodge of Benin

Burkina Faso
- Grand Lodge of Burkina Faso
Burundi
- Droit Humain
Cameron
- Grand Lodge of Cameron
- Grand Orient and United Lodges of Cameron
- Droit Humain
Congo
- Grand Lodge of Congo
- Grand Orient of Congo
- Droit Humain
Gabon
- Grand Lodge of Gabon
Guinea
- Grand Lodge of Guinea
Ivory Coast
- Grand Lodge of the Ivory Coast
- Droit Humain
Liberia
- Grand Lodge of Liberia
Mali
- National Grand Lodge of Mali
- Droit Humain
Madagascar
- *National Grand Lodge of Madagascar*
- Droit Humain
Mauritius
- Droit Humain
Morocco
- Grand Lodge of the Kingdom of Morocco
South Africa
- Grand Lodge of South Africa
- Droit Humain
Senegal
- Grand Lodge of Senegal
- Droit Humain
Togo
- Grand Lodge of Togo
- National Grand Lodge of Togo
Zaire
- Droit Humain

NORTH AMERICA

CANADA

- Droit Humain (Canadian Federation)
- National Grand Lodge of Canada (men only, women only, and mixed Lodges)

Alberta
- Grand Lodge of Alberta A.F.&A.M.
- Prince Hall Grand Lodge of Alberta

British Columbia and Yukon
- Grand Lodge of British Columbia and Yukon A.F.&A.M.

Manitoba
- Grand Lodge of Manitoba A.F.&A.M.

New Brunswick
- Grand Lodge of New Brunswick F.&A.M.

Newfoundland and Labrador
- Grand Lodge of Newfoundland and Labrador A.F.&A.M.

Nova Scotia
- Grand Lodge of Nova Scotia A.F.&A.M.

Ontario
- Grand Lodge of Canada A.F.&A.M. in the Province of Ontario
- Prince Hall Grand Lodge F.&A.M. of the Province of Ontario and Jurisdiction

Prince Edward Island
- Grand Lodge of Prince Edward Island A.F.&A.M.

Quebec
- Grand Lodge of Quebec A.F.&A.M.

Saskatchewan
-Grand Lodge of Saskatchewan

UNITED STATES OF AMERICA

- American Federation of Human Rights (Co-Masonry)
- Droit Humain (American Federation)
- Grand Lodge Symbolic of Memphis-Mizraim for the U.S. and its Jurisdiction
- National Grand Lodge, Prince Hall Origin (National Compact)

Alabama
- Grand Lodge F.&A.M. of Alabama
- Prince Hall Grand Lodge F.&A.M. of Alabama
- King Solomon Grand Lodge A.F.&A.M.
- St. James Grand Lodge of Alabama, Inc.
- Progressive Free and Accepted Masons of the U.S.A
- Mt. Olive Grand Lodge, Prince Hall Origin
- National Grand Lodge of F.&A.A.Y.M. of U.S.A.
- Brotherly Love Grand Lodge

Alaska
- Grand Lodge of F.&A.M. of Alaska
- Prince Hall Grand Lodge F.&A.M. Alaska and its Jurisdiction
- King Solomon Grand Lodge A.F.&A.M.
- Sons of Solomon Grand Lodge A.F.&A.M. of Alaska

Arizona
- Grand Lodge of Arizona F.&A.M.
- Prince Hall Grand Lodge F.&A.M. Arizona
- St. John Grand Lodge of Arizona
- Ezra Grand Lodge A.F.&A.M.
- Golden Eagle Grand Lodge

Arkansas
- Grand Lodge of Arkansas F.&A.M.
- Prince Hall Grand Lodge F.&A.M. of Arkansas
- Alpha Grand Lodge
- St. John's Grand Lodge
- King David Grand Lodge
- St. James Grand Lodge

California
- Grand Lodge F.&A.M. of California
- Prince Hall Grand Lodge F.&A.M. of California
- King Solomon Grand Lodge F.&A.A.Y.M.
- St. John Grand Lodge F.&A.M.
- St. John's Grand Lodge A.F.&A.M. of Canada and California
- Pyramid Grand Lodge A.F.&A.M.
- Sons of Light Grand Lodge A.F.&A.M. of California
- Mt. Nebo Grand Lodge, Prince Hall Origin
- Eureka Grand Lodge F.& A.A.Y.M.
- King David Grand Lodge of California
- Enoch Grand Lodge A.F.&A.M.
- Esoteric Grand Lodge of America
- Hiram of Tyre Grand Lodge A.F.&A.M.

Colorado
- *Grand Lodge of A.F.&A.M. of Colorado*
- *Prince Hall Grand Lodge of Colorado, Wyoming and Utah*
- *Hiram Grand Lodge (Prince Hall Origin)*
- *Ivanhoe Grand Lodge A.F.&A.M.*

Connecticut
- Grand Lodge of Connecticut A.F.&A.M.
- Prince Hall Grand Lodge of Connecticut F.&A.M.
- Hiram Grand Lodge
- St. John's Grand Lodge A.F.&A.M.

Delaware
- Grand Lodge of Delaware A.F.&A.M.
- Prince Hall Grand Lodge F.&A.M. of Delaware

District of Columbia
- Grand Lodge F.A.A.M. of the District of Columbia
- Prince Hall Grand Lodge F.&A.M. of the District of Columbia
- King Solomon Grand Lodge A.F.&A.M.
- Eureka Grand Lodge, Prince Hall Origin
- George Washington Union
- St. John's Grand Lodge A.F.&A.M.

Florida
- Grand Lodge of Florida F.&A.M.
- Union Grand Lodge F.&A.M. Prince Hall Affiliated
- St. James Grand Lodge F.&A.M.
- Meridian Grand Lodge

Georgia
- Grand Lodge of F.&A.M. for the State of Geogia
- Prince Hall Grand Lodge F.&A.M. of Georgia
- St. John Grand Lodge
- Traveling Masons of the World
- Smooth Ashlar Grand Lodge, Prince Hall Origin
- Lazarus Grand Lodge of Georgia

Hawaii
- Grand Lodge of Hawaii F.&A.M.
- Prince Hall Grand Lodge of Hawaii

Idaho
- Grand Lodge of Idaho A.F.&A.M.

Illinois
- Grand Lodge of Illinois A.F.&A.M.
- Prince Hall Grand Lodge F.&A.M. of Illinois
- Hiram Grand Lodge
- St. John Grand Lodge A.F.&A.M.
- St. James Grand Lodge A.F.&A.M.

Indiana
- Grand Lodge of Indiana F.&A.M.
- Prince Hall Grand Lodge F.&A.M. of Indiana
- King Solomon Grand Lodge of Indiana
- Indiana Grand Lodge, Prince Hall Origin

Iowa
- Grand Lodge of Iowa A.F.&A.M.
- Prince Hall Grand Lodge of Iowa
- Daniel Grand Lodge

Kansas
- Grand Lodge of Kansas A.F.&A.M.
- Prince Hall Grand Lodge of Kansas F.&A.M.
- St. John's Grand Lodge of Kansa A.F.&A.M.

Kentucky
- Grand Lodge of Kentucky F.&A.M.
- Prince Hall Grand Lodge of Kentucky F.&A.M.
- Eureka Grand Lodge

Louisiana
- Grand Lodge of the State of Louisiana F.&A.M.
- Prince Hall Grand Lodge F.&A.M. for the State of Louisiana
- St. John Grand Lodge A.F.&A.M. of Louisiana
- St. Andrew's Grand Lodge of Louisiana
- King George Grand Lodge A.F.&A.M.
- Universal Grand Lodge A.F.&A.M. of Louisiana

Maine
- Grand Lodge of Maine A.F.&A.M.

Maryland
- Grand Lodge of A.F.&A.M. of Maryland
- Prince Hall Grand Lodge F.&A.M. State of Maryland
- Luxor Grand Lodge
- Maryland Grand Lodge, Prince Hall Origin
- Harmony Grand Lodge in the Great State of Maryland

Massachusetts
- Grand Lodge of A.F.&A.M. of the Commonwealth of Massachusetts
- Prince Hall Grand Lodge F.&A.M. of Massachusetts
- Hiram Grand Lodge A.F.&A.M.

Michigan
- Grand Lodge of Michigan F.&A.M.
- Prince Hall Grand Lodge F.&A.M. of Michigan
- Bethany Grand Lodge of Michigan A.F.&A.M.
- Pride of the East Grand Lodge, Prince Hall Origin
-Sinai Grand Lodge A.F.&A.M. of Michigan
- King Darius Grand Lodge, State of Michigan

Minnesota
- Grand Lodge of Minnesota A.F.&A.M.
- Prince Hall Grand Lodge of Minnesota and Jurisdiction
- North Star Grand Lodge, Prince Hall Origin

Mississippi
- Grand Lodge of Mississippi F.&A.M.
- Stringer Grand Lodge F.&A.M., Prince Hall Affiliation
- Prince Hall Grand Lodge F.&A.M. of the Jurisdiction of Mississippi
- King Hiram Grand Lodge A.F.&A.M.
- King David Grand Lodge A.F.&A.M. of Mississippi

Missouri
- Grand Lodge of A.F.&A.M. of the State of Missouri
- Prince Hall Grand Lodge F.&A.M. of Missouri
- St. Mark Grand Lodge A.F.&A.M. of Missouri
- St. Andrew's Grand Lodge, Prince Hall Origin

Montana
- Grand Lodge of Montana A.F.&A.M.

Nebraska
- Grand Lodge A.F.&A.M. of Nebraska
- Prince Hall Grand Lodge F.&A.M. of Nebraska
- St. Stephan's Grand Lodge, Prince Hall Origin

Nevada
- Grand Lodge of F.&A.M. of the State of Nevada
- Prince Hall Grand Lodge F.&A.M. of Nevada
- King James Grand Lodge A.F.&A.M.
- St. Mark Grand Lodge A.F.&A.M. of Nevada

New Hampshire
- Grand Lodge of New Hampshire F.&A.M.

New Jersey
- Grand Lodge of New Jersey F.&A.M.
- Prince Hall Grand Lodge F.&A.M. State of New Jersey

New Mexico
- Grand Lodge of New Mexico A.F.&A.M.
- Prince Hall Grand Lodge F.&A.M. of the State of New Mexico
- King Solomon Grand Lodge A.F.&A.M. of New Mexico

New York
- Grand Lodge of New York F.&A.M.
- Prince Hall Grand Lodge of the F.&A.M. of the State of New York
- King Solomon Grand Lodge A.F.&A.M. of New York
- Omega Grand Lodge A.F.&A.M.
- La Serenisima Gran Logia de Lengua Espanolo
- Alpha Grand Lodge of New York
- Enoch Grand Lodge of New York

- Rose of Sharon Grand Lodge I.F.&A.M.M.
- Sons of Zebedee Grand Lodge A.F.&A.M.
- Mt. Nebo Grand Lodge of New York
- Mt. Ephraim Grand Lodge

North Carolina
- Grand Lodge of North Carolina A.F.&A.M.
- Prince Hall Grand Lodge of F.&A.M. of North Carolina and Jurisdictions
- St. James Grand Lodge, Prince Hall Origin

North Dakota
- Grand Lodge of North Dakota A.F.&A.M.

Ohio
- Grand lodge of Ohio F.&A.M.
- Prince Hall Grand lodge of Ohio F.&A.M.
- Hiram Grand Lodge A.F.&A.M. of Ohio
- St. John's Grand Lodge A.F.&A.M.
- International Grand Lodge of Masonic Brotherhood

Oklahoma
- Grand Lodge of Oklahoma A.F.&A.M.
- Prince Hall Grand Lodge F.&A.M. Jurisdiction of Oklahoma
- Eureka Grand Lodge, Prince Hall Origin

Oregon
- Grand Lodge of Oregon A.F.&A.M.
- Prince Hall Grand Lodge F.&A.M. of Oregon
- King James Grand Lodge of Oregon A.F.&A.M.
- St. Joseph Grand Lodge of Oregon

Pennsylvania
- Grand Lodge of Pennsylvania F.&A.M.
- Prince Hall Grand Lodge of Pennsylvania F.&A.M.
- Keystone Grand Lodge A.F.&A.M. of Pennsylvania
- Widows Son Grand Lodge of Philadelphia

Rhode Island
- Grand Lodge of Rhode Island F.&A.M.
- Prince Hall Grand Lodge F.&A.M. of the State of Rhode Island

South Carolina
- Grand Lodge of South Carolina A.F.M.
- Prince Hall Grand Lodge of F.&A.M. of the State of South Carolina
- International F.&A.M.
-New Hope Grand Lodge
- Palmetto Grand Lodge, Prince Hall Origin
- James O. Dugan Grand Lodge of South Carolina

South Dakota
- Grand Lodge of South Dakota A.F.&A.M.

Tennessee
- Grand Lodge of Tennessee F.&A.M.
- Prince Hall Grand Lodge F.&A.M. of Tennessee
- Hiram Abiff Grand Lodge A.F.&A.M. State of Tennessee
- Traveling Masons of the World

Texas
- Grand Lodge of Texas A.F.&A.M.
- Prince Hall Grand Lodge of Texas F.&A.M.
- Abraham Grand Lodge of Texas
- Eureka Grand Lodge of Texas
- Mt. Carmel Grand Lodge of Texas
- Sinai Grand Lodge of Texas
- Scottish Rite Grand Lodge of Texas A.F.&A.M.

Utah
- Grand Lodge of Utah F.&A.M.

Vermont
- Grand Lodge of Vermont F.&A.M.

Virginia
- Grand Lodge of Virginia A.F.&A.M.
- Prince Hall Grand Lodge of Virginia
- King Solomon Grand Lodge of Virginia
- Harmony Grand Lodge of the State of Virginia
- Consolidated Hiram Grand Lodge A.F.&A.M. of Virginia

Washington
- Grand Lodge of Washington F.&A.M.
- Prince Hall Grand Lodge F.&A.M. of Washington
- Sons of Haiti Supreme Council

West Virginia
- Grand Lodge of West Virginia F.&A.M.
- Prince Hall Grand Lodge F.&A.M. of West Virginia

Wisconsin
- Grand Lodge of Wisconsin F.&A.M.
- Prince Hall Grand Lodge F.&A.M. of Wisconsin

Wyoming
- Grand Lodge of Wyoming A.F.&A.M.

CENTRAL AMERICA AND CARIBBEAN ISLANDS

Bahamas
- King Edward Grand Lodge
- Prince Hall Grand Lodge F.&A.M. of the Bahamas

Barbados
- Prince Hall Grand Lodge of the Caribbean
Costa Rica
- Grand Lodge of Costa Rica A.F.&A.M.
- Droit Humain
Cuba
- Grand Lodge of Cuba A.F.&A.M.
Dominican Republi
- *Grand Lodge of the Dominican Republic*
- Droit Humain
El Salvador
- Grand Lodge Cuscatlan of the Republic of El Salvador
Guatemala
- Grand Lodge of Guatemala
Haiti
- Grand Orient of Haiti
Honduras
- Grand Lodge of Honduras A.F.&A.M.
Nicaragua
- Grand Lodge of Nicaragua A.F.&A.M.
Mexico
- York Grand Lodge of Mexico F.&A.M.
- Grand Lodge Valle de Mexico
- Grand Lodge of the State of Baja California
- Grand Lodge of the State Baja California Sur
- Grand Lodge of the State of Campeche
- Grand Lodge of the State of Chiapas
- Grand Lodge Cosmos of the State of Chihuahua
- Grand Lodge Benito Juarez of the State of Coahuila
- Grand Lodge Sur-Oeste of the State of Colima
- Grand Lodge Guadalupe Victoria of the State of Durango
- Grand Lodge of the State of Hidalgo
- Grand Lodge Occidental Mexicana of the State of Jalisco
- Grand Lodge Lazaro Cardenas of the State of Michoacana
- Grand Lodge of the State of Nayarit
- Grand Lodge of the State of Nueva Leon
- Grand Lodge Benito Juarez Garcia of the State of Oaxaca
- Grand Lodge of the State of Queretaro
- Grand Lodge of the State of Quintana Roo
- Grand Lodge El Potosi of the State San Luis Potosi
- Grand Lodge of the State of Sinaloa
- Grand Lodge Del Pacifico of the State of Sonora

- Grand Lodge Restauracion of the State of Tabasco
- Grand Lodge of the State of Tamaulipas
- Grand Lodge Unida Mexicana of the State of Veracruz
- Grand Lodge Oriental Peninsular of the State of Yucatan

Panama
- Grand Lodge of Panama A.F.&A.M.

Puerto Rico
- Grand Lodge Soberana of Puerto Rico
- Grand Lodge Mixed of Puerto Rico

Virgin Islands
- International F.&A.M.

SOUTH AMERICA

Argentina
- Grand Lodge of Argentina
- Droit Humain
- Women's Grand Lodge of Argentina

Bolivia
- Grand Lodge of Bolivia

Brazil
- Grand Orient of Brazil – Brazilian Masonic Federation
- Droit Humain
- Masonic Grand Lodge of Acre-Gleac- (Brazil) "Serenissima"
- Grand Lodge Mixed of Brazil
- Women's Grand Lodge of Brasil
- Grand Lodge of the State of Alagoas A.F.&A.M.
- Masonic Grand Lodge of the State of Amapa
- Masonic Grand Lodge of the Amazonas-Glomam
- Masonic Grand Lodge of the State of Bahia
- Grand Lodge of Brasilia A.F.&A.M.
- Masonic Grand Lodge of the State of Ceara A.F.&A.M.
- Masonic Grand Lodge of the State of Espirito Santo
- Grand Lodge of the State of Goias A.F.&A.M.
- Grand Lodge of Maranhao A.F.&A.M.
- Masonic Grand Lodge of the State of Mato Grosso
- Masonic Grand Lodge of the State Mato Groso do Sul
- Masonic Grand Lodge of Minas Gerais
- Masonic Grand Lodge of Para A.F.&A.M.
- Masonic Grand Lodge of the State of Paraiba
- Grand Lodge of Parana
- Grand Lodge of Pernambuco
- Grand Lodge of Piaui A.F.&A.M.

- Masonic Grand Lodge of the State of Rio de Janeiro
- Grand Lodge of the State of Rio Grande do Norte A.F.&A.M.
- Masonic Grand Lodge of the State of Rio Grande do Sul A.F.&A.M.
- Masonic Grand Lodge of the State of Rondonia- Glomaron A.F.&A.M.
- Masonic Grand Lodge of the State of Roraima A.F.&A.M.
- Grand Lodge of Santa Catarina A.F.&A.M.
- Masonic Grand Lodge of the State of Sao Paulo
- Masonic Grand Lodge of the State of Sergipe A.F.&A.M.
- Masonic Grand Lodge of the State Tocantins

Chile
- Grand Lodge of Chile A.F.&A.M.
- Women's Grand Lodge of Chile
- Grand Orient of Chile
- Grand Lodge Mixed of Chile
- Droit Humain

Colombia
- National Grand Lodge of Colombia
- Grand Lodge of Colombia
- Grand Lodge of the Andes
- Serenisima National Grand Lodge of Colombia
- Occidental Grand Lodge of Colombia
- Grand Lodge Oriental of Colombia- "Francisco de Paula Santander"
- Grand Lodge "Benjamin Herrera"
- Droit Humain

Ecuador
- Grand Lodge of Ecuador
- Grand Lodge of Guayaquil
- Grand Lodge of Quito
- Equinoxial Grand Lodge

Paraguay
- Symbolic Grand Lodge of Paraguay

Peru
- Grand Lodge of Peru A.F.&A.M.
- Droit Humain

Uruguay
- Grand Lodge of Uruguay
- Droit Humain

Venezuela
- Grand Lodge of the Republic of Venezuela

INTERNATIONAL MASONIC ORGANIZATIONS

General Grand Chapter Royal Arch Masons International

Organized October 24, 1797, General Grand Chapter Royal Arch Masons International is the Supreme governing Body of Royal Arch Masons in the world, having under its control over sixty Grand Chapters in the US, Europe, Latin America and elsewhere. http://www.ramint.org/

World Conference of the Masonic Grand Lodges

The World Conference of the Masonic Grand Lodges is an international consulting body of the regular Masonic Jurisdictions meeting annually.

CLIPSAS

CLIPSAS (Centre de Liaison et d'Information des Puissances maçonniques Signataires de l'Appel de Strasbourg) is an international group of Masonic Grand Orients and Grand Lodges that adhere to Continental Freemasonry and signed the "Strasbourg Appeal". Members include the Grand Orient de France, the Grand Orient of Belgium and the Grand Lodge of Italy, of which the first two left the group between 2000-2010 The newest member is the Grande Oriente Ibérico. Since 2011 it has had Special Consultative Status at the UNESCO. **www.clipsas.com**

International Masonic Union Catena
The organization was created in 1961 by the Nederlandse grootloge der gemengde vrijmetsalerij, Humanitas – Freimaure-großloge für Frauen und Männer in Deutschland and Österreichischer Universaler Freimaurerorden - Humanitas. It is only for mixed Masonic organizations. The Catena is open only to lodges that acknowledge a Supreme Being (Great Architect of the Universe). **www.catena.org**

The International Secretariat of the Masonic Adogmatic Powers - Secrétariat international Maçonnique des Puissances Adogmatiques (SIMPA)
The International Secretariat of the Masonic Adogmatic Powers (ISMAP) - *Secrétariat international Maçonnique des Puissances Adogmatiques* (SIMPA) is an international organization of Masonic jurisdictions of Masonic lodges. The jurisdictions involved are considered irregular by the United Grand Lodge of England (UGLE) and most other Anglo-Saxon Grand Lodges, because they accept women, or do not require Masons to have a belief in a Supreme Being. The organization was founded on December 26, 1998 in Brussels, Belgium. The organization was founded after the Grand Orient de France and the Grand Orient of Belgium left CLIPSAS.

MASONIC LIBRARIES AND MUSEUMS

Library and Museum of Freemasonry
- Freemasons Hall, 60 Great Queen St. London, WC2B 5AZ, U.K.

Museum of the European Freemasonry (And Library of the Grand Orient of France)
- 16, rue Cadet, 75009 Paris, France

Library and Museum of the Grand Lodge of France
- 8, rue Puteaux, 75017 Paris, France

The German Masonic Museum and Library in Bayreuth
- Im Hofgarten 1, 95444 Bayreuth, Germany

Cultural Masonic Center Prince Frederik (Museum and Library)
- Grand Lodge of Netherlands, Prinsessegracht No. 27, Hague, Netherlands

Library of the Grand Orient of Brazil
- Avenue W5, Sul-Quadra 913, Conjunto H- CEP, 70390-130, Brasilia, Brazil

Scottish Rite Library
- House of the Temple, 1733-16th Street, Washington DC 20009, U.S.A.

Carl H. Claudy Memorial Library
- Masonic Service Association of North America 8120 Fenton Street, Silver Spring MD, 20910, U.S.A.

Masonic Library and Museum of the Grand Lodge of Pennsylvania
- Masonic Temple, 1 North Broad St. Philadelphia PA, 19107, U.S.A.

Allen E. Roberts Masonic Library and Museum of the Grand Lodge of Virginia
- 4115 Nine Mile Rd. Richmond, VA, 23223, U.S.A.

George Washington National Memorial Library
- 101 Callahan Dr. Alexandria, VA, 22301, U.S.A.

Library and Museum of the Grand Lodge of Canada in the Province of Ontario
-363 King Street, West Hamilton, Ontario, L8P 1B4, Canada

Museum of Our National Heritage - Library and Museum
- A.A.S.R. Northern Jurisdiction for U.S.A.
33 Marrett Road, Lexington, MA, U.S.A.

Chancellor Livingston Masonic Library and Museum
- Grand Lodge of New York F.&A.M.
71 W 23rd Street, New York, NY, 10010 U.S.A.

MASONIC RESEARCH ORGANIZATIONS

Quatour Coronati Lodge of Research (Premier Lodge of Research in the world)
- 19 Great Queen St. London, WC2B

Canonbury Masonic Research Center
- Canonbury Tower, Canonbury Place, London,
N1 2NQ U.K.

The Cornerstone Society
- 68 Foxley Lane, Purley, Surrey,
CB8 3EE U.K.

Villard de Honnecourt Lodge of Research No.81 (G.L.N.F.)
- 131, 133 rue de Saussure, 75017 Paris,
France

American Lodge of Research (Grand Lodge of New York)
- Harvey A. Eysman, The Secretary
15 Stonehenge Road, Great Neck, NY 11023,
U.S.A.

Australian and New Zealand Masonic Research Council
- Kent Henderson, The Secretary
PO Box 332, Williamstown, Vic 3016, Australia,
e-mail kent@netlink.com.au

The Philalethes Society
- Wallace E. McLeod FPS, Executive Secretary,
Victoria College University of Toronto, 73
Queens Park Crescent
Toronto, Ontario, Canada M5S 1K7

Scottish Rite Research Society
- 1733 16th Street, NW, Washington DC, 20009, U.S.A.

The Phylaxis Society
- Tommy Rigmaiden FPS, The Secretary 808 LaFitte Drive, Alexandria LA, 71302, U.S.A.

MASONIC MAGAZINES, PERIODICALS, AND WEB SITES

Ars Regia
Polish Masonic Journal (Ideas and History of Freemasonry)
www.wlnp.pl/Arsregia.htm

AQC (Ars Quatuor Coronatorum)
Annual Transactions of the Quatuor Coronati Lodge of Research No. 2076 (U.G.L.E.)
www.quatuorcoronati.com

El Taller.
Revista de Estudios Masonicos - In Spanish
www.geocities.com/tallermasonico/

Freemasonry Today – Magazine
The Independent Voice of Freemasonry
www.freemasonrytoday.com

Freemasonry for the Next Generation
Independent electronic magazine published bimonthly (PDF file)
www.phmainstreet.com

Freemasonry.FM
All the links a Freemason needs. Excellent source of references
www.freemasonry.fm

Franc-Maçonnerie Française.
An outstanding website with valuable information regarding French Freemasonry
www.fm-fr.org

Heredom
The Annual Transaction of the Scottish Rite Research Society
www.srmason-sj.org

Le Journal de la Grand Loge de France
A monthly magazine with always interesting content
www.gldf.org

Masonic Forum Magazine
Exceptional material from Romania (Monthly)
www.masonicforum.ro

MQ
Masonic Quarterly Magazine, official publication of the UGLE
www.mqmagazine.co.uk

Northern Light
A window for Freemasonry
Published quarterly by the Supreme Council A.A.S.R., N.J., U.S.A.
www.supremecouncil.org

Philalethes
Bi-monthly magazine published by the Philalethes Society
www.freemasonry.org

Phylaxis
Magazine published by the Phylaxis Society
www.freemasonry.org/phylaxis

Pietre-Stones Review of Freemasonry
Outstanding papers with prominent contributors
www.freemasons-freemasonry.com

? (Point d'Interrogation)
Official Magazine of the Women's Grand Lodge of Belgium
e-mail- wolfy@scarlet.be

Points de Vue Initiatique
A quarterly magazine of the Grand Lodge of France
with excellent content
www.gldf.org

Renaissance Traditionnelle
One of the best Masonic research periodicals
worldwide (most of the articles in French)
www.renaissance-traditionnelle.org

Rough Ashlar
An outstanding online Masonic magazine from
Quebec (Canada)
www.roughashlar.com

Royal Arch Mason
A quarterly magazine of the General Grand Chapter
R.A.M. International
www.members.aol.com/GGCHAPTER/Magazine

Scottish Rite Journal
A monthly magazine published by the Supreme
Council A.A.S.R., S.J., U.S.A.
www.srmason-sj.org

Zenit.
An Italian Masonic review
www.zen-it.com

BIBLIOGRAPHY

Hall, Manly P. – The Secret Teachings of All Ages, Los Angeles, CA, Philosophical Research Society, 1928

Mackey, Albert J. -Masonry Defined, New York, Masonic Supply Co. 1926

Newton, Joseph Fort. -The Men's House, Kingsport, TN, Southern Publishers, 1923

Steinmetz, George H. -Freemasonry, its Hidden Meaning, Richmond, VA, Macoy Publishing and Masonic Supply Co. 1979

Wilmshurst, W. L. The Meaning of Freemasonry, (originally published in 1922), New York, Barnes &Noble Books 1999

Beresniak, Daniel – L'Apprentissage Maconnique Une Ecole de L'Eveil, Paris, France, Editions Detrad a.V.s. 2004

Daudin, Jean-Frederic – L'ABCdaire de la Franc-Maconnerie, Paris, France, Editions Flammarion, 2003

Beresniak Daniel – Symbols of Freemasonry, Paris, France, Editions Assouline, 1997

Claudy, Carl H. – Introduction to Freemasonry, Washington, DC, The Temple Publisher, 1959

Fontana, David – The Secret Language of Symbols, San Francisco, CA, Chronicle Books, 1994

Hall, Manly P. – Lost Keys of Freemasonry, Los Angeles, CA, The Philosophical Research Society, 1928

Haywood, H. L. – Symbolic Masonry, Kingsport, TN, Southern Publishers, 1923

Macnulty, W. Kirk – Freemasonry, A journey through Ritual and Symbol, London, UK, Thames and Hudson Publishers, 1991

Mlodinow, Leonard – Euclid's Window, New York, Touchstone, 2001

Roob, Alexander – The Hermetic Museum: Alchemy & Mysticism, Bonn, Germany, TASCHEN GmbH, 2001

Schneider, Michael S.- A Beginners Guide to Constructing the Universe, New York, HarperCollins Publishers, 1994

Stewart, Thomas M. – Symbolic Teachings of Masonry and its Message, Cincinnati, Stewart & Kidd Co. , 1917

Chevalier, Jean & Gheerbrant, Alain – Dictionnaire des Symbolles, Paris, France, Editions Robert Laffont, S.A. and Editions Jupiter 1969, 1982

Denslow, Ray V. – Masonic Rites and Degrees, USA, Published by the Author, 1955

Jones, Bernard E. – Freemason's Guide and Compendium, revised edition, London, UK, 1957

Kleinknecht, C. Fred – Forms and Traditions of
the Scottish Rite, Washington, DC, Published for
the Scottish Rite Research Society by the Supreme
Council 33. S.J., USA, 2000

Mackey, Albert G. – An Encyclopedia of Freemasonry,
Vol. I & II, Chicago, IL,
The Masonic History Company, 1921

Pike, Albert – Morals and Dogma of the Ancient
Accepted Scottish Rite of Freemasonry, Washington,
DC, Supreme Council AASR, Southern
Jurisdiction of the USA, 1963

Beresniak, Daniel – Rites et Symboles de la
Franc-Maconnerie, Paris, France, Editions
Detrad a.V.s., 2004

Mainguy, Irene – La Symbolique maconnique du
troisieme millenaire, Paris, France,
Editions Dervy 2001

Baigent, Michael and Leigh, Richard – The Temple
and the Lodge, New York, NY,
Arcade Publishers, 1989

Churton, Tobias – The Gnostics, USA, Barnes &
Noble Inc. 1997

Knoop, D. & Jones, G.P.- The Genesis of Freemasonry,
London, 1947, 1978

Leadbeater, C.W. – Freemasonry and its Ancient
Mystic Rites, New York, NY,
Theosophical Publishing House, 1986

Lomas, Robert – Freemasonry and the Birth of
Modern Science, Gloucester, MA,
Fair Winds Press, 2003

McLeod, Wallace – The Old Gothic Constitutions,
Bloomington, IL, published by The Masonic Book
Club, 1985

Robinson, John J. – Born In Blood, The Lost Secrets
of Freemasonry, New York, NY,
M. Evans and Company, Inc. 1989

Yates, Frances A. – The Rosicrucian Enlightenment,
USA, Barnes & Noble Inc. 1996

Anderson, James – The Constitutions of the
Freemasons, 1723 (and) The New Book of Constitutions...
1738, Facsimile reprint, London, 1976

Gould, Robert Freke – The History of Freemasonry,
Vol. I-IV, New York, NY,
John. C. Yorston & Co. Publishers, 1886

Jacob, Margaret C. – Living the Enlightenment,
Freemasonry and Politics in
Eighteenth-Century Europe, New York, Oxford
University Press, 1991

Rebold, Emmanuel – A General History of Free-
Masonry in Europe, Cincinnati,
American Masonic Publishing Association, 1868

Stillson, H.L. , Hughan, W.J. and a Board of Editors
– History of the Ancient and Honorable Fraternity of Free and
Accepted Masons, and Concordant Orders,
Boston, MS, The Fraternity Publishing Company, 1910

Hamill, John and Gilbert,Robert – Freemasonry,
A Celebration of the Craft, London, GB,
Greenwich Editions, 1998

Hamill, John and Gilbert,Robert – World Freemasonry,
An Illustrated History,
London, 1991

Poole, Herbert (Editor) – History of Freemasonry,
Vol. I – IV, London, UK,
Caxton Publishing Company, 1954

Pick, Fred L. & Knight, G. Norman – The Pocket
History of Freemasonry, London, 1991

Combes, Andre – Histoire de la Franc-
Maconnerie au XIX siecle, Paris, France,
Editions du Rocher, 1998, 1999

Le Forestier, Rene – La Franc-Maconnerie Templiere
et Occultiste aux XVIII et XIX siecles, Vol
I and II, Second Edition, Paris, France, 1987

Coil, Henry Wilson – Coil's Masonic Encyclopedia,
Richmond, VA, Macoy Publishing and Masonic
Supply Co. , 1961, 1996

Fox, William (Editor), Valley of the Craftsmen,
Scottish Rite Freemasonry in America's
Southern Jurisdiction 1801-2001, Washington,
DC, published by the Supreme Council
A.A.S.R. , S.J. , USA, 2001

Henderson, Kent & Pope, Tony – Freemasonry
Universal, Vol. I and II., Australia,
Global Masonic Publications, 1998 and 2000

Newbury, George Adelbert & Williams, Louis
Lenway – A History of the Supreme Council
A.A.S.R. for the Northern Masonic Jurisdiction of the USA,
Lexington, MS, published by the Supreme Council
A.A.S.R., N.M.J., 1987

Singer, Herbert T. and Lang, Ossian- New York
Freemasonry, A Bicentennial History,
1781-1981, New York, Published by the Grand
Lodge of F.&A.M. of the State of NY, 1981

Brodsky, Francoise (Editor)- W:.L:. Universalis
No.21, New York, pamphlet published by the
Lodge for their tenth anniversary, New York, 2002

Buisine, Andree- La Franc- Maconnerie Anglo-
Saxonne et les Femmes, Paris, France,
Editions Guy Tredaniel

Buisine, Andree- La Grand Loge Feminine de
France- Autoportrait. Paris, France,
Editions Guy Tredaniel, 1995

Hivert-Messaca, Gisele et Yves – Comment la
Franc-Maconnerie vint aux femmes: deux siecles
d'adoption feminine et mixte en France, 1740-
1940, Paris, France, Editions Dervy

Andrews, Richard and Schellenberger, Paul – The
Tomb of God, London, G.B.,
Little, Brown and Company, 1996

Baigent, M., Leigh R. and Lincoln H.- The Holy
Blood and the Holy Grail, New York,
Dell Publishing Group, Inc., 1989

Knight, Christopher and Lomas, Robert- The
Book of Hiram, London, U.K.
Published by Century, 2003

Sadler, Henry- Masonic Facts and Fiction, England,
The Aquarium Press, 1985

Wallace-Murphy,Tim and Hopkins, Marilyn –
Rosslyn, Guardian of the Secrets of the Holy
Grail, New York, Barnes & Noble, Inc. 2000

De Hoyos, Art and Morris, S. Brent – Is it true
what they say about Freemasonry, The Methods
of Anti-Masons, Silver Spring, MA, Masonic Information
Center, 1997

Leazer, Gary – Fundamentalizm & Freemasonry,
The Southern Baptist Investigation of the Fraternal
Order, New York, M. Evans & Co., 1995

Whalen, William J. – Christianity and American
Freemasonry, Milwaukee, USA,
The Bruce Publishing Co., 1958

Beresniak, Daniel – Les Bas-fonds de
L'Imaginaire (Fascisme, Integrisme, Esoterisme
et manipulation), Paris, France, Editions Detrad aVs

Piatigorsky, Alexander – Who's Afraid of Freemasons,
New York, Barnes & Noble, Inc. 2005

Roberts, Allen E. and McLeod, Wallace – Freemasonry
and Democracy, Its Evolution in North
America, Highland Springs, VA, Anchor Communications
Roberts, Allen E. – The Search for Leadership,
Highland Springs, VA, Anchor Communications, 1987

Roberts, Allen E. – Key to Freemasonry's Growth, Richmond, VA, Macoy Publishing and Masonic Supply Co., 1969

Nisand, Leon – Celebration Humaniste, Paris, France, Editions Detrad aVs, 2004

Zeller, Fred – Trois points c'est tout, Paris, France, Editions Robert Laffont

Bauer, Alain – Address to the 2002 California Masonic Symposium by the Grand Master of the Grand Orient of France, Sacramento, California, Published by the Burbank Masonic Lodge No.406, 2002

Bradley, Don – Freemasonry in the Twenty First Century, California,
Published by Native Planet Pub., 1995

Cecius, Jacques – Le Reve Citoyen d'un Franc-Macon, Paris, France,
Editions Detrad aVs,2004

Verdun, Jean – Lumiere sur la Franc-Maconnerie Universelle, Paris, France,
Editions Detrad aVs, 2002

ABOUT THE AUTHOR

About the Author

Stevan V. Nikolic was born in Belgrade, Serbia in 1958 and moved to New York, USA in 1987. He began his literary career as a poet before turning to non-fiction and fiction. As a writer, he spent last fifteen years studying various forms of esoteric spirituality. Stevan V. Nikolic is the author of nine books: Royal Art (2006), The Purpose of Freemasonry (2008), Astrology (2010), Alchemy (2010), Kabbalah (2010), Ancient Mysteries (2011), Freemasonry in Serbia (2011), Spiritual Guide to the Secret of Birth (2012), and a novel Star - The Book of Life (2013). He published his articles and papers in Freemasons Press Magazine (New York), Ars Quatuor Coronatorum (London), Transactions of A.L.R. (New York), Lodge Singidunum Annual Transactions (Belgrade), Builder Magazine (Belgrade) and numerous other publications. A fluent speaker, he lectures on different esoteric traditions and history of Freemasonry. He lives in New York and Belgrade and works in POD and web publishing as a freelance editor, copywriter, and a web-designer.

www.ingramcontent.com/pod-product-compliance
Lightning Source LLC
Chambersburg PA
CBHW031403290426
44110CB00011B/244